Anna's Shtetl

JUDAIC STUDIES SERIES

Leon J. Weinberger
General Editor

ANNA'S SHTETL

Lawrence A. Coben

THE UNIVERSITY OF ALABAMA PRESS
Tuscaloosa

Typeface: Sabon

∞
The paper on which this book is printed meets the minimum requirements of
American National Standard for Information Sciences-Permanence of Paper for
Printed Library Materials, ANSI Z39.48–1984.

Library of Congress Cataloging-in-Publication Data

Coben, Lawrence A.
    Anna's shtetl / Lawrence A. Coben.
        p.   cm. — (Judaic studies series)
    Includes bibliographical references.
    ISBN-13: 978-0-8173-1527-6 (cloth : alk. paper)
    ISBN-10: 0-8173-1527-6
    1. Dien, Anna Spector, b. 1905. 2. Jews—Ukraine—Korsun'-Shevchenkivs'kyi—
Biography. 3. Korsun'-Shevchenkivs'kyi (Ukraine)—Ethnic relations. 4. Korsun'-
Shevchenkivs'kyi (Ukraine)—History—20th century. I. Title. II. Series: Judaic studies
series (Unnumbered)
    DS135.U43D543 2006
    947.7'6—dc22
    [B]
                                                                        2006013110

To the memory of Anna Spector Dien

Those things from my childhood when I was 9, 10, 11, 12—I mean those things spontaneous [sic] I can tell you because I have little pictures, I have pictures in my mind, and I can tell you. Then if you go it [sic] over, and if I made a mistake, I can recall a name or something, but the place and the event that happened at that particular time cannot be changed in my mind, because it's indelible. That's the way it happened! . . . So if we will, if we would go only on that, you know, from the time my dad—we were standing outside our house, and my dad left for America. . . . That is when my childhood started, because that was the time of my deprivation. You see, my father went to America with such wonderful—it was such a wonderful idea. He'll [sic] come to America.

  —Taped interview with Anna Spector Dien, March 10, 1995

Sometimes they gave me some pieces of wood that was [sic] lying around [in the forest]—they let me pick up. I wasn't alone; we had sacks—five or six children—burlap sacks for the wood that the peasants would let us take. Once I was by myself—a beautiful evening with a pink sky, the sun was shining, the water on the branches kinda melted a little. Then when the sun went down, everything got ink and the frost got colder and froze and when the wind shook it, it was just like a violin. It was music.

  —Interview with Anna Spector Dien, December 17, 1995

Contents

Preface

Anna Spector, at eighty-nine, had a clear memory of her father, dressed in his best, stepping into a carriage that would take him out of town on his way from the Ukraine to America. She was seven years old when he left in January 1913. She would not see him again until she was sixteen. Before her father's departure relatively little of her life had remained in her memory. From that day on, though, her memory was fully awake. She would later say that it felt almost as though she could recall every day of her life in the small town of Korsun once her father went away. When he left, she said, her childhood ended.

Anna's memory was remarkable, but not only because she could recall so many incidents, people, and objects. What set her memory apart was that many of her recollections were in the form of scenes—visual images, often including color, and sometimes made even more realistic by sound, aroma, motion, or emotion. As Anna said emphatically about some things that happened during her childhood in Korsun, "I have pictures in my mind . . . the place and the event that happened at that . . . particular time cannot be changed in my mind, because it's indelible. That's the way it happened!"

If Anna could describe a particular incident because she was able to see it, she could often pick out other parts of the scene that might not have anything to do with the main subject of the incident. She might mention an old sleigh summering on the roof of a pigsty; the puddle of ink on the floor near an open ink bottle during a pogrom; or the words on a German soldier's belt buckle. So from these mental tableaus also came small background details—pungent, trivial, revealing, mundane—bearers of reality.

Anna's family and many others who shared the slow deprivations of wartime and the sudden assaults of pogroms found ways to endure. Anna's intelligent curiosity, her interest in other people, and her venturesome na-

Figure 1. Korsun and environs, to show towns and cities mentioned in the text and notes. In large gray type are the names of provinces. Population figures, in thousands, are from the 1897 all-Russian census (Troinitskago, N.A. *Naselennyiya mesta Rossiiskoi imperii. . . . 1905a;* Troinitskago, N.A. *Goroda i poseleniya. . . . 1905b*)[1]. Inset: The Western European portion of the Russian Empire, to show the location of Kiev in relation to other relevant Russian cities.

ture provided her awakened memory with a store of information that may bring us closer to understanding why and how they managed. Over the course of many interviews, I asked Anna how ordinary life was arranged in her shtetl, Korsun—in kitchen and bedroom, in marketplace and school. I asked her how people made a living; how they shopped and cooked and ate; how they washed their clothes and where they slept, and what kind of light they had at night.[1]

Anna's childhood, however, had not been merely a catalog of furniture. She had lived through interesting times—World War I, the Bolshevik Revolution of 1917, and part of the ensuing Russian Civil War. Korsun had also endured three pogroms. Much of what Anna had seen and experienced had remained coiled in her memory. Only when we began to concentrate on Anna's personal experiences did the scenes hidden for so long unwind into the story of her childhood. She was a keen observer. It was the telling of her story that cast the most light on shtetl life.

Although some of the recollections pained her, she looked forward to our conversations as much as I did. If she related an incident, we often came back to it in later talks, confirming details, allowing more of its sights and sounds to float to the surface of her memory. Wherever possible, I checked her recollection against the written record of history.

In Anna's Korsun, the Jewish community was stifling in its social intolerance and its religious zealotry, while the Gentile community was tainted by its anti-Semitism. In her Korsun, pettiness was too prevalent, perhaps because too many were struggling to survive in poverty. For Anna, who came of age in Korsun, her hometown became a place better left behind.[2]

But in Korsun she also had friends, both Jewish and Gentile. She thrived in an integrated high school. Her memories of personal experiences with individual Christians were largely positive. It was not unusual for her to be treated fairly or kindly. She saw humor where it was to be seen. Having an artistic soul, she thrilled to the sight of a flowering acacia tree, the aroma of lilac blossoms, and the mystery of uncountable stars; but except for nature, Korsun could show her little of beauty.[3]

Allowed at last by the Bolshevik army to leave Korsun with her mother and sisters, Anna spent two exciting years in Moscow and Petrograd (St. Petersburg), waiting for a chance to emigrate to America. Although she lived in refugee camps, her aesthetic sense could now feast on the theater, ballet, painting, architecture—all the cultural treasures of those two grand cities. Having arrived in Moscow as a small-town girl, Anna left Petrograd two years later with a store of knowledge about the ways of a modern metropolis, an interest in the world of art that would inform her life, and with renewed hope that her family would finally reach America.

Acknowledgments

For editorial advice and criticism, I am indebted to many people. The members of the nonfiction section of the 1997 Summer Writers Institute at Washington University in St. Louis, Missouri, under Dr. Rockwell Gray, were congenial and helpfully frank. Of this "Dirty Dozen," the two who lasted longest under the steady drip of revisions were Deborah Meister and especially Mary Ellen VanderLinden, who (almost) never met a compound sentence she didn't prefer to split.

Literary agent Elise Goodman rejected an earlier version of the manuscript for good reason, and was kind enough to tell me why.

My sister, Dorothy Ferster (aided by her husband Paul Ferster), and my niece, Judith Ferster, both fine writers, suffered through various chapters and various arguments about style. Dorothy had the good sense to insist early that Anna's story was paramount.

I am indebted most especially to my wife, Sandy Coben, who never gave up. She encouraged, guided, and edited, and she shaped the final version of the manuscript. Our children, Rachel, Josh, Anna, and David, were also unable to escape reading chapters. I thank them for their help.

Many people kindly helped in my search for historical and other details to corroborate or explain some of Anna's recollections, as follows: Anna's children—Jane Rogul, Anna's daughter (site of the Iowa photograph and dates of Anna's arrival in America and marriage); Albert Dien, Anna's son (photographs of Anna); Saul Dien, Anna's son (his birth date and place)— Norma Vavra (tape of her 1985 interview with Anna, as well as a copy of the essay she wrote about Anna); Klavdia Kolesnikova, of the Korsun-Shevchenkovsky historical cultural preservation park (invaluable Korsun history); Professor Paul Robert Magocsi, University of Toronto (rights of Korsun's princess); and Professor Michael Hamm, Princeton University (the word "oblavy").

Nuntius Russia, Apostolic Nunciature of Moscow (Izmailovsky Trinity Cathedral [*Troitsky Sobor*]); Gregory Ofman (definitive photographs of Petrograd's Lion Bridge and information about the White Nights); Reverend Robert Bohdan S. Piorkowski, Pastor of St. Mary Assumption Ukrainian Catholic Church, St. Louis, Missouri (the word "*Ros*"); Professor David Engerman, now at Brandeis University (Russian history); Vladimir Feldman (matters Ukrainian, especially language, Kiev, Bulgakov, and material on Russian passport laws); Michael C. Finke, Associate Professor of Russian, Washington University in St. Louis, Missouri (Lermontov's poem "Borodino"); and Dr. Alla Sokolova, St. Petersburg Jewish University (Petrograd).

For help on Russian law and the Russian census: Professor ChaeRan Freeze, Brandeis University; Anna Rakityanskaya, Librarian, Slavic Division, Widener Library, and the staff of the Phillips Reading Room, Harvard University; Reference Librarians Leena Siegelbaum, Yuliya Bir, and David Ferris (Rare Books), of the Harvard University Law Library; Reference Librarians Molly Molloy and Carol A. Leadenham, Hoover Library, Hoover Institution; and Helen Sullivan, Manager, Slavic Reference Service, University of Illinois Library.

For information about natural phenomena: Leon Havill, Mandalea Limited, Rangiora, New Zealand (honey and mead); ZoeAnn Holmes, Nutrition and Food Management, Oregon State University, Corvallis, Oregon, and Joanne McGuire, Malt Products Corporation, Saddlebrook, New Jersey (molasses); Dr. Stephen Kaffka, Associate Specialist, Agronomy and Range Science, University of California–Davis, Roger Ruslund, Agronomist, Monitor Sugar Company, Bay City, Michigan, and Dr. Adolph Steiner, Institute of Plant Breeding, University of Hohenhem, Stuttgart, Germany (Napoleon's beet seeds); Missouri Botanical Gardens (black locust tree, *Robinia pseudoacacia*); Professor Terry Prouse, Canada Climate Impacts on Water Resources, University of Victoria, British Columbia, Canada, and Michael G. Ferrick, Research Hydrologist, U.S. Army Engineer Research and Development Center, Hanover, New Hampshire (the term "ice breakup"); and Fred Espenak, Planetary Systems Branch, Code 693 NASA/ Goddard Space Flight Center, Greenbelt, Maryland (eclipses).

Professor Jeffrey Veidlinger, Indiana University (*A Thousand and One Nights*); Professor Curt Leviant, Center for Jewish Life, Rutgers University; Mrs. Aliza Shevrin (Sholem Aleichem's "hooligan"); Professor Holger Nath, Heinrich Heine University, Duesseldorf, Germany (material on Nahum Stiff); and the late Donn O'Meara of Israel (help with a Yiddish expression); Gunnar Berg, archivist at UIVO (copies of the *Oytobiographye* and the obituary of Nahum Stif); Dina Byelikova, Hebrew Immigrant Aid Society (HIAS), Chicago.

Aaron Gardner, Access Services of the Northern Regional Library Facility of the University of California–Berkeley (arranging for me to see and photocopy Alexander Berkman's book, *The Kronstadt Rebellion*); Ronald Goldfeder, staff member, Transport Museum, St. Louis County (showing me real trains and pertinent photographs of trains).

For help with the "American correspondent" mystery: Dr. Bernard Crystal, Curator of Manuscripts, Rare Book and Manuscript Library, Columbia University Library (information on Sam Spewack); Daniel Schorr, National Public Radio; Nicholas Daniloff; and Robert Korengold.

The library staff at Olin Library and the School of Medicine Library, Washington University in St. Louis (help and interlibrary loans); St. Louis Public Library map section staff (finding and copying the 1953 U.S. Army Map Service map); Alexander Tague (designing and creating the map of Anna's region).

Finally, for invaluable translation help: Professor Albert Dien, Stanford University (Russian); Professors Emeritus Solon Beinfeld and Seymour Pollack, Washington University in St. Louis (Yiddish); and Mrs. Lyuba Ryback (both).

Note on Transliteration and Pronunciation

Russian and Ukrainian words are presented according to the modified Library of Congress system of transliteration. Yiddish words are presented according to the YIVO system.

The letter combination *kh* is used in Yiddish, Russian, and Ukrainian words to indicate the sound that is absent in English, but is present in the *ch* sound of the Scotch word *loch* and the German word *nach,* as well as in the Russian name of pianist-composer Sergei Rachmaninoff.

Other Yiddish transliterations are:

oy (Yiddish letter combination *vov, yud*) as in *boy* is presented as *oy.*

a as in *date* is presented as *ey.* Thus the name of Anna's grandmother Beyla rhymes with *sail uh* (and *Venezuela*). Also, the name of Anna's mother Leya rhymes with *say uh* (and *Malaya*).

i as in *ride* is presented as *ay.* Thus the name of Anna's sister Mayna rhymes with *mine uh* (and *Carolina*).

Anna's Shtetl

I

The Two Shevchenkos

Eighty years later, Anna Spector still remembered the Ukrainian girl who was her best friend in high school: She was such a lovely girl. I don't remember her first name. We always just called her Shevchenko.

On the first day of high school, Anna Spector had sat next to Shevchenko because a teacher made a mistake. The art teacher wrote "Shpector" when Anna gave her name. He was a Czechoslovakian and couldn't pronounce the letter *S* properly in Russian.[1] The desks were assigned alphabetically, so Shpector sat next to Shevchenko from that day in 1916 all through high school. Once they got to know each other, it didn't seem to matter that Shevchenko was an average student, while Anna made top grades, or that Shevchenko was well-to-do and Orthodox Christian, while Anna was poor and Orthodox Jewish. They became friends because they both liked embroidery and despised injustice, and because they just took to each other.

Shevchenko liked to take the side of the underdog. Two boys with poor grades accused someone in the class of copying work from another student. No one in the class liked what these two troublemakers did, but Shevchenko was the only one brave enough to do something about it. She argued vigorously to defend the innocent student. Shevchenko's arguments carried weight. She came from a prosperous family employed by the princess, and she didn't hesitate to speak up and stand her ground.

Another time, Anna was the injured party, needing someone to stick up for her. A family had given her a velvet bag to decorate with embroidery. Closed by a drawstring, and meant to hold prayer implements, such bags were commonly given as gifts to young men. The family wrote out a particular young man's name in Hebrew letters for Anna to copy in embroidery on the bag. At that time her family lived just across the street from the dressmaking and needlework shop of a woman named Dina, where Shevchenko often came with her mother and older sister to have their winter clothes made. Anna would meet them there by chance while she was embroidering the letters.

Proud that her lettering had turned out so well, she brought the finished bag to school to show to her home economics teacher, Nina Constantinovna. The quality of the needlework was so good that the teacher didn't believe Anna had done it, and told her so. Shevchenko jumped to Anna's defense, furious at the teacher for calling Anna a liar. No one but Shevchenko would dare to stand up to a teacher that way. Nina Constantinovna had to back down, and the teacher never again doubted Anna's word.

Shevchenko lived about four miles east of Korsun in the woodland. Her father was the managing director of the princess's forest. Anna saw their grand house when the class went on a picnic nearby, and her friend's mother came out to greet them, bringing cookies and a drink. Another time, when Shevchenko invited Anna to her home, her older brother proudly showed them some squirrels he had shot, making Anna squeal in repugnance at the gruesome sight. That was in her first year of high school, two years into the world war, when life at school, and in the town, was still relatively tolerable.

In the next two years, Anna's life in Korsun, like the lives of most people in Russia, became increasingly hard. Russian people spoke of the bad years, the years when the upheaval of World War I and the Bolshevik Revolution stretched into the Russian Civil War, as "the time of troubles." The winter of 1918–1919 was the worst winter of all. That was during Anna's third year of high school, when the poverty, the wars, the typhus epidemic, and the pogroms of "the time of troubles" had reduced her family to despair.[2]

The family's need for food became most urgent in the summer of 1919. Another pogrom hit Korsun, and the looters who invaded Grandmother Beyla's house, where Anna's family was now living, stole every scrap of food. Grandfather Avrum needed to soothe his ailing stomach with food many times a day. Gaunt and pacing in pain from his cancer, he was actually crying for something to eat. Anna decided that it was up to her to bring home food. She went begging.

Anna chose small farms as the most likely source of food. Korsun, a backwater in the enormous empire that had been ruled by the tsar until the recent revolution, was a small town resting on the fertile, black-earth soil of the Ukraine, famous for its yields of produce. In normal times the peasant farmers in the Korsun area would eat as many of their tomatoes as they could, then feed the rest to the pigs. Now, however, most of the pigs were gone, as were most of the livestock and most of the men. Those animals not taken during the world war were now being taken during the civil war by the several contending armies, whose soldiers had also commandeered or stolen most of the fruits, vegetables, and grain that had been so abundant in peacetime. Still, if anyone had food it would be the farmers. The farmers lived in the villages surrounding Korsun, each village a cluster of ten or twelve houses spaced less than a mile apart, each house with its own farmland within walking distance.

Never having ventured into most of the villages, and not knowing exactly where to go, fourteen-year-old Anna crossed the wooden bridge over the Ros River and headed east. Her sister Mayna, only seven years old, stayed home, but Gussie, at eleven, was old enough to come along and help carry anything they might find. Barefoot, wearing whatever remnants of skirts and blouses the *pogromshchiki* had not taken during their looting, the two girls walked until they saw a village surrounded by low hills. Anna led the way to the group of peasant houses.

At each house she just opened the door—people didn't knock—and walked in. She walked into one house and saw three half-naked children. Their mother was harvesting in the fields, one of the children told her. When Anna asked if they might spare any food, the oldest child brought out two pieces of rusk—bread prepared by prolonged drying in the oven. They went to other houses and then walked to the next village to continue begging. Often they found infants and small children in the care of an older child. Many of the babysitters, who were the same age as Anna and Gussie, felt sorry for them and gave whatever food they could, until the two beggars had filled a bag with pieces of dried bread and cooked potatoes.

They kept walking, two brown-eyed beggar girls in tatters, Anna the brunette and Gussie the blonde, each with her hair pulled back in two braids meeting behind her head. When Gussie said she was tired, they sat and rested, but by now Anna was lost. The girls recrossed the Ros River at a narrow place, stepping carefully on a flimsy bridge built for goats. Although they were trying to find their way home, they were far to the south of the cobblestoned road and the planked bridge where they had first crossed the river to look for the peasant villages. Not knowing where they were, they kept walking westward.

Finally, plodding through open fields, they came upon a barefoot peasant woman, digging potatoes with her son. She saw how tired the girls were and gave them some milk and a few pieces of bread while they rested. After they had eaten, the woman asked them to help with the harvest, offering to pay by giving them some potatoes to take home. Anna was delighted. The woman knelt on the black earth, doing the hard work of digging out the potatoes. Anna and Gussie did the easy job of cleaning the potatoes of dirt and putting them into a sack. The son, about fourteen, helped his mother dig, then lifted the sacks into a wheelbarrow and took them away in a horse-drawn wagon.

The woman's first name was Domakho. Although neither had recognized the other, Anna later realized that she was the milk lady who used to come to their house before "the time of troubles." Her husband and two older sons had been taken into the army, leaving her with the youngest son and a daughter about eight years old. The authorities had also taken away most of her animals, leaving her with one horse and one cow. She was making do with what she had.

During a rest period, Anna told Domakho that eight people in her family were all living in her grandmother's house, and that the *pogromshchiki* had stolen whatever food they had left. After more digging, Domakho kindly gave Anna and Gussie each a sack to fill with potatoes. She pointed them in the right direction, and they found their way home, dragging the heavy sacks along the ground. That evening was like a holiday, as the family feasted on rusk and potatoes.

The two girls went back several days that week, until the potatoes were all dug and cleaned. Each day they helped Domakho, and each day she told them to take as many potatoes as they could manage. Each potato was almost enough to make a meal for one person, and by the time the harvesting was finished, Anna's family had accumulated a month's supply. Moreover, Domakho told Anna that if she would come to her house—only a short walk from where Anna was living—she would give her some milk. Anna went to the warmhearted peasant woman's house several times, carrying the only container that the looters had not stolen in the pogroms—a two-handled pan with white enamel on the inside and blue enamel on the outside. From a container that Domakho kept in the small shed just outside the barn door, she would pour a half cup of milk for Anna to drink, then fill the enameled pan for her to take home. In those times of scarcity, nobody could believe that Anna was able to get milk. Her family had not tasted it for nearly a year.

The walk from her grandmother's house on the hill, not far from the Ros River, the eastern boundary of town, to the milk lady's house had become routine for Anna—down to the bottom of the hill, then east on the cobblestones sloping gradually downward toward the river, past the blacksmith shop, past the houses of the elementary Hebrew school teacher and the rope maker, turning to the right at the telephone building, crossing the cobblestoned street, and stepping onto the dirt road that led south to the cemetery, and on the way, to the milk lady's. Anna was on a first name basis with Domakho's dog, whose Ukrainian name was *Shag*—"Half-penny."

One day when Domakho was on her way to the market, she happened to meet Anna, and said, Come over and bring your pan on Sunday. I'll have some milk for you. On that Sunday, Anna left her grandmother's house on the hill, intending to go to Domakho's for milk. She was carrying the enameled pan. She walked down the hill, headed east toward the river, and began to notice that the cobblestoned main street was unusually quiet. No one was about, not even a scratching chicken or a scavenging pig. She had heard gunfire all night, the sound of fighting between two armies near the town, so people were probably fearful of coming out in the daylight.

She passed the blacksmith's house, then the Hebrew teacher's, then the rope maker's, and came to the last building, the telephone exchange. Turning to the right, she crossed the cobblestoned street, stepping onto the road that led south to the cemetery. The dirt road on which she was walking was wide enough for several animals to stroll abreast, hemmed in by a low wooden fence on either side. In these outskirts of the town, where every family had a cow or a herd of sheep or goats, several families would hire a shepherd to guide all of their animals along this road to and from the pasture. Wagons, too, occasionally creaked along here, but the road was just wide enough for one wagon to pass. A person on foot would have to press against the fence when one came along.

As Anna approached Domakho's house, which was less than a block to the south, she saw about twenty young women and half again as many young men coming toward her. They looked like peasants coming from a wedding. Because they were yelling, Anna began to watch them as they came on, although they were still some distance away. A young man in his early twenties was ahead of the group. Seeing her, he began to run, yelling at her in Russian. He had a gun in his hand.

Anna recognized him at once. It was Shevchenko's brother. He didn't recognize Anna, who had grown up in the few years since their only meeting. Many people in Korsun, peasants and Jews alike, were afraid of this Shevchenko. People had been talking about him because he was the leader of a small gang of young men who hid in the forest and terrorized the town. They called themselves the Protectors, and in the civil war they were guerillas fighting on the side of the "Whites"—the White Army—who were trying to overthrow the new Bolshevik government. The Bolsheviks called them bandits. When Shevchenko's men ran out of food, they would raid a farm, sometimes even in broad daylight, taking away everything the farmer had—chickens, a cow—whatever they could take or carry. The young men in this wedding party were Shevchenko's guerillas. Each one was wearing a pistol. Shevchenko was yelling, Who is in Korsun? Who is in town? He was aiming his gun at her.

Anna stood aside, backing into the fence. Shevchenko wanted to know if the Bolsheviks had taken the town. They were somewhere near, but Anna didn't know if one of the armies was actually in Korsun. She told him she didn't know. He thought she was refusing to tell him. He called her ugly names, and he accused her of knowing but not telling him because she was one of the Bolsheviks.

They had all been drinking, the girls and the boys, but they kept shouting at him to leave her alone. With one hand, the tipsy Shevchenko reached toward Anna, and with the other he pointed his gun at her face. He was about to grab her blouse, but his friends grabbed him from behind, and in that fraction of a second she got away.

She darted around him and ran toward Domakho's house. It sat on the right side of the dirt road, in the center of a large yard on a hill. She threw herself over the fence, ran up to the house, and pounded on the door. Domakho came to the door, looked out, saw the mob of armed young men, saw Shevchenko with the gun in his hand, and slammed the door in Anna's face.

The Jews were not alone in fearing mobs in those days of the civil war and of the pogroms. Although some Korsun peasants became *pogromshchiki*, attacking Jews and looting their homes and businesses, many others did not. Like the Jews, these peaceful peasants were in danger from lawless bands—marauders from an army, and the local *pogromshchiki* who joined them. Knowing this, Anna didn't blame Domakho for slamming the door on her, but it made her jerk back and hesitate momentarily, her first plan thwarted.

She fled up a hill between the house on her left and a pigsty on her right, stretching her legs to match the long spaces between the crude footholds notched into the hillside, until she came abreast of the roof of the sty. Lying on the weathered roof was an old sleigh, waiting for winter to come again, so close that she could have reached over and touched it. Although it had nothing to do with what was happening to her, the image of the sleigh remained frozen in her memory.

The hillside steps took her up into a garden full of fruit trees. Anna caught sight of raspberry and gooseberry bushes grown thick and tall in the summer sun. Behind her, Shevchenko was running and looking for her, but she could tell that he had not located her yet, so she scrambled under the berry bushes to hide and catch her breath. She could see him between the branches, but he couldn't see her. After a time, he lowered his gun and walked the other way with his friends. Lying under the bushes, Anna heard the noise of the mob fade. She waited long enough to be absolutely sure that they would not see her, then left the bushes and ran again.

She started to run west, away from the house and the pigsty, but not far from her hiding place the land fell away in almost a straight drop, as if a giant cleaver had chopped off the end of the garden. Anna teetered on the edge, looking down, worrying that Shevchenko might come back and find her, wanting to keep going, needing to get farther away from him, wanting to jump, but knowing that it looked too far down. In a glimpse of soft green leaves below, and a glance at the tree roots sticking out of the side of the cliff near her feet, her decision made itself. She grasped at the roots and started down the face of the cliff, grabbing and scrambling and jumping and falling, and she landed with a soft bounce.

Anna found herself in a ditch partly filled with the leafy tops of sugar beets. The soft leaves on their long flexible stalks had cushioned her fall. When she turned so that the cliff wall was behind her, she saw that the other wall of the ditch was not nearly so high as the cliff. Where it leveled off, she could see people sitting near the edge, looking down at her. Some of them were using little hatchets to slice off the tops of cone-shaped sugar beets as big as melons. She was too far down in the ditch to climb up to them by herself.

She saw two girls standing with their palms pressed to their cheeks, looking concerned, afraid she had hurt herself. They began to scream. Some of the women crossed themselves. Someone yelled, Get a *koromisl*, get a *koromisl*, until one of them brought the shoulder yoke used to carry buckets of water. Grasping one end of the wooden yoke, a peasant woman pushed the other end down to Anna and told her to hold on to it. A few young men had come over to help, and as soon as Anna had gripped the yoke with both hands, they began to pull her up.

Meanwhile, a boy about twelve had climbed down to help, and Anna thought she felt him push her feet up, but she was in such a hurry to run home that she was not sure if that really had happened. Her rescuers didn't ask her why she had been running. There was little time to ask, because as soon as the beet harvesters had pulled and pushed her up from the ditch, she flew away, catching sight, as she ran, of a woman lopping off the head of a sugar beet with one swing of her hatchet.

A dirt road led in the direction of the fairgrounds, and Anna knew that the fairgrounds were not far from her grandmother's house. She ran all the way home, crossing the cobblestoned street, running up the hill, and bursting into the house. Barely able to catch her breath, she rested until she had recovered enough to tell the family that Shevchenko had been chasing her with a gun. Her mother, Leya, and her grandmother had no reaction to her story. Leya did notice that Anna was no longer carrying the milk pan. She asked where it was, upset because it was the last pan she had left. Anna could have been killed, but her mother could only let herself worry about the lost milk pan.

Anna never walked to the farm of Domakho for milk again, nor did she ever again see the beet harvesters. Less than a week after she was chased by the partisan leader Shevchenko, the town was occupied by the Bolsheviks that he had been so eager to learn about. Having earlier captured Kiev, Ukraine's capital, eighty miles to the north, they had finally reached Korsun.[3]

Leya was desperate to escape after nearly five wartime years of struggling to survive and keep her family safe. She had long been preparing to flee Korsun. Her only hope lay in being able to take her daughters to America. Early in September 1919, in the same week when Shevchenko had chased her, Anna left Korsun with her mother and her two sisters, on their way to America.

They were still waiting for the train when a young man came over to Anna. She didn't know him, but he told her he was a member of a self-defense organization formed to protect Korsun's Jews from pogroms.

He said, You must be the Spector girl that Shevchenko ran after.

Then Anna heard the young man say, Don't worry, he'll never run after anybody again. We killed him.

Eighty years later, Anna still remembered how she felt when she heard that the older brother of her best school friend, Shevchenko, had been killed. I felt sorry for her. Oh, now I remember! Nadia was her name. Nadia Shevchenko, such a lovely girl.

2
The Town

Anna's hometown of Korsun was too large to be called a village (a *dorf* in Yiddish), and too small to be called a city (a *shtodt*), but it was large enough to be called a small town, a *shtetl*. Korsun was a typical shtetl—a small market town in which Jews form a substantial proportion of the population.[1]

Korsun was a town of scattered, small hills, as though its two bordering rivers—one on the east and another on the west—had squeezed the earth between them, thrusting the land upward here and there. The town was home to some ten thousand people. Its population was evenly split—about as many Jews as Gentiles.

The land was also split, into four roughly equal quadrants or quarters, by the two major roads—one running east to west, the other north to south—which met to form the crossroads at the center of the town. The cobblestoned main street ran from east to west. It started at the Ros River, which formed the eastern boundary of the town, and it ran to the smaller, unnamed river forming the western boundary.

The north to south road, the palace road, led from the twin-towered palace of Korsun's princess at the northern edge of town to the Christian cemetery at the southern edge. This palace road was paved with cobblestones only from the palace to the crossroads; its southern half was a dirt road.[2]

Shops, stores, and public buildings lined both sides of the main street, as well as the cobblestoned part of the palace road, and, more sparsely, the dirt section of the palace road. The large homes—built of timber and stucco in white, or occasionally light green or pink, and having wood floors—of most of the wealthy families, both Jewish and Gentile, were also distributed along both streets.

Neither of the cobblestoned streets was quite wide enough for two carriages. If a carriage going one way met a carriage coming the other way, it
usually had to stop. If Anna was walking on the street and heard a carriage
coming, she had to step off the cobblestones onto the dirt to get out of
the way.

3
Grandmother Beyla

Even though Anna's Grandmother Beyla seemed healthy when she was born, her parents gave her a double name, Khaya Beyla. The name Khaya, meaning "to live" in Hebrew, was often given to girls when they became seriously ill, to ensure recovery. Her parents' purpose in adding the name Khaya was to provide an amulet to keep away the Angel of Death, who had already carried off so many of Beyla's infant brothers and sisters. The amulet worked. She survived.

The parents had only two children who outlived childhood—Beyla and her brother Mendel. So important was Mendel to his parents that they would not send him to the elementary school, the *kheyder*, where he would normally have received a Jewish education. They had already sent their first two sons to that school. Each son in turn was exposed to a fatal infectious disease and died at age four or five years. The parents came to associate *kheyder* with death. Despite their piety, they could not risk yet another son to a religious education. Mendel grew up with a knowledge of Jewish religious practices so slim that when Beyla married, her husband would sneer that her brother might as well be a goy, a non-Jew.

Beyla was born and grew up in her parents' big house on the hill overlooking the east-west cobblestoned street, the main street of Korsun. She spent much of her married life in a duplex nearby, but when a fire partly destroyed it in 1912, she and her husband moved to the house on the hill, and there she died in 1923, when she was in her early sixties.

Her father was an important Hasid in Korsun, a member of the Hasidic branch of Judaism, and Beyla's mother was the daughter of a Hasidic spiritual leader, a *rebbe*, so Beyla grew up with all the Hasidic rituals and practices. It was unusual for a girl to go to *kheyder*, or to be given any formal education. Beyla taught herself to read Hebrew and Yiddish.

Her parents arranged her marriage to Avrum Steinberg, a young Hasid whose religious learning made him a suitable match for their daughter. Wed in her mid-teens, she soon delivered the first of her thirteen boys and girls, only six of whom survived infancy, all daughters.

Because she was very ill with a high fever after she delivered the first surviving daughter, Beyla could not nurse the little girl. The family finally found a gypsy who had a baby of her own and who agreed to nurse the new Steinberg baby, Khana. One day, when the woman's milk supply seemed not enough, she improvised a procedure that stilled Khana's crying. She took one of Beyla's goats that was nursing a kid, made the animal lie down next to the doorstep, and put Khana to the goat's nipple. The infant sucked successfully, and with a source of milk assured, thrived. The dam became accustomed to this routine and would lie down at the threshold of the house when the baby was carried out. Khana loved this particular goat. Even when she was three years old, and had stopped nursing long ago, the animal would come and lie down at the threshold. Whether it had anything to do with her diet of goat's milk, no one knew, but Khana turned out to be the healthiest of the six children.

Beyla's husband, Avrum, taught biblical commentary (*Gemara*), to the more advanced students in a religious school, the local free *kheyder* called the Talmud Torah, but his salary was small. Beyla bore not only the children, but also the burden of earning enough money to feed and clothe her husband, herself, and their six daughters. Her father left her some money, and she turned herself into a businesswoman, buying wholesale lots of merchandise, mainly foodstuffs from farmers, and selling them to Korsun's princess. The palace social calendar included birthday parties, wedding feasts, and holiday celebrations for the royal family and for the retainers. Beyla's reputation for honest dealing earned her a busy career as a purveyor.

While she carried on her wholesale business, Beyla reared her six daughters and saw each one marry in turn. Khana, who had been nursed by the goat, married and moved thirty-six miles away to her husband's hometown, Tarashcha, and there she raised a family of five children.

Beyla's second daughter, Mekhli, was a more modern woman than her mother. Her inability to read Russian did not stop her from reading Tolstoy and other Russian writers translated into Yiddish, and she also read the emerging popular Yiddish literature, the stories of the pen-named masters, Mendele the Bookseller (Sholom Yakov Abramovitsh) and Sholom Aleichem. Mekhli and her next sister, Sura, were able to emigrate to New York to live with their new husbands, because Beyla gave each of them a dowry of money specifically intended to pay the passage of husband and wife to America. Both young men, soon to be of military age, had married primarily for the dowry that would take them forever out of the reach of the tsar's army, a decision that was common and sensible.

Compulsory military service was a longstanding problem for the Jewish community. To eradicate the Jews of Russia, Tsar Nicholas I began in 1827 to conscript Jewish boys into the army at age twelve, transport them to remote camps (cantons), and torture them to force them to convert to Christianity. Many boys died on the long trip to the camp. Of the survivors, many converted.

Russian law held the governing council (the *kahal*) in each Jewish community responsible to meet quotas, forcing the Jewish elders to send the children to possible apostasy or death. "Catchers" (*khapers*), themselves Jewish, were paid to take children from their mothers, even those under the lawful age of twelve.[1]

Only after thirty-one compulsory years in the army did the surviving men, called *Nikolai soldaten* ("Nicholas's soldiers"), return. Purposely deprived of any Jewish education, they did not know what "kosher" meant. Some could no longer speak Yiddish; others had even forgotten the town of their birth. They were treated as outcasts. Even the poorest religious family in Korsun would not give a daughter in marriage to one of Nicholas's soldiers.[2]

Seven years after the first *Nikolai soldaten* edict, a rumor held that a new law would ban all Jewish marriages, thereby leaving every Jewish male open to conscription. Until the law took effect, the unfounded rumor said, Jewish males would be allowed to marry and avoid conscription. Jewish parents rushed to marry their children in their early teens. The conscription of *Nikolai soldaten* ended in 1856, but in Anna's day the bride and groom were still commonly in their early teens, and both might even be twelve. The marriage contract could place the couple in the home of the bride's parents, fully supported, for a specified number of years.

Beyla's fourth daughter, Feyga, who married Beryl, a vendor of honey and beeswax, lived in a small house about a quarter of a block from Beyla's big house on the hill. Feyga's house had a thatched roof and looked, to Anna, like a warehouse, probably the warehouse in which Beyla had stored her merchandise when she was in the catering business. Anna and her sisters often visited there, assured of a warm welcome by their aunt.

The fifth daughter was Anna's mother, Leya. Like Beyla, she would become the strength and support of her family.

Meyndl, Beyla's sixth and youngest surviving daughter, lived with her parents, and kept house for them. Her husband, Yankl, had been taken into the Russian army. Eventually Meyndl received a telegram saying that he was missing in action. He never returned.

Though Beyla had successfully reared six daughters, and had built a business that had supported the family, she believed that her life had value because she was the wife of a man of religious learning. Her tradition taught her that she was married to a man who was carrying out that most important *mitzveh,* the commandment of the Torah to spend his life studying and teaching the word of God. She was participating in the holy work by freeing him to study. For the honor of participating, she bore her burdens willingly. She looked forward to the promised reward that when they died and went to heaven, Avrum would sit among the elite, and she would be a footstool under his feet.[3]

Almost the entire population of the town lived in the two northern quarters of Korsun. The northeast quarter, called "Old Town," contained two sections, side by side. The predominantly Jewish section extended from the palace road eastward. Beyla and Avrum lived here. Where the Jewish section ended, the predominantly Christian section began, extending from there to the Ros River.

In the Christian section of Old Town, several landowners lived in attractive houses with fine gardens, some extending to the Ros River. In the rest of this section, a larger number of poor peasants rented smaller houses, with small garden farms. Many of these tenant farms made up the outskirts of the town, near the edge of the granite cliff where irregular, stair-step rocks led down to the sandy beach of the Ros River. Several Jewish families lived in this Christian section of Old Town.

In the Jewish section of Old Town stood an irregular cluster of the five prayer buildings of the Jewish community. Most of the houses in the Jewish section were small, but several larger ones were scattered among them. In most of the homes, both small and large, lived Jewish families, but in one of the larger ones, for example, lived the young priest of the Orthodox Church. He lived closer to the five Jewish houses of prayer than to his own church with its onion-bulb spires immediately south of the palace. Four doors away from the young priest lived Anna's Grandmother Beyla, in the house overlooking main street. From her big house on the hill, Beyla could look out on the comings and goings on the cobblestoned road, much as she looked out on the Jewish community of Korsun.

Beyla did not sit idle while she awaited her place in heaven. She was busy with her own holy work as a leader, counselor, arbiter, intermediary, and religious role model in her community. Although a woman traditionally consulted the rabbi for guidance in religious matters, many women in Beyla's community preferred to take their personal and private concerns to Beyla. Troubled women would come to her house, where they would sit and talk with her, sometimes inside, other times on the porch. Although Anna knew that she was not to intrude when her grandmother had a visitor, she would catch a glimpse here, a snatch of conversation there, and she would see a woman start to cry as she told her story to Beyla. Eventually Beyla would say to the woman, God will help. The woman would seem to feel comforted when she left the house.

Quarreling vendors also came to see Beyla. Arguments were bound to happen in the marketplace. Women did much of the selling, and when two women could not resolve a difficulty by themselves, they brought the problem to Beyla for her advice.

The conflicts might be more serious. When a young Jewish woman was keeping company with a young Gentile man, the parents would ask Beyla to talk her out of it. A young Jewish woman fell in love with a young Gentile neighbor, and the two were about to elope when her parents found out and rushed to Beyla for help. Beyla, who knew the young man's parents, was able to establish communication between the two families, so that the marriage could be called off. Beyla knew a number of Christians of her own age, and they respected her, making her an apt intermediary.

Early in the war, when many people fled from the German invasion of Russia, Beyla took in three refugees from a town near Minsk, the capital city of the neighboring province. Grandfather Avrum moved beds into the formal living room, allowing the refugees to live there for a year.

Another time, a destitute old woman needed a place to live. She had married a widower, taking on the responsibility for his children, but after the husband died and after his children had grown up and left, she was alone in the world, searching for a way to support herself. Beyla took the widow in, giving her a small room with a bed and a table. The widow began to make poppy-seed candy, selling it in front of the fancy stores in the open area of the marketplace where women sold whatever they could, spreading their wares on a blanket or on the ground. After she had been selling it for a time, a man who bought ready-made candy began competing with her. The widow was losing too much income. Beyla saw this as unfair. Anna did not know whether Beyla spoke to the authorities or went directly to the man, but the next week he closed his stand in the market, leaving the old woman to sell her candy in peace.

As much as Beyla was loved and admired for these virtues by many in the Jewish community, she was feared and even despised by others. Those who loved and admired her had good reason, for she was a generous woman whose honesty, piety, and religious conformity set a high standard. But Beyla was a zealot for the strict observance of the biblical commandments. Those who feared or despised her also had good reason, for she insisted that everyone live up to the example of her behavior.

Beyla kept one eye on the women of her congregation to spot any deviations from strict observance. If a housewife discovered a neighbor's lapse from keeping a strictly kosher kitchen, she told Beyla, who had a word with the culprit. If Beyla was informed that a woman didn't go to the ritual bath, the *mikveh*, every month, she considered it a terrible sin and told the sinner so.

One Friday afternoon, when Anna was at the house of a friend, the girl's mother was upset because the family's preparations for the start of the Sabbath were going too slowly. The mother anxiously told her daughter to hurry, because Beyla would soon pass by the house and see that they had not yet lit the Sabbath candles. Until that moment, Anna had only known and admired her grandmother as a pillar of the community. Now she was embarrassed, seeing at first hand how Beyla wielded power and inspired fear. Beyla was a sun to her community, a sun whose light nourished many lives but whose heat was so intense that it was in danger of withering others.

The children in her family, however, saw a softer side of Beyla. Anna's love of reading was fostered by her grandmother, the only one in the family who told the children stories or read aloud to them. Anna especially admired Beyla for having taught herself to read.

Beyla was a busy woman who didn't seem to have much time for the children, but Anna remembered fondly the times spent with her. As Beyla's life could not be separated from her religion, so the activities that Anna shared with her grandmother were almost always a part of the religious life, but they usually involved storytelling. Curiously, the only nonreligious activity also involved storytelling.

On Saturday afternoons—on the Sabbath day of rest—Beyla would nap after the noon dinner, the "warm meal." On awakening she would gather her five grandchildren who still lived in Korsun, and she would read to them the chapter of the Bible prescribed for that week. Anna drank in the Bible stories of the Torah, the Five Books of Moses, and convinced herself that she never had to read them again because she remembered everything that came to her in the voice of her grandmother.

Beyla upheld the old ways in religion—she would not read the modern Yiddish stories by Sholom Aleichem and his peers—but sometimes she would gather her grandchildren to tell them tales from *The Thousand and One Nights*—those tales that include Sinbad the Sailor, Ali Baba and the Forty Thieves, and Scheherazade. How Beyla had even been exposed to these stories of the "Arabian Nights," tales so distant from her religious tradition, was a delightful mystery to Anna.[4]

Anna was allowed to accompany Beyla to shul on four or five occasions, each time sitting next to her grandmother. Beyla led the women in her shul, all of whom sat upstairs in their own gallery, by tradition segregated and hidden from the glances of the men downstairs, but able to hear their voices reading in Hebrew. Having taught herself to read both Hebrew and Yiddish, Beyla was the only one able to read the prayer book and the Bible. She was the "sayer," the *zogerin,* for the thirty or forty women in the congregation. They sat on their chairs, listening as she read aloud to them in Yiddish from the *Sedra,* in a women's Torah volume.

In spite of Beyla's high position among the women in shul, she was also a close friend to several of them. One of these was Oodl Slivnik, the mother of the wealthiest Jewish man in town. Oodl and Beyla were both about the same age as the princess, all of them members of the older generation. Oodl ran her own prestigious store that catered to the wealthy women of the princess's estate. She traveled to Poland and to other countries to import fancy clothing accessories.

Though Beyla and Oodl could have worn silks and fine woolens, they both preferred simple, dignified clothes. Beyla had a varied wardrobe, but typically might be dressed in a navy blue blouse with pearl buttons and a matching skirt long enough to hide every part of her black, high-buttoned shoes except for the toes and the "spool" heels. Like most women of her age, she had stopped wearing a wig to shul, but she still kept her cropped gray hair hidden under a white muslin nightcap, made with an elastic band to keep any stray locks of hair from showing. A strip of lace at the front of the cap hid her brow as well. Draped across the top of the cap to cover the upper part of the lace strip, and tied under her chin, was a triangle of delicate, off-white silk, worked in an elegant, flowered brocade pattern. Only Jewish women wore this scarf.

Beyla had never been a beauty—in fact the opposite. Now, like most women in their fifties, she was outwardly old, but if life had turned her hair gray, stolen her teeth, and deeply lined her face, it had not sapped her energy or dulled her spirit. The two friends, Beyla and Oodl, each an inch or two over five feet tall, both of them pious women and successful entrepreneurs, would walk to shul together, engrossed in conversation.

Leya, with her daughters, had already been in America for a year when she received a letter telling of her mother's death and funeral in Korsun, but the story of the arrangements for Beyla's burial had begun many years before. Young adults customarily prepared for their own burial. Buying a length of beautiful linen, Beyla had brought together her women friends for a shroud-making party. They ate, and they sewed, and then she danced in her new-made shroud. Afterward, she stored it in the attic. This was in the good times. Then in the time of the pogroms, Oodl Slivnik was murdered, and they had to bury her on a Friday at noon. There was no time to make a shroud, because otherwise they would have to keep her until Sunday. They went to Beyla's house on the hill, and she gave them her own shroud for Oodl.

Afterward, Oodl's son, a merchant who traveled widely, brought back for Beyla the most beautiful linens she had ever seen. And they had another party and sewed another shroud for her. And when another pogrom came, the first thing the looters took was her linen shroud. And she said, Let them take it; I am still here. And when she died, they had to bury her in a burlap sack.

4
Grandfather Avrum

Anna's Grandmother Beyla married Grandfather Avrum not for love, but for *yikhes*. *Yikhes* meant pedigree, the history of a "good" family. A family was judged good by the Jewish community if it could boast a religious scholar (or a philanthropist) in its lineage. The greater the number of generations of such scholars, and the greater their renown, the greater the *yikhes*. However, a man could acquire his own *yikhes* if he was a religious scholar or a benefactor.

Avrum, chosen by Beyla's parents through a matchmaker, had his own *yikhes*, that of a student at a yeshiva, a Hebrew religious college. Beyla's father had acquired a certain degree of *yikhes* for himself by marrying the daughter of a rabbi. Besides, he was a wealthy man, and wealth allowed him to acquire his own *yikhes* by giving to charity and by supporting religious learning in the community. Such a man commonly added to his store of *yikhes* by finding a learned man—such as Avrum—to marry his daughter.

Avrum married Beyla and took up his life as a husband, going to live in his bride's town, as did many newly married men. He found work as a schoolteacher, a *melamed,* at Korsun's free school. His pupils were the sons of families too poor to pay for a private school education, and his small salary was paid by the Jewish community organization, which financed the free school. The school was located in the poorhouse, the *hekdesh,* another local institution supported by the charity of the Jewish community.

The Korsun poorhouse was neither ramshackle nor run-down like those in many other towns, but a decent building, adequately built to take care of a social need. Although most of the Jews in Korsun were poor, the beggars were the poorest of the poor, the homeless people of those times. They had usually come to Korsun from another town to beg in anonymity, knowing that the poorhouse would give them shelter.

Avrum was not one of the unlearned variety of *melamed*, men of whom it was often said that they teach the ABCs to the youngest boys because they can't make a living doing anything else. When Avrum first arrived in Korsun, he taught biblical commentary, *Gemara*, to boys eight to twelve years old in the free school. By the time Anna was in high school, he had risen to the highest position in his field, teaching at the Korsun yeshiva, the religious academy where young men from age thirteen to twenty studied rabbinic literature as well as the Talmud. Of those who studied at a yeshiva, some would leave school as well-educated laymen, just as Avrum had done. Others would be ordained, earning the title of "rabbi," a title meaning "my master" in Hebrew, and designating a man qualified to decide questions of Jewish law.

Most parents could not afford to send their sons on to a yeshiva, sending them out instead to find work as soon as they had finished school. Some gave their sons over to artisans as apprentices to learn a trade. Others brought them into a family business, but since that business was likely to be barely enough to live on already, it was like inviting a guest to share a meal of stale bread and plain hot water.

Avrum's daily routine was well established by the time Anna was old enough to notice it. He left the big house on the hill for the morning prayers before the darkness of night had faded, walking the four or five blocks to the house of prayer and yeshiva, then coming home, as most men did, for the noon meal, the most substantial fare of the day. In the afternoon he walked back for more teaching and prayers. With his blond hair and full blond beard, Avrum reminded Anna of the pictures she had seen of a saint, even though his blond mustache was mixed with gray in his old age and was slightly discolored on one side, the mark of a snuff taker. He was a Hasid. The Hasidic branch had been founded as a revolt against excessively scholarly Judaism. It held that the religiously ignorant were no less worthy than the learned, and that although prayer and the keeping of the commandments were proper goals, a pure heart was to be preferred over study. It prescribed joyful worship, with dancing and the singing of songs, because evil desire can be bested only by joy, and man can be brought close to God by melody.[1]

Avrum did not agree with the more modern Hasidim, who had taken to wearing western-style suits and might even hide their long earlocks by combing them behind their ears. Even worse were those men who shaved off both beard and earlocks. He was a Hasid of the old-fashioned kind, letting his earlocks drop alongside his cheeks, one spiraling curl in front of each ear, and wearing the standard Hasidic attire, copied by the first Hasidim in the eighteenth century from the historic dress worn by Polish noblemen.

Anna found her grandfather always to be neat and well dressed. Everything he wore was black except for his white shirt and socks—black hat, black vest, black cravat, black trousers held up by black suspenders, black above-ankle-length frock coat, and black shoes. In summer the black shoes were made of elastic, rubberized cloth. In winter Avrum wore black boots made of good leather, boots that were pulled on by grasping the strap, or "ear," that grew out of the highest part of the boot on each side. From this kind of boot, Anna would later learn, came the English expression "pulling yourself up by your bootstraps."

His vest buttoned down the front. On either side of the buttons were pockets, in one of which Avrum kept his pipe tobacco. In another he carried a fancy snuffbox, made especially for the powdered tobacco used to induce a pleasurable sneeze. In a third vest pocket he kept his gold-cased pocket watch, anchored by its gold chain, a standard pair of engagement gifts to a groom from his in-laws-to-be.

The long frock coat, the *kapote,* was made of either alpaca wool or gabardine to wear well. The two tails of the *kapote* fell from the level of two cloth-covered waist buttons at the back, one on either side but close to the midline, and in each tail was an oversize pocket, invisible from the outside. Avrum kept a large handkerchief, about two feet square, in one of the pockets. When he went to a joyous ceremony such as a circumcision, a bris, he would slip cookies into these pockets to bring home for Anna and her two sisters.

Like other Orthodox Jewish men, Avrum always wore a yarmulke, a skullcap, from the moment he awoke until the moment he went to bed. On weekdays in summer, a visored cap of thin, porous fabric covered the skullcap. On Saturday, the Sabbath, Avrum, like other common folk, wore a plain derby hat of stiff, black felt. In contrast, the fur-trimmed *shtrayml* was only worn by the officials of the Hasidic community such as the *rov* (the town rabbi), the *rebbe* (a "righteous man," leader of a dynasty of Hasidim), and perhaps the *dayan* (the judge of the community's religious court). The *shtrayml* consisted of a skullcap (like a yarmulke) of cloth or velvet, from whose rim rose a band of fur—beaver, mink, or even sable— five inches tall, hugging the head all around.

Anna knew almost nothing about Avrum's family except for one story. Avrum's mother had been invited to a wedding in another town. The occasion must have been important to her, probably the wedding of a close relative, because she was prepared to attend even though it took place in winter, when snowstorms were unpredictable, and when the only way to get there was by horse-drawn sleigh. She left town in a sleigh driven by a coachman, but never returned. In the spring, she and her driver were found in the sleigh, lost and frozen to death.

Teaching neither occupied all of Avrum's time nor satisfied all of his yearnings, which were both artistic and altruistic. He had good hands as well as a good head, and he used both to serve the poor. One of his good deeds was to serve as a scribe. Every Jewish community had an official scribe, who was one of the seven paid functionaries hired by the Jewish town council, the *kahal,* an organization of wealthy men who ran the community. One of the scribe's duties was to restore the integrity of the small parchment scroll that every Jew displayed, as the Bible commanded, on the doorposts of his house in the mezuzah, a metal or wooden case. Two passages from Deuteronomy were written on the scroll. Twice in every seven years a scribe was to inspect the scroll to make sure that time had not smudged or erased any of the Hebrew writing. The poor people of Korsun preferred to come to Avrum rather than go to the official scribe, because Avrum did not charge for this service.

Another of Avrum's good deeds was to write prayers for women in childbirth, who commonly used paper amulets to keep the Angel of Death away from their newborns. The prayers were especially important if the woman had lost other infants, as was often the case. Anna saw this practice when her aunt Meyndl was in labor. The women of the family pushed the bed against a wall, then hung sheets from ceiling wires to make a privacy curtain for the other three sides. On the sheets they hung pieces of paper, each containing a *molitva,* the Russian word for a prayer.

Avrum wrote these prayers gratis. When a relative of an expectant mother came to the big house on the hill asking for a *molitva,* he would write out a standard prayer, adding the name of the woman in labor in the proper place, thereby letting the Angel of Death know that this particular woman was to be spared. Once Anna saw a boy of about twelve years consult Avrum, bringing a piece of paper with the name written on it. Avrum became angry when the boy spoke the name, because the boy said something different from the name on the paper. The writer may have made a mistake, and Avrum, who could not be sure which name was correct, was upset at the possibility that he might be writing a blessing with the wrong name in it, for in that case the Angel of Death would not know that this mother was to be spared.

Anna would see Avrum in the formal living room, sitting at his table, which served as a desk, writing these blessings with his quill pen. She and her generation were already using the replaceable metal pen tip, the nib, whose arciform shank was inserted into an identically curved slot in the tip of a wooden penholder. Avrum, however, never used a pen of metal, making his own from the quill of a goose feather, painstakingly sharpening one end into a point with the blade of his pocketknife.

But he was not only a scribe. Yet another of his good deeds was the carving of inscriptions on tombstones for people who could not afford to pay. He began the work on each monument at home, plotting on paper the words and the designs to be carved. That done, he took the paper and his tools to the Jewish cemetery to do the carving. He did most of his work on summer afternoons, when the longer daylight gave him more time after his pupils left school for the day.

Nor was he only altruistic. The best expression of Avrum's artistic side was his hobby of engraving designs such as birds and fruits on a pane of glass, then adding a background of colored candle wax until he had entirely disguised the glass surface, transforming it into a picture. Anna never saw that kind of work again. He must have given all the panes away, because even though he kept making more, they did not accumulate in the house. To Anna, who found the glass pictures beautiful, it was inconceivable that no example of Avrum's artistry ever graced her grandmother's house, but it was a house in which the only decoration hanging on the walls was a single picture of the Baal Shem Tov, the revered founder of Hasidism.

Through his glass picture hobby, Avrum became a good friend of Alter Koslov, who had been his pupil in biblical commentary studies and who was now an artist of wide reputation. Later, shortly after Avrum had died, Koslov's standing helped Anna's family when they needed a good deed.

Avrum had a nook at one end of the attic of his house, a place where he could stretch out on the floor, a place where he could enjoy solitary relaxation. Sometimes in the early afternoon, after he had finished teaching for the day, he would climb the ladder to his nook, to read or perhaps take a nap. The attic was so hot during the summer that Avrum hired workmen to remove the tin roof, replacing it with unglazed tile to keep it cooler.

When Grandfather Avrum was in the attic, his grandchildren were not to go near the ladder, for fear of disturbing him. Although the children had no trouble clambering up the crude rungs resembling pieces of mop handles, Anna wondered how her grandfather, at his age, was able to manage the ladder time after time without injuring himself. Having reached the attic, Avrum had to crouch under the slanting sides of the roof unless he was more nearly under the peak, but the attic was as long and as wide as the house itself, giving him plenty of space for his nook at the front end, where a large window in the triangular upper part of the outside wall let in enough light for him to read his books.

The books were illegal. He kept them in a box that he covered with rags and straw to disguise and hide them. Everybody in the family knew that his box in the attic contained banned books. Avrum owned books of Jewish mysticism called Kaballah, as well as the writings of Josephus, a general in the first-century Jewish revolt against Rome, who authored a history of the Jews.

Anna didn't know who had banned Josephus and Kaballah, or why, but she knew that her grandfather hid them because in the tsars' times the police arrested people for having them. If there were to be a raid, all the men who owned these illegal books knew about it in minutes, mysteriously, without using telephones. One time, for example, the house suddenly became dark. Men were in the house, moving things, hiding the books in the cellar. The raiders did not come to search the house.[2]

During the German occupation of Korsun in 1918, one of their wounded soldiers from the hospital, a Jewish boy, came to visit Grandfather Avrum in the summer, on a day when the doors of the big house on the hill were open. It was after the revolution, so the two of them were not afraid of a police raid as they crawled up into the attic. When Avrum gave the soldier some Kaballah books to take back to the hospital to read, he was so interested and excited that he couldn't thank Avrum enough.

It was not strange that Avrum should treasure the books of the Kaballah. They were central to the beliefs of the Hasidic sect, founded in the first half of the 1700s by the saintly Israel ben Eliezer. Israel had earned the epithet "Baal Shem," meaning "Master of the Name," signifying that through the mystic ideas of Kaballah he had been able to master the secret and unutterable name of God. From this mastery, Israel gained the power to work miracles.

As important as Avrum's upstairs activities were, though, the whole attic could not be given over to him, because Grandmother Beyla kept geese there. Other women also thought an attic was a convenient place to keep fowl. Khayka, the woman who ran the notions store at the center of town, told Anna that instead of letting her chickens go in and out of the house, she kept them in the attic, where it was easier for her to find the eggs they laid.

Besides serving as Avrum's sanctuary and the home of Beyla's geese, the attic was used for general storage and for drying clothes. Wet clothes were hung in the attic in the winter and, if necessary, in the summer. Rope clotheslines were strung from hooks inserted into the wooden framework, a common practice because no one had outdoor clotheslines. In summer, clothes were dried on rocks at the riverside before being brought home. Some clothes were then hung on a fence at home, or on a neighbor's fence. If more time was needed for drying, the clothes were moved from the fence to the attic. In winter, clothes were washed only once or twice. They were washed at the river, wrung out, and then taken home to be placed in the attic, where they were draped over the clotheslines. No one had clothespins. When Anna would go into the attic a few days after a batch of clothes had been hung in winter, she would find them frozen stiff. Eventually in the warmth of the house lent by the generous kitchen oven, the clothes thawed, and in about a week they were dry.[3]

The storm windows were stored either in the attic or in the shed during the warm weather. Also kept in the attic were the dishes that had been made kosher for Passover, together with the *zhlikta,* the hollowed tree-trunk segment in which the table linens, towels, and certain garments for that holiday were cleansed with boiling water. Not every family had a *zhlikta*, but those who did were generous in lending them to neighbors when preparations for the holiday began.

Avrum had a workbench with his stone-carving tools at his end of the attic. Several suitcases and trunks of different sizes were stored nearby, old-style trunks made of woven branches. Almost all the townspeople packed this kind of trunk when they traveled, for modern trunks were not used in Korsun yet. Some of the woven trunks came with leather belts fitted with keyed locks, but Beyla's trunks, in which she kept feather-stuffed mattresses and blankets, had no locks.

Avrum never sat and talked with the women in the house, keeping busy instead with reading and writing, or with his good deeds and hobbies, meanwhile smoking his pipe. His one contribution to the day-to-day management of the household, as Anna saw it, was that he took care of the chiming wall clock, checking it now and then to keep it in good working order. Taking it down from the wall and placing it on the table in the formal living room, he would wind it, set it to the correct time, and adjust the hanging weights. If the clock stopped, he took it apart, made it run and ring properly, and put it back together. The grandchildren knew that nobody was supposed to go into the living room while he was doing the complicated work on the clock.

Avrum and Beyla seldom expressed their emotions, except during their frequent arguments. They fought mostly about his habit of hiding money. Korsun had a bank, viewed by Beyla, the successful businesswoman, as the place where money should be held in safekeeping. Instead, Avrum hid his money in books. He housed the books in a bookcase, locked the case, and kept the key. He divided the money—a few ruble notes in this book, a few in that one. (One ruble was worth fifty-one American cents.) These were not prayer books, of course, since neither money nor pictures are suitable for a holy book.

The arguments seemed one-sided, because Avrum would yell at Beyla, but Anna never heard Beyla raise her voice. Anna wondered whether there was more to the arguments than the fact that Avrum entrusted his teaching wages to a book instead of a bank. Perhaps it was his failure to contribute his earnings to the household, except when he had to give up some money because one of his daughters was being married. Avrum spent his money on other things, she thought, donating to his Hasidic *rebbe*, his spiritual leader. When the pogroms began, Avrum's hiding places were discovered, because the looters knew enough to shake books until the ruble notes fell out. By that time, however, the paper money had become worthless.

Anna saw another kind of confrontation between Avrum and Beyla. During the world war, when Russian young men were hiding from the army, Avrum's sister, who lived in another town, was looking for a place to hide her son. She sent him to Grandmother Beyla, who told him she couldn't hide another fugitive safely because she was already hiding her son-in-law Yankl and her nephew Zavl. Avrum wanted to help the young man, but what could he do? He was contending with both his daughter Meyndl—it was her husband, Yankl, who was hiding in the house—and his wife. In this instance Beyla had the last word.

Having long been ill and in pain, growing thinner and thinner from stomach cancer, Avrum died in the summer of 1919. Not long before Avrum died, Anna was given a job tilling the garden of the priest, for which she was paid a loaf of bread each day. Although she had been deeply affected by her beloved grandfather's suffering, she was also worrying about Mayna, concerned that her little sister might become ill or even die from starvation under the severe conditions of the civil war. One day she saw Avrum holding a piece of the bread that she had earned with her digging, bread she had hidden to save for Mayna.

She grabbed the bread from her grandfather and gave it to Mayna, who had nothing to eat. Anna knew instinctively that a child had a greater claim on scarce food than an old man who was dying. She would continue to believe that she had made the correct decision, but the sadness of the situation would haunt her.

5
Aaron and Leya

Anna's mother, Leya, was an ordinary woman. She was the fifth surviving daughter born to Avrum and Beyla, and the fifth daughter to wed. She was married in Korsun at age nineteen to Aaron Spector, who was five or six years older.

Although both of Leya's parents were Hasidim and Aaron was not, he was a pious young man. He was not wealthy, or even mildly prosperous, but he was continuing his father's business as a jobber of glassware, selling the three glass objects in common use—drinking glasses, chimneys for coal oil lamps, and beer bottles. He paid peasants to drive him to the Alita factory near Kiev, wrap the glassware in straw (some of the wares broke on the trip anyhow), and deliver them to towns in the Korsun area, where Aaron sold them to stores. The beer bottles went to the Jewish-owned brewery in Korsun. He also sold his glassware for a time from a stall in the Korsun marketplace.

Aaron left his hometown of Vinograd, thirty-four miles southwest of Korsun, and the newlyweds moved into the other half of Grandmother Beyla's duplex. Beyla had established, as a dowry, the custom that each of her daughters should live rent-free in the duplex for a time, moving in when they married, and moving out as soon as the next sister married. During six years in the duplex, Leya gave birth to two of her three daughters—Anna in 1905, and Gussie three years later. Although the affairs of the Jewish community were administered by its own governing body, the birth of each Jewish child was registered both by the tsar's government and by the Jewish community. The father told the details about his newborn child to the crown rabbi—an official of the tsarist government whose duties included issuing marriage licenses and divorces, registering births and deaths, and swearing in witnesses at trials—who then registered the birth with the Russian government at the Korsun courthouse.[1] The infant was given its Yiddish name on the Sabbath at shul, where the beadle (the *shammes*) inscribed the name in the record sooner or later.[2]

In the summer of 1910, when Meyndl, the youngest of Beyla's daughters, married and took over the dowry half of the duplex, Leya and Aaron found a room in the house of Sura (Sarah), a young dressmaker whose husband was in the army. Sarah's house was not in the northeast quarter near Beyla's duplex, but in the northwest quarter, in the other predominantly Jewish neighborhood. Caring for one baby and expecting another, Sarah was managing by adding the rent money to the little she earned by sewing for peasants. Anna helped her by turning the wooden wheel that powered the sewing machine, stopping whenever Sarah reached over to touch her arm. While she turned the wheel, Anna tried to learn how to sew by paying attention to what Sarah did.

At the end of the second year with Sarah, Leya gave birth to Mayna, her third and last Korsun-born child. Mayna's Yiddish name was Mekhli, but Sarah said she needed a fancy Russian name and began to call her Mayna.

Leya was still in bed—women were usually confined to bed for ten days after childbirth—when, through her window, she heard someone yelling that Avrum and Beyla's duplex was on fire. Although no one was hurt in the fire, one unit of the house was badly damaged. Since it was summer, Avrum, Beyla, and their son-in-law and daughter were able to live in the half of the house that was less damaged, for more than a month before moving into the big house on the main street where Beyla had grown up. Beyla bought the house from her brother, who had inherited it from their parents but who now made his home twenty miles away in the town of Boguslav. Avrum and Beyla would remain in this house for the rest of their lives.

Aaron's income, never large, had been dwindling for a long time. Over the years, the railroads had added stops at small towns, allowing businessmen to have their goods delivered by train from manufacturers in Kiev.[3] Aaron's services as a jobber were less and less in demand. Even before Mayna was born, he could only occasionally find a job lot of merchandise to bring in from Kiev, hiring a few peasant wagons to distribute it to other small towns. Then, in late 1912 he made some money unexpectedly, when Germany began to pay high prices for beet seeds.

Like many of the townsmen, Aaron scrambled to get his hands on as many seeds as he could in as short a time as possible. It was as though gold had been discovered, and everyone hurried to stake a claim. Aaron, though, having transported glassware for years, knew where to rent wagons and horses and how to pick up and deliver goods. He made more of the quick money than most.[4]

The beet seed money gave Aaron a nest egg—enough money that he and Leya could now realistically discuss their two dreams. In one dream he would stay in Russia, and they would buy a house of their own in Korsun. In the other dream Aaron would immigrate to America, make more money there, and then send for his wife and their three girls. The First Balkan War had begun, heightening fears of a general European war, a war in which Russia seemed ready to fight as an ally of Serbia against Turkey. Aaron and Leya decided that he should go to America to avoid serving in the tsar's army.[5]

Meanwhile, they could afford to leave Sarah's room, renting their own half of a duplex nearby in the last months of 1912. Their new home had a clay floor in the kitchen-dining room, but it had the distinction lent by a "quarry tile" floor in the bedroom. Aaron's beet seed money was not enough, though, to take him to America as well as to provide for Leya and the three girls until he could send money to them. His oldest brother, Meyer, a wealthy man, gave him enough money to make up the difference.

This was not the first time that Aaron's family had helped him to avoid the tsar's draft. When he married in 1904, the disastrous war with Japan had begun in February and would last until September of the next year. Aaron was in his mid-twenties then and would have been in the tsar's army were it not for his father. When Aaron had reached the age of registration for induction into the Russian army, his father, Moyshe (Moses) Spector, had traveled to the induction center in Kanev, forty *versti* (twenty-seven miles) away. Instead of Aaron, though, Moyshe took along a crippled young man whom he had hired to deceive the authorities. He told them that the young man was his son. The authorities filled out a blue passport, stating that Aaron Spector was not eligible for the army. Many other fathers were doing the same for their sons.

Threatened by an informer, Moyshe managed to pay extortion money to prevent exposure, and Aaron remained safe from the draft. Moyshe carried out the same deception to prevent the induction of each of his four sons. By the time Aaron had earned his nest egg selling beet seeds to the Germans, however, his father had died, another war loomed, and no one could be sure that Aaron would be safe from a draft for this new, larger war.

Aaron was able to leave Korsun for America without arousing suspicion. He and his stepbrother, who was also distancing himself from the army, dressed themselves in their best clothes and stepped into a carriage in the daytime, when anyone could witness what they were doing. They had hired the carriage to take them out of town. When a neighbor asked where they were going, Leya said they were going to a wedding. Anna started to say, No, they're going to America, but Leya shushed her in time.[6]

In the spring of 1913, a few months after Aaron had left, Leya took the girls to the photographer on the palace road, the first shop north of the crossroads. The photographer had filled his window with sample pictures

Figure 2. A formal 1913 portrait of seven-year-old Anna
(standing on her mother Leya's right); her sister Gussie
(standing on Leya's left); and her sister Mayna (on Leya's
lap). (Courtesy Dien Family)

to attract customers, but Leya needed no inducement. She wanted to send
a picture to Aaron in America.

Leya, now twenty-seven, sat in the center, holding nine-month-old Mayna
on her lap. Wearing one of her two wedding dresses—the black one, in
which she had gone to religious services the day after her wedding—Leya
was enveloped from her neck to her toes. Her dark hair was pulled close to
the head and drawn back behind her ears. Blonde Mayna, her hair cut
short, with bangs, wore a long white dress and white shoes.[7]

The two older girls stood with their arms at their sides. Seven-year-old Anna was on her mother's right, and four-year-old Gussie on her left, each wearing plum-colored velveteen dresses with elbow-length sleeves, and with white silk trim at collar and elbow. They had worn these dresses to a wedding several months earlier. They both wore long black stockings and the customary high-button black shoes. Gussie's blonde hair was not as light as Mayna's, but was cut like hers. Anna's dark, wavy hair, also cut in bangs, fell at her ears to below her shoulders, with a white bow above each ear. No one smiled. The photographer had told Anna to smile, but she was thinking about her father in America, so her serious expression did not change.

Unseen in this formal picture are the little bags of camphor that Anna and her sisters wore on strings around the neck to protect them from illness at a time when it was not uncommon for mothers to lose half or more of their young children to infectious disease. A child whose mother had already lost infants might wear a second string holding a coin blessed by the rabbi.

A year and a half after Aaron had escaped to America, the big war began. Every week, another handful of Jewish men walked toward the railway station, on their way to be inducted into the army. Anna stood in the street to watch the first groups leave as women walked with their husbands and sons, or ran after them, crying. Anna's uncle and her two cousins were taken by the army, and so were Mr. Alushka, the master shoemaker, and other men whom Anna knew. They all disappeared in the direction of the induction center in Kanev.

Meanwhile, Anna's father was living safely in America, out of reach of the tsar's army, and had sent money back for several months. Then his letters and the money stopped. Anna's mother had no other income. After less than a year in the duplex with the quarry tile bedroom floor, she ran out of rent money. They moved in with Yenta Koslov.

6
The Surprise (1914–1916)

Yenta Koslov was not an ordinary woman. A good friend of Anna's Grandmother Beyla, Yenta was a well-to-do widow whose children had all grown up and moved out. She welcomed company in her house. Everyone benefited from the new arrangement when Leya and her three daughters moved in with Yenta. Leya and her daughters had a roof over their heads, while Yenta had another woman to talk to, as well as a house filled with the chattering of three little girls. Yenta treated all three girls as substitute grandchildren, but her favorite was Mayna, who was still a babe in arms.

Anna's family stayed with Yenta Koslov for three years, until the summer of 1916. Yenta lived in a European-style duplex on Korsun's main street. Built of wood, and with wooden floors, the house had the added luxury of a parquet floor in the living room. Leya and the three girls shared Yenta's kitchen but slept in their own large bedroom, while Yenta slept on a sofa in the living room. Her half of the duplex had no foyer, only a lean-to in which they kept the kitchen utensils.

Although no one was living in the other half of the duplex, its large foyer was still being used. It contained the workshop of Yenta's deceased husband, a wheelwright. Yenta's son-in-law, also a wheelwright, had taken over the business. He and his two helpers made wagon wheels of wood encased in rims of iron.

Yenta was not only a friend of Beyla, but also a neighbor. Their houses sat on hills opposite each other—Beyla's on her hilltop, Yenta's part way up her hill. One of Yenta's daughters lived farther up the slope. Yenta could walk out her back door into a beautiful garden, and from there to the daughter's house. Leya's family sometimes ate with Yenta, but for most of their meals they walked down the slope, crossed the cobblestoned street, and climbed all the way up the hill to Grandmother Beyla's house.

Anna never knew of another woman in Korsun like Yenta Koslov. For one thing, she was the cleanest woman in Anna's experience, then and later. Although she had neither running water nor washing machine, she always seemed to be wearing clothes that had just been washed and ironed, and everything that she touched was spotless. All the Hasidic women of her generation wore white muslin caps to cover their hair, but hers was the whitest and cleanest of all. In later years, whenever Anna saw something clean and folded and accurate, she thought of Yenta Koslov.

Already toothless and old enough to be called "Alta"—"the old one"—when Anna's family moved in, Yenta was still energetic, and she always seemed to add her own special touch to whatever she did. She kept exotic plants in a corner of her living room, including three trees—a date, a lemon, and a palm. From Yenta, Anna learned to love plants, and in Yenta, Anna first saw that a woman could arrange her life to her own taste.

Of Yenta's five children, three were also individualists. One of her two daughters, Reyzl (Rosie [little Rose], in Yiddish), was a designer who had created clothes for the entourage of Korsun's princess before moving to Kharkov, the second largest city in the Ukraine, where she was making high-fashion clothes for Gentile women. Yenta's oldest son, Alter, a painter famous in the Ukraine, had his studio in Kiev. Anna never met the middle son, who was apparently brilliant, because he was a career officer in the tsar's army, a rarity for a Jew, and a source of pride for the town of Korsun.

Yenta's daughter who lived in the house just up the hill was married to the wheelwright who had taken over her father's business. Wheelwrights were considered highly skilled, which gave her a certain social standing. Yenta's youngest son was a would-be sculptor. He visited Korsun once or twice a year, and was well dressed when Anna saw him. When he was taken into the army, Anna began to write postcards to him for Yenta, who was illiterate. Anna took dictation from Yenta, writing in Yiddish. Yenta would begin with the standard formal and flowery opening used by religious Jews, praising the reader, assuring that the writer was in good health, and praying that the reader was also free of illness. After that, Yenta would jump from one subject to another, without any connection that Anna could make out.

Once, Yenta was so full of things to say to her son that before long Anna told her that all the lines on the postcard were filled. Yenta pointed out that there were spaces between the lines. Anna filled the spaces with Yenta's words. This evidently made reading the card difficult and irritating, because when the son came to town for a visit, he brought the postcard with him and scolded Anna for writing between the lines. Anna was just as irritated with him, and thought him unfair, since she had only done what his mother had wanted. Also, since he had trouble figuring out how to read the postcard, she decided he was not as bright as his successful brothers and sister.

Anna had learned to read and write Yiddish soon after moving in with Yenta. She taught herself by studying an unusual calendar that hung on Yenta's wall. Jokes and sayings were printed in Yiddish on the back of each page in two scripts, block letters and cursive, or as Anna put it, "one for writing and one for reading," each in its own column. Yenta was the first of a list of women for whom Anna wrote letters to children and husbands in faraway cities.

In the last year of her stay with Yenta, Anna played almost every day with a girl named Sonya, who lived on the other side of the main street near the Ros River. At Sonya's house was a Turkey carpet, the only Turkey carpet Anna ever saw on a Korsun floor, and the only carpet Anna set foot on while she lived in Korsun. Sonya's family was fairly well off, because her father was the town's rope maker, and her mother made extra money by selling the eggs laid by her flock of chickens.

Even before going to Sonya's house, though, Anna knew the habits of chickens. Many women in Korsun kept a hen or two, not as a business, but to provide eggs for the family. In addition, a housewife like Anna's mother sometimes bought a chicken to fatten for a Sabbath meal, feeding it and keeping it for a few days under the oven. The chickens were allowed to roam the street and yards during the day, but they went in to roost at dusk each night. They even went to roost when it became cloudy during the day.

It was the behavior of chickens in the street that alerted Anna to the most surprising thing to happen while she was living with Yenta Koslov. Anna was sitting on the steps of the house with her mother, Leya, her two sisters, and Yenta when the sky began to turn cloudy. After a time it grew darker, and the chickens seemed upset. They were flapping and fluffing their wings, running here and there, and squawking in a frightened, confused way. The sky kept getting darker. Anna knew that the chickens were acting strangely, but she had no idea why they were so upset. It was becoming clear that the sky was acting strangely, too. It was not just clouding over. The darkness was looking more and more like nighttime, even though it was still the middle of the day. No one explained to Anna what was happening to the sunlight.

Seeing the chickens running this way and that in the street, the women scrambled to catch them in the gloom and took them into the proper houses. The sunlight finally disappeared. Still, neither Leya nor Mrs. Koslov told Anna anything. Only afterward did she find out that she had experienced a total eclipse of the sun.[1]

7
The Marketplace

Anna's eclipse of the sun occurred on August 21, 1914, twenty days after Germany had declared war on Russia. Eclipses in those days, as for hundreds of years before, were often regarded as predictors of dire events. If anyone in Korsun regarded the blotting out of the sun as an omen, though, it was not mentioned on that August day so soon after the beginning of war.

In Korsun, far from the battlefields, it was easy to ignore the possibility of dire events. Even though men were being taken into the Russian army, everyday life was little changed. One center of everyday life in Korsun was the marketplace, where farm met town and Christian met Jew.

The farmers in the hamlets and villages in the countryside surrounding Korsun were Christian peasants. Half of the townspeople were Jewish, most of them poor. At the marketplace, the Jews bought farm produce from the Christian peasants, who then had money to spend in town. The peasants spent the money in the shops and stores along the main street and the palace road, almost all of them Jewish-owned. Thus, the money spent by the Jewish women to buy farm produce came back to them and their husbands, at least in part. Of course, this did not change the fact that most of the Jews were poor. The farmers depended upon the town-dwelling Jews to sell them the goods they did not grow or make for themselves—the processed foods, such as sugar, salt, and tea; the manufactured goods, such as cloth and soap; and the refined products, such as kerosene.[1]

The marketplace sat in Korsun's southwest quadrant, nestling close to the crossroads of the main street and the palace road. It consisted of a row of three parallel, long rectangular areas, their long sides running north to south. The first area, closest to the crossroads, made up the eastern edge of the marketplace and was occupied by a wooden building containing both booths and stores. The next rectangle to the west was not a building, but open ground. Finally, next to the open ground was a rectangular area containing a dozen individual wooden stands.

The wooden building, a long rectangle, consisted of a row of small, open-fronted booths facing east, sharing a long, common back wall with a row of large stores whose doorways faced west. In the booths, vendors sold pickled or dried fish. Each earthen-floored booth was only about three feet wide and four feet deep. Its open front was closed at night by pulling down a corrugated metal wall and locking it at the bottom. Anna passed these booths every morning on her way south to the high school. Their open fronts were only a step from the dirt section of the palace road, which ran past the school, and she would sometimes buy the sardine-sized dried smelt, which she would take to school to eat for lunch, together with a piece of bread from home.

At these fish booths, the peasants bought nonkosher fish, such as catfish, while the Jews bought kosher fish, such as herring and the smelt that Anna liked. The Jews also bought *kaptshonkes*—the whitefish given an artificial gold color and dried until they were as stiff as the winter wash hanging on clotheslines in the attic. A whitefish was safe to keep unrefrigerated for a week, and most people overcame its rigidity by cooking it to softness with potatoes. Hanging from nails in the booth were strings, each holding five or six dried fish pierced through the eye sockets. Many of the fish were imported from the Volga River delta, where a factory processed lox, herring, and dried whitefish for sale all over Russia. Several Korsuners worked in this factory, coming home a few times a year for the holidays. Each of these half-dozen fish booths sold the same kinds of fish. The vendors made a small profit each week, but only because the booths were so small that the rent was minimal.

Back to back with the booths were the large stores. All of the stores opened onto a wooden walkway that ran the length of the building and was protected from the rain by an overhang. To reach the walkway, customers walked up from ground level on two wooden steps that also ran the length of the building. The princess's retainers and other customers shopped for textiles, clothing, and accessories at the row of Jewish-owned stores. In the store of Beyla's friend Oodl Slivnik, women bought imported hats, gloves, scarves, and fancy shoes, while in the shop of Oodl's son, four or five doors away, they found fine fabrics, to be made into clothing fit for the wealthy. Peasant women, too, shopped at the stores, buying simpler dry goods such as muslin for skirts and jackets. In the next rectangle, the open area, peasant women arranged their farm-fresh vegetables, fruits, chickens, eggs, butter, and cheese on sacks or tablecloths spread on the ground.

If Anna was up early, she saw these women walking into town, barefoot on the harsh cobblestones, carrying baskets or shouldering buckets filled with fresh food. Of the many different farmwomen who sold produce, only fifteen or twenty came to town on any given day. Since many of their customers were Jews, the farmwomen knew that Jews were forbidden to eat food that had touched nonkosher containers or utensils. Knowing this, they wrapped their butter and their cheese—a hard cottage cheese formed into a loaf—in an unripe cabbage leaf. The leaf, despite its unpleasant woody taste, made a kosher container.

However, for food to be kosher, the process by which it was made had to be kosher also. The peasants' butter, for example, was judged by Jews to be certainly kosher and was freely bought, since it was made in a churn touched only by the hot water that washed it between batches. On the other hand, the peasants' cheese was only deemed probably kosher, and many Jews, Leya and Grandma Beyla among them, preferred to make their own cheese, because the peasant's wooden cheese paddle may or may not have touched other food.

Anna once saw a woman sitting in the open area, displaying a bag of second-hand tealeaves. A palace worker had noticed that the princess used her tea only once at a party. Instead of throwing the tea away, he took it home to his wife. She took it to market to sell, assuming that people would buy the princess's used tea. She was right.

A small offshoot of the open area lay between the fine store building and the main street, alongside what would have been the sidewalk if Korsun had had any sidewalks. In this area, the wife of Korsun's only weaver sold her husband's scarves, and the wife of the *vattenmakher* sold her husband's cotton batting mats, which were used as lining for winter coats and bed quilts. During the summer, a Christian woman from the town stood there, selling delicious ice cream made with pure cream. She sold it by the teaspoon.

Next to the open area were the individual stands. Most were rented by Jewish vendors who catered mainly to middle-class Jews and Christians. Each narrow stand was about six feet long, with a dirt floor. It had two wood-lattice sides (but no front or back), and its roof was supported on four poles. The vendor displayed her produce on top of a cupboard in which she locked her valuables at night—mainly her hand-held balance scale and weights, or in a few cases, a more modern scale.

Most of the stands sold fruit or vegetables. At the fruit stands, strings of dried figs were sold for a holiday, but the mainstays were imported lemons, oranges, and apples, each displayed in a pyramid pile. (Korsun's apples were tasty, but often wormy, and were mostly made into applesauce or *kvas*, a fermented drink.) Poor Jews, who seldom had a taste of these imported fruits, had a saying that if a Jew eats an orange, either the Jew or the orange is rotten.

Women yelled and bargained at the stands, just as they did at the booths and at the open area, the customers insisting on picking out the exact fish or the piece of fruit they thought looked best, and haggling with the seller over the price. Anna was uncomfortable with the haggling when she first went shopping with her mother, but as she grew older she found that everyone, Jews and non-Jews alike, haggled, and usually without hard feelings.

Later, during the war, less than half of the stands might be open at a given time. Oranges and lemons were unavailable. Neither the Jewish nor the Gentile bakers in Korsun were able to bake bread. When a peasant woman had enough flour and enough wood to fire her oven, she baked and took four or five loaves to market to sell from an unoccupied stand. In normal times it was considered a sin to buy nonkosher food, but in wartime the Jews bought the peasants' bread, feeling lucky to find bread of any kind.

At the two stands nearest to the main street, fresh fish swimming in tubs of water were sold on Thursdays and Fridays. (On other days, vendors sold other foods at those two stands.) The fish stands sold fish from both the Ros and the smaller river. The best and most expensive were the fat, salmonlike fish stocked in the smaller river that bounded the town on the west. These fish were raised by two peasant families who lived rent-free near the river as part of their payment for managing the fish stock. They harvested fish at night on Wednesday and Thursday, then sold them by the cartload to the stand vendors in the morning.

The other fish caught in the smaller river on Wednesday and Thursday night were smelts—slim fish about three inches long. Smelts were almost as cheap as crayfish, which were so common that the fishermen often threw them back into the river. Poor Russians used to say, If you can't afford any fish, well then crayfish is also a fish. Placed on the vendor's scale alive, the smelts were bought to be prepared in any of three ways. Many were dried, some were pickled whole, and others were rolled in flour (after the head had been pinched off) to be cooked and eaten as finger food, bones, tail, and all. From the Ros River, still other peasants caught several kinds of small fish at night, fish also affordable by the poorer people in town.

Like most women, Leya bought her perishables daily, since she had no refrigeration. The dugout cellar of her house was cold enough for carrots, cabbages, potatoes, and apples, but not for eggs, fish, or meat. If she had very little money, she might wait until late in the day, hoping for a better price when the peasants were eager to get home. Otherwise, though, the best time to arrive at the crossroads was at first light, when she had her pick of the produce just in.

She might buy the vegetables for a borscht soup in spring or summer, choosing from the cabbages and white sugar beets, or she might buy the makings for a pot of beans. Cheese, never eaten as it came from the market, was made into a dish such as blintzes (thin pancakes wrapped around a filling) or *kreplekh* (known more commonly as kreplach, or filled dumplings). One day a week, a housewife bought a chicken, or if money permitted, she went to one of the several stores on the street of butchers for a pound of beef. A portion of butter or a few eggs were luxuries. She could choose among abundant fruits—fresh cherries or plums, delicious pears, all kinds of berries by the bucket, and local apples.

Only the very poor shopped on Friday, delaying their Sabbath purchases until the last minute, perhaps hoping to scrape up another few kopecks to spend. (One kopeck was equal to one-half of an American penny.) All Jewish-owned places of business at the market and elsewhere were closed by noon, or at most by 3:00 PM on Friday, in preparation for the Sabbath, since no self-employed Jew, whether vendor, tailor, shoemaker, or other handcraftsman, worked on the Sabbath, beginning Friday at sundown.

Among the few Saturday renters of stands were peasants who sold pork, hams, and hogs' heads, displaying them on a large sack covering the cupboard. Strings of liverwurst and other sausages hung from the stand. Other peasants sold a variety of breads, advertising their stands by hanging out strings of doughnut-shaped bread rolls, each loop of cord passing through the center of about ten—a Russian dozen—of the *bublichki*. Peasant bakers also made a larger size, the *bubliki*. Anna believed that the *bublichki* were a peasant invention that had been copied by the Jews, who gave their copies the Yiddish name "bagel."

Practically the only customers in the marketplace on Saturday were the local Gentiles who worked in the town, for the town, or for the princess's estate. Village peasants did not come into town to shop at the market or elsewhere on Saturday, knowing that most places of business were closed for the Jewish Sabbath.

Sunday, the Christian Sabbath, was an ordinary workday for Jews in Korsun. Jewish boys spent all day in school, Jewish stores were open for business, Jewish tailors stood at their tables, and Jewish shoemakers sat at their benches. Peasants came into town on Sunday not so much to sell their produce, but instead to attend church services or buy needed supplies.

When Anna and her family were living at the Koslov house on the main street early in the war, she had a good view of the peasant women coming into town from the Ros bridge, walking to the crossroads, and then turning north on the palace road to reach the church. They wore their Sunday best, walking along together almost as though they were a chorus marching in an opera, the color or design of each woman's headscarf indicating her home village beyond the Ros.

These village peasants would not think of wearing the modern, western-style clothes worn to church by the town peasants and by the wealthier town Gentiles. Each of the women walking into town wore the same traditional peasant costume. The dark-colored heavy cotton skirt, gathered tightly to the waist (never pleated, a modern fashion) and sweeping down to the ankles, had deep side pockets. Sometimes decorated with a small pattern, the skirt was embellished by a white half-apron. The linen slipover blouse, generously embroidered on the long, full sleeves and ornamented with beads, had no buttons or hooks; the opening down the front was tied closed with two attached ribbons. The vest, worn even in summer, was distinguished from that of a man by the "poplin" hanging from its waist— about a foot of flared, poplin fabric, ruffled all around except in front where it buttoned. A married woman rolled her braids on top of her head and covered them with a scarf. Some women wore their boots, but others tied them together across their shoulders and went barefoot on the way into town.

Sunday was a good business day at the crossroads notions shop of Khayka, a friend of Anna's family, because the peasant girls, scattering to all the stores after church, often came to her for ribbons, beads, and cloth. When war came, some of the peasant men in the army addressed their letters to Khayka's shop, not only because the women could conveniently pick up letters during their frequent visits to the shop, but also because she was known and trusted.

In winter the village peasants came into town mainly to buy supplies. A husband and wife in their sleigh brought little to sell at the marketplace except for dried fruits and vegetables—dried beans, apples (cut into circles before drying), plums, pears, and currants, as well as unpitted cherries. Leya often bought the dried fruits to cook a winter *tsimmes*, a stew of cherries, prunes, apples, and pears.

Peasants made home deliveries of items too heavy or too inconvenient for a housewife like Leya to carry home from the market or the fair.[2] A peasant woman came into the house with fresh milk early each morning. Leya usually bought one cupful for each of her three girls. Adults drank tea. Leya, like most women, knew that raw milk might carry disease, so she always boiled it before using.

Peasants carried home deliveries into the foyer (the *hoyz* in Yiddish), which was a large, almost barnlike entry chamber attached to the outside of the house, usually on the long side nearest the street. It served not only as the antechamber or vestibule to be entered before opening the door to the interior of the house proper, but also as a storage area, as the place of entry for both the cellar and the attic, as a place to keep animals, and, in the houses of some craftsmen such as shoemakers and tailors, as a work area. The floor had the shape of a long rectangle whose short side was wide enough to allow a peasant to drive his wagon, pulled by one or two horses, completely inside. To allow the wagon to enter, the foyer had a large doorway consisting of a pair of large doors, wide and tall like barn doors, opening outward into the yard. In contrast, a person would usually enter the foyer through a smaller single door, which in some foyers was separate, but in others was an inset in one of the larger doors. The foyer, having no ceiling, was in open communication with the attic of the one-story house.

Although a peasant would usually park his wagon on the street, there were times when he would drive it through the yard and into the foyer. In winter, if he arrived at the house late in the afternoon, as darkness was falling, or if it was raining or snowing, he might prefer to spend the night in the foyer, rather than to try to find his way back to his village in the dark.

8
Nobility and Obscurity

The peasant who delivered firewood was poor, but like Anna's family, still above the lowest social level, which was occupied by beggars and servants. Similarly, the wealthy families, whether Jewish or Gentile, did not belong to the highest class, which was reserved for royalty.

In the twin-towered palace of Korsun lived Princess Olga Valerianovna Lopukhina-Demidova. Her deceased husband was descended from the first wife of Peter the Great (Tsar Peter I). Anna believed that the princess owned not only the town, but also the surrounding villages and everything produced by the peasants there, from sugar beets to cows. Whether this was true or not, the princess was certainly influential.[1]

The princess seemed both benign and just in her treatment of the town and its people. She was liked by most townspeople, and much of the town could be said to make its living from the palace. The children of the princess often lived abroad, favoring Germany or France, but that was no more than the privilege of royalty. Anna's day-to-day existence had little to do with the lives of this royal family. Occasionally though, she was an observer at the margin of the princess's world.

The tsar's mother, dowager Empress Maria Fyodorovna, visited Korsun in the summer of 1916 to raise money for the war. Arches of flowers festooned her route in greeting as her ornate, four-horse carriage arrived from the railway station, bumping along the paving stones of the main street and turning north at the crossroads. The whole town stood at the side of the cobblestoned palace road—Korsun had no sidewalks—craning to catch sight of the royal visitor, who waved back to everyone. Anna was standing a block from the palace, near the two-story building housing the town's fancy delicatessen on the first floor and the dentist on the second. The dentist and his wife had hung an oriental rug from their balcony, the way people in big cities did to welcome visiting dignitaries.

It was a week or two before school let out for the summer, and for this occasion the girls from the high school were told to wear their school uniform if they still had one to wear. With Russia at war for almost two years, not everyone had the proper uniform. Anna was wearing hers on that day, the brown pinafore with its high collar, long sleeves, and pleated skirt. The full-length white apron reserved for festive occasions fell from the ruffled shoulders of the brown dress. Anna's mother, Leya, had made Anna's apron out of a curtain.

A visitor to the palace some time later had brought an automobile to Korsun. Stopping the car, the chauffeur got out to tinker with the engine. A crowd gathered, staring at his military-style uniform with expensive boots, and at the outlandish machine. The passengers sat patiently in the car until the chauffeur, having finished his repair, climbed back into the driver's seat to continue his progress toward the palace. Anna had seen an automobile in Kiev during a trip with her mother. For most Korsuners, though, it was the first one they had ever seen.

On another occasion, Anna's Aunt Meyndl took Anna to see a funeral procession for a member of the princess's retinue. Standing among other townspeople on a granite bluff, they looked across the Ros River at the procession walking slowly along the bluff on the other side. This was not an ordinary funeral of a middle-class Christian. The Orthodox priest in charge of this distinguished funeral wore his colorful, magnificently embroidered vestments, while as many as ten young priests flanked the path, chanting psalms, carrying icons on poles surmounted by cloths adorned with pictures of saints and the Virgin Mary.

Other Jewish townspeople had more direct contact with the palace. The dentist (the same one who had hung out the rug in honor of the visiting dowager empress) not only catered to the royal household, but also dealt directly with the princess. So did Mr. Shmilyosel and Mr. Spector (no relation to Anna), who were the only Korsun tailors talented enough to design and make clothes for the princess.

The princess's staff bought premium foods at the fancy delicatessen or at a delicatessen on the street of butchers near the marketplace. These stores carried out-of-season fruit such as oranges and pears. Anna was once in the fancy delicatessen near the palace when a wealthy woman, perhaps a retainer, bought pears and carefully counted them into her fourteen-year-old daughter's shallow, tall-handled basket to make sure that the girl wouldn't eat one on the way home. Members of the princess's household bought woolen fabrics to be made into their clothes from Mr. Slivnik's quality store at the marketplace, and retainers of the princess patronized a particular hand laundry on the main street.

On a different level were the people salaried by the princess. The best

known of these salaried employees was Mr. Kobek. Anna saw him once in
the stationery store. Her attention was attracted by a man in a fine cutaway
coat and a gray cylinder hat—last-century clothes now worn only by a man
neither shy nor lacking in flair. The clerk said to him, Will that be all,
Mr Kobek? Anna recognized the name as that of a Korsun celebrity.

That was the only time Anna saw him, but she saw his work many
times. Mr. Kobek's job was to design and produce fireworks for the princess. He put on a display a half dozen times a year, for occasions such as a
birthday or a national holiday. The princess would invite her friends to a
party in her garden, and Mr. Kobek would entertain with his fireworks.

People would say, Come on, it's time for Kobek's fireworks. The family
would go outside to watch them, even keeping the children up past their
bedtimes to enjoy the show. His designs were more sophisticated than anything Anna would later see in America. He might produce fruit trees made
of fireworks or a scene of a mother duck swimming in water with her
ducklings. Anna heard that the princess paid Mr. Kobek a salary so large
that he could afford to live in a fine house with a huge yard and a picket
fence, ride in a carriage, and need no other job to support his wife and
daughter.

Mr. Shevchenko, father of Anna's school friend, oversaw the princess's
forest, including the hunting of its animals. From this royal forest to the
east came the branches that the princess sent as firewood to the families of
soldiers during the war. The princess also operated a factory in the forest, making shopping bags and traveling cases woven from the acres of a
rattanlike fiber grown nearby. Anna did not see the factory until after the
revolution, and then only because she went into the forest looking for firewood. That was long after the factory had been looted and left abandoned
during uprisings by peasants against the landowners. The peasants had stolen the baskets, hoping to sell them, but nobody had money to buy them.

At the other end of the social scale from royalty were servants and beggars. Anna was astonished once to overhear a peasant maid address the
well-to-do Jewish woman for whom she worked as "*barina.*" The woman
told the maid not to call her *barina*—mistress—a word by which commoners addressed nobility or landowning gentry. The maid did not understand
that her employer was embarrassed to be treated as such a lofty personage.
Just as the peasants continued to wear their customary clothes long after
they had been legally emancipated from serfdom, they continued their
forms of address as well as their subservient attitude toward the other
classes.

Although the serfs had been freed in Russia by Tsar Alexander II in
1861, more than a year before President Lincoln's Emancipation Proclama-
tion, true freedom took many decades to evolve. Social equality did not

begin until the end of 1917, when the Bolsheviks, as they took power, abolished all titles except "Citizen" and "Comrade," and issued decrees declaring the legal equality of men and women, nobles and commoners.[2]

Although Anna saw the lives of the royalty only from a distance, she had firsthand experience with servants. Anna never had a chance to know servants in her own home. Even before her father left for America, they were not well off. Through her grandmother, though, Anna knew other well-to-do families who had servants.

Anna got along well with maidservants, and learned from them. She met one maid while preparing for the high school entrance examinations during the war. Anna shared a tutor with three of the wealthy Shapiro children, whose mother had hired a teacher to board with the family. He was not only the best teacher in Korsun, he was also a very good teacher—so good, people said, that his pupils almost did not need to take the entrance examinations for high school. With help from the tutor, and from Mrs. Shapiro, who was a high school graduate, Anna passed the examination. Leya tried to give Mrs. Shapiro money for the lessons, but she would not take it.

During the tutoring, Anna became friends with Khveodora, the maid who did all of the gardening, cooking, and washing for the Shapiro family. Whenever Anna came into the Shapiro house, Khveodora talked amiably with her, and when the maid was working in the garden, she let Anna tag along. Anna learned the names of gardening tools by fetching them from the shed for Khveodora. She also learned good planting technique by watching the maid set up tomatoes and cabbages.

Khveodora eventually lost her job when the Shapiros abandoned their house after it was attacked in a pogrom during the Russian Civil War. Still later, Anna, who by then was about thirteen years old, heard that Khveodora was ill. Jewish girls did not usually visit peasant girls, but wanting to see her friend, Anna found out that Khveodora was staying with a sister and went there.

The sister lived at the edge of town, in one of the houses where peasants worked small garden farms close to the Ros River, with strutting chickens and, at one side of the house, the pigsty. The house and garden faced the river. Khveodora's illness turned out to be a still-bandaged, infected finger, not a trivial matter in those days. After they had talked, and while they were standing in the garden as Anna was getting ready to leave, Khveodora offered to give her some fresh flowers. Anna asked for one particular blossom. When Khveodora cut it from its stem, her ten-year-old niece in the house began to cry. The girl had planned to include this very flower, one of the best in the garden, in the bouquet she would carry to church on Sunday.

Another servant was Polashke, who had begun working for Grandmother Beyla long before Anna was born. Coming into the household as a young girl in the era when peasant girls were often given away by their parents into a life of virtual slavery, Polashke had lived with and served Beyla for much of her life. Like many peasant girls, Polashke grew up as a maid in a Jewish household, speaking Yiddish. It was Polashke who taught the Jewish morning prayer to Anna's mother and to Beyla's other daughters.

When Anna was being tutored at the Shapiro's, Polashke was already an elderly woman. As the war continued, some of those people who had managed on their own in peacetime were no longer self-sufficient. Although Anna's Grandmother Beyla had a large house, she could turn away neither relatives who needed housing nor a friend paralyzed by a stroke. She took them all into her home and gave Polashke's room to the friend. Anna never saw the servant again, nor did she know what became of her.

Anna thought the hardest household chores of all were done by peasant women, and specifically by those hired to do laundry. Women in Korsun washed and rinsed clothes in the river, scrubbing them with soap and water. Only a few people had a washboard, a new invention not as amazing as the telephone, but more efficient than the rocks at the river. Jewish women washed clothes and linens in bulk at the river only two or three times in a year, but especially in spring, at Passover. These large washings were done by landless peasants from the outskirts of town, some of whom were so poor that they were happy to take a few kopecks for such chores.

Anna knew that peasant women were hard workers who did not talk much. She once spoke to a washerwoman, though, asking her if she would be happy when Passover was over so that she would not have to work so hard. The woman laughed. She told Anna that when she was at home, her calf might fall into the ditch beside the road. She would have to put a rope around that calf's neck and pull it out, even though it didn't want to get out. That would be what she called heavy work! Washing clothes, for her, was like taking a rest, she said, and she even got paid for doing it.

Anna had little contact with peasant beggars. She saw them only at the fairs and at the church. On Sundays peasants and landowners attended services at the Russian Orthodox church next to the palace. The beggars came to the church, but did not attend the services. Lining up in two rows outside the church, they sang songs. The landowners and peasants, when they came out of church after the service, customarily gave money to the singing beggars. Anna heard a story, after she had left Korsun, that Tchaikovsky was once struggling to compose a theme for a work he was writing. Hearing the beggars singing outside a church, he recognized that their melody was the theme he needed. Grateful for the tune, he took all of the loose change from his pocket and gave it to the beggars.

Unlike the peasants lined up outside the church each Sunday, Jewish beggars might walk into any Jewish home at any time. They counted on the fact that the giving of charity was one of the commandments of the Jewish religion. It might even be said that the beggar was doing a favor for other Jews by giving them the chance to obey a commandment. Although most of the Jews in Korsun were poor, the beggars were the poorest of the poor, the homeless people of those times. Beggars would accept either money or food. They didn't mind begging from poor people, who would usually not have a kopeck to spare, but who would give them a piece of bread.

Most beggars had come to Korsun from another town, knowing that the poorhouse would give them shelter. Korsuners rarely knew the family background of a beggar, or the nature of the ill fortune or problems that had led her into a life of begging.

Anna was alone at home when she met her first Jewish beggar. A woman let herself in through the back door. She wore a heavy woolen shawl against the winter cold, and in her arms she carried a baby. She had come for a handout. Anna's father had not yet left for America, and the family was still able to afford a rented house. Her mother had baked a potato for seven-year-old Anna. Anna felt sorry for the beggar and her infant. She took the potato from the oven and handed it to the woman.

Five years later, when Anna, her sisters, and her mother were living with Khayka, who ran the popular notions store at the crossroads, another beggar let herself in. The beggar was dressed better than Anna's mother. She was carrying a glass jar, and she asked for a little jelly. She claimed that a sick person in the poorhouse needed to take a bitter medicine. The jelly was to take away the bitter taste.

This time Khayka's seventeen-year-old daughter, named Donya, was looking after Anna and her two sisters, as well as her own sister and two brothers. It was Saturday morning, the Sabbath. The adults were in shul. Donya and the children were bewildered by the beggar's request. Earlier in the war, when people could still make jelly, it was not a luxury. A piece of black bread with jelly and a glass of tea was a supper. Now, though, there was certainly no jelly in the house. The war had been going on for three years. The fuel shortage was still severe, and Khayka was the third person to give Anna's family shelter since the beginning of the war. The beggar's glass jar would remain empty.

9
At Alta's House (1916–1917)

Anna had gone to one rally celebrating a Russian victory in a battle with the German army. The Korsun police and public officials had arranged a bonfire in the center of town, and speakers had told the crowd about the valor of the Russian soldiers. That was early in the war, though.

By the summer of 1916, the effects of the war on life in Korsun had become serious. The day had passed when Korsuners had known a market-place overflowing with food and had seen wagonloads of firewood. More and more families had no firewood to heat their houses, and the authorities were forcing them to move in with others who had fuel. A rumor went around that the police had finally been shocked into taking this action after going into a household that had no wood and finding a baby frozen to death.

The police moved Leya and her three daughters in with a husband and wife, Oora and Alta, who had an extra room now that both of their sons were away. Since one son was in the tsar's army, the couple had enough firewood, a gift to the families of servicemen from the princess.

The couple's house, like most of the poorer ones, had walls of clay, an old-fashioned roof of thatch, and no outhouse. It was the last house at the north end of the Jewish section of Old Town, and just beyond stood a row of fenced-in peasant gardens.

Alta and Oora had their own bedroom next to the kitchen and gave the big extra room at the back of the house to Leya, who moved in one of her two black-lacquered, gold-trimmed beds, leaving her wardrobe and her other furniture behind. Alta prided herself on her clean house. When Anna washed the dishes and tidied up after Leya had cooked a meal, she cleaned the kitchen as though the princess were coming for tea, partly to avoid Alta's anger, and partly out of pride, lest Alta think them a slovenly family. Since her mother paid no rent, Anna already felt like an intruder. Alta made it clear that only she and Oora would use the little room off the kitchen where the couple ate their meals.

Alta's mother had been a servant in a wealthy household for many years, and when the mistress died, she bequeathed her a set of seed pearls, graduated in size, smaller and smaller, five or six strands of them. In turn, Alta's mother left them to Alta, who told her son that when he married, she would give the pearls to his wife. In the meantime, even though she didn't need to pawn them, Alta left her pearls with a pawnbroker most of the time, because she trusted him to keep them safe from loss and theft. Not that theft was common in Korsun. In fact, it was rare to hear of a robbery, partly because most of the people were too poor to own anything of major value. Alta's pearls were among the exceptions.

Once every year or two she redeemed her pearls from pawn to clean and enjoy them, always preserving enough pawn money for the next time. Since she told her neighbors and friends weeks beforehand that she would be bringing the pearls home, everybody looked forward to their homecoming.

The ransoming of the pearls was at hand when Anna came home one day to find the front door locked, which was so unusual that she looked in at the front window. She saw a niece and a few of Alta's friends sitting around the table. Going in through the back door and peeking from the kitchen, she saw that Alta had locked the front door to bar intruders because she had laid her pearls out on the dining room table, cushioned on a towel. Anna watched the women cutting the strands, collecting the tiny pearls, and washing them, trying not to lose any.

None of the older women wore eyeglasses. The work was tedious, coaxing each pearl onto the thread, then looping a tiny knot into the strand. Exasperating though it was, it was not real work like the cooking and baking, washing and cleaning that they did daytimes, or the mending and knitting they did evenings by the glimmer of an oil lamp. Even though it took a few days to finish the restringing of the pearls, the gossip and the joking made it more like a party, and the old faces around the table became younger in their laughter.

Alta was not the only woman who pawned valuables. Korsun had no pawn shop, as Anna knew from running errands all over town, so pawning was not done in public, but her mother, Leya, for example, had given up a pair of beautiful silver candle holders. Leya had used the candlesticks, a gift from her own mother, during the first few years of her marriage, but then had been forced to exchange them for money. She was never able to redeem the candlesticks, and while Anna never saw them, she heard about them often. Alta, though, finally redeemed her pearls one last time, when she had the double pleasure of seeing her son marry and of giving the strands to his bride as a wedding present, just as she had promised.

Alta's husband, Oora, was a maker of sheepskin coats, but most of his customers were poor peasants who could only afford to have him patch their old coats over and over. By night an oil lamp lit his work. By day, when Anna passed the open door of his small workroom, she saw him sitting near a window to catch the sunlight, a small man pushing his stout needle into the sheepskin. Although a number of tailors and seamstresses in town had Singer sewing machines, Oora did all of his stitching by hand.

One week, a few peasants might bring their coats to the house to have a torn place mended or a worn section replaced, and Oora might even make a whole new sleeve if the fur inside was too worn to keep its owner warm, but the next week he might have no one at his door and nothing to do. Sometimes in the slack periods Oora used all of his skills to make new coats, turning the fur side of the sheepskin to the inside for warmth, and sewing green braid along the seams—a ready-made braid of a conventional zigzag design, bought by the roll—giving the sleeves a touch of elegance. These he sold to the peasants who drove their horse-drawn wagons or walked from the outlying villages to the vast field of grass near the center of town every other week for the fair, men who had money in their pocket after selling the vegetables from their farms. Oora also made and sold many pairs of mittens. Anna watched him work, learning his pattern and his procedure so well that many years later she was able to make mittens for her own children.

Oora was also a part-time furrier. The town had several cap makers who supplied the demand for the fur caps worn during the harsh winters, but no one in Korsun knew how to soften the skins they needed except Oora. He soaked them in the slop bucket overnight.

He smoked more than was good for him, and being a poor man he rolled his own cigarettes from the cheapest grade of tobacco, called *makhorka* in Russian, made mainly from the skeleton of the leaf after the good part had been removed. He saved the money he might have wasted on the luxury of the soft, ready-made cigarette papers by arranging the tobacco on a rough rectangle he cut from ordinary, coarse paper.

Oora had a big sore on his lip when Anna and her family first lived with him, but he was not in great pain. Later, he sat in his workroom, a homemade cigarette dangling from one side of his mouth, his hand holding a leaf pressed to the cancer on the other side. Most of the time in the later months of her stay, however, she saw him without a cigarette, pressing the medicinal leaf to his mouth, moaning, Ahh, ahh, ahh, and crying tears. In those days no one had any thought of being cured of cancer, and all one could wish for the sufferer was a quick release.[1]

Oora was not only a small man, but he was also so emaciated that it hurt Anna to look at him. He usually had little to say to her, except for one time when he invested in two whole Persian lambskins. He brought the expensive skins home to make into coat collars. He put them into the slop bucket in the kitchen to soften.

That night, Anna went into Alta's kitchen to clean up. Leya had cooked the meal on the floor of the oven mouth, in a pot on a long-legged tripod positioned over a small fire, a way to use much less wood than by firing the whole oven. Grasping the long-handled, iron-tipped coal poker standing in the corner, Anna shoved the wood coals far back into the oven, where they could be used again, put the poker back in the corner, pulled the metal ash bucket out from under the oven, took the *flittervish*—the part of a goose wing containing the twenty or so long outer feathers—and swept the ashes into the bucket.

She put back the bucket and the goose-wing brush, then washed and put away the few dishes, pouring the water into the slop barrel, the *pomoinitsa*. Even in the daylight, the water in the barrel was always murky, hiding the potato skins, carrot tops, or herring heads that swam in it. Carrying the small barrel out to the open ground behind the house in the dark, she went as far from the house as she could, emptying it onto the ground near the fence of the neighboring peasant garden.

Oora came into the kitchen the next day to take his lambskins out of the water, but they were gone. Ordinarily, if the barrel was filling up, it was emptied in the evening before dark, or early the next morning; but if not, it could wait. Wanting Alta to think well of her family's cleanliness, Anna emptied it sooner rather than later, and Oora had come back too late.

Crows, stray dogs, and roaming pigs took the place of garbage collectors in Korsun, but they did not grow fat in this neighborhood, where poor people ate almost every scrap. Animals had apparently discovered the lambskins dumped with the slops, and had carried them off.

Oora's anger was as great as the value of the lambskins, but he stopped short of threatening to throw Anna and her family out of his house. Anna did not talk back to her elders, but she knew that the loss of the skins was not her fault. Her mother agreed and did not punish her for it, which helped, but even so, the lambskins were gone, and no one could expect Oora to be happy about it.

The run-in with Oora didn't last long. Ordinarily he was not difficult to live with, but Anna also had to get along with his wife, Alta, and that was a horse of a different color. Alta could not stand to have children living in her house. Even the three small children living next door annoyed her. The children lived with their grandmother, and Alta didn't get along with her, either. The two women irritated each other, each a pebble in the other's shoe. They chafed and bickered until their emotions boiled over, and during a terrible argument late in the summer Alta shoved the neighbor so hard that she fell to the ground.

Naturally, the son of the next-door grandmother was unhappy after she told him that she had been attacked. He argued about it with Alta's son, who happened to be visiting at home when the incident occurred, but the only thing the two sons could agree on was to bring the matter before the secular Russian court, rather than the *dayan,* the judge of the Jewish community's religious court.

Although no one living in Alta's house had witnessed the fight between the two grandmothers, Alta's husband and her son believed they would need a witness if she were to win her case. They decided to persuade eleven-year-old Anna to testify that the neighbor had kicked Alta, thus provoking her to push her neighbor down. Even Anna's mother said she should testify for Alta. Anna was pulled in different directions. On the one hand, she and her sisters and their mother were living in Alta's home, obliged to her because they were dependent on her for shelter and heat. Besides, Leya had told Anna to testify for Alta, and a child neither argued with a parent nor disobeyed her wishes. On the other hand, it was Surka's grandmother whom Alta had shoved, and Surka was a friend with whom Anna walked to school every day, so she did not like the thought of having to accuse Surka's grandmother, even if she were guilty. After thinking the matter over, she decided that her conscience told her not to lie, and certainly not to a judge in a court of law.

The court sent a letter to each grandmother, notifying them to appear on a certain date at a house not far out of town, across the Ros River to the east, where the circuit-riding judge would hear cases. It was decided that the two feuding women would go to court accompanied by their sons and by the two supposed witnesses, Anna and a teen-age boy who was said to have seen the fight. No other relatives would be allowed in court.

The next-door son was a coachman, an *izvozchik,* but he could not fit the six people into his passenger carriage. Like all coachmen, however, he also had a wagon in which he hauled goods, or carried sheep or goats to the slaughterhouse.

On the appointed day, heartsick at being told to lie, but unable to defy her mother openly, Anna got ready for the trip to court, putting on her school uniform, a dress of brown antique cotton with a black apron. Going outside, she joined the two sons and the two grandmothers to climb up the pair of steps at the rear of the wagon. The last of the six passengers was the boy of perhaps fifteen years who would be a witness for the next-door grandmother. He worked as a groom in the stable of her son.

They sat facing each other silently on the low bench seats, the next-door grandmother with her two supporters on one side of the wagon, Alta with her two supporters on the other side. Meanwhile, sitting with their backs to the outward-slanting wooden sides of the wagon, they had to watch where they placed their feet on the floor among the livestock droppings.

The two horses pulled the wagon to the nearby main street, followed the cobblestones to the plank bridge over the Ros River, headed out of town, and brought the two trios of opponents to the courthouse early, in time to watch the case that was being tried before theirs.

A Jewish merchant alleged that he had sold some merchandise to a Gentile couple, but had allowed them to take the goods on credit. Now the debtors were arguing that they had paid for the goods. The merchant replied that he would have given a receipt if they had paid.

The judge eventually ruled in favor of the Jewish merchant. Fuming at the defeat, one of the losers called the judge a Jew lover. The judge told the man that he would end up in jail if he spoke that way again. He ordered the couple to pay the merchant right away. They swallowed their anger, paid their debt, and left in silence. Listening to the judge, Anna was encouraged to be in the court of a Russian who was not an anti-Semite. This judge was an example of a good person.

Having finished that case, the judge was ready to hear the charges against Alta. The stable boy testified that he had seen the fight, and that Alta had pushed the innocent next-door grandmother down. Alta, in turn, showed her leg to the judge, to demonstrate that the other woman had kicked her. Alta was showing her varicose veins. Anna had seen the same veins on her grandmother and other older women. When the judge saw the veins, he laughed. Calling Alta "Grandmother," he told her that these veins were not what you get when someone kicks you. Old people get them. Then he asked Alta where her witness was. He was told that Anna was the witness. She stood up. The judge looked at her and asked whether she had seen Alta kick the other grandmother. Anna told the judge that she had not even been there.

The judge picked up a piece of paper, and he brought it to her. Since many people couldn't write, and somebody had to be a witness when they made their mark, he called over a person to be a witness in case Anna didn't know how to write.

The judge asked Anna her name. She told him. He gave her the paper that recorded what she had testified, and asked her to sign her name to it. She wrote her name in careful, clear handwriting, with the name of her school. He looked at what she had written, and at her brown uniform, and said that he was happy that she was going to school.

He asked if she went to the town school. She said that she did. He said that going to the town school was a good thing, and that she should keep it up. He told Anna that she had pretty handwriting. Then he thanked her very much, and he winked at her.

So Anna spoiled the whole thing for Alta. The old woman was furious with her, but Anna wasn't sorry about telling the truth. Still, when she came home she expected she'd be yelled at and punished, but nobody said a word.

Eighty years later, however, Anna remembered her conflicting feelings. Her mother, feeling obliged to Alta, had told her to say something that wasn't true. Anna was still ashamed about that. It was the only time she could remember disobeying an elder. She was proud that despite being a mere school child, she had stood up before all the old people and had done what her conscience had dictated. That was the day she met the wonderful Russian judge who did not hate the Jews, and who was a just person. He respected her for telling the truth. That was the day Anna met an adult she could admire.

Anna's Prize (1916–1917)

At the end of the first summer living with Alta and Oora, Anna passed her high school entrance examination and began her first year as a student in the fall of 1916. In her tutored preparations for the examination, she had learned arithmetic, geography, and how to read, write, and speak Russian, but she brought an additional skill to high school. She had already taught herself to embroider by watching her aunt Meyndl when the women sat outside, knitting or embroidering in the sunlight.

Anna finished the first small piece of handwork assigned in school in only a few hours and with such flair that the home economics teacher, Nina Constantinovna, asked if she would like to attempt a major project, a linen dresser scarf. Anna had to explain that she had no money for materials. The teacher offered to buy the linen and thread, but only on the condition that she would own the finished scarf. Anna agreed.

Almost every woman in town owned a dresser scarf, and Anna knew she wanted to make one like Aunt Meyndl's, only better. She liked the traditional red and black Ukrainian pattern, but she knew she could improve on her aunt's inept embroidery. She even decided to use a more difficult technique than the ordinary stitchery in her aunt's scarf.

After Nina Constantinovna gave her the new white linen, Anna began to search for the best thread, the English red. Young girls embroidering their trousseaus usually bought all the English red they could find, because its color didn't bleed, but Anna found enough for her scarf in a market stall at the crossroads. She also bought black thread, but the ordinary kind, since it didn't bleed.

A Christian friend at school, seeing Anna's skill with the needle, asked to be taught how to embroider. They bought some Russian-made red thread at the same stall at the center of town where Anna had found her own imported red, and took it to the girl's house. Anna embroidered a simple pattern, working slowly, explaining as she worked. Then she handed the needle and cloth to her friend, patiently watching her reproduce the design again and again, staying until she saw that her student was progressing well.

Next day in school, the friend told how her mother had washed the scarf, only to see the red thread bleed onto the white linen, but the girl didn't blame Anna. A few weeks later when they were walking home from school, the two girls were so wrapped up in their conversation that they passed Anna's street and came to the house of the friend, who asked if Anna wanted to see her new litter of kittens.

While they were playing with the kittens, the girl's mother came in. The friend introduced Anna to her mother, reminding her mother that Anna had taught her how to embroider. The mother said that if Anna was the one who had taught the embroidering, she must also be the one who had stuck them with the thread that had bled all over, ruining their scarf. Anna apologized, feeling responsible even though she was not to blame, but the apology did no good. The woman told her daughter that she should have known better than to deal with Anna. After all, Anna was nothing but a *zhidovka*.

Anna stood still for a moment. The friend's mother had just called her a kike, a dirty Jew. The venomous word *zhidovka* hung in the air. Then Anna took herself out of the woman's house and never visited there again. In school, her friend was too embarrassed to look her in the face.

Anna worked on her embroidery through the late October change of season as the cold rain began and people prepared their houses for winter. Even the poor families put storm windows up and upholstered the outside of their door with straw-filled burlap sacks in the hope of keeping the coming winds from whistling into the house through the cracks. Soon after, the hard frost that signaled winter sealed the earth.

When the snow came and the long nights stole the natural light from the late afternoon, Anna fashioned a little lamp from a potato she begged from her mother. She stood it on its cut end and poured a spoonful or two of the local sunflower seed oil into a thumb-sized well she scooped out of the top. Twisting a wick from a strip of lining she tore from an old coat, she submerged most of its length in the oil and lit the upper end with a wooden match. Anna went on with her stitchery through the winter evenings, sitting close to her flickering lamp. She knew that her mother approved. Leya never said so, but she would sometimes stand and watch silently, and even though she did complain about how hard it was to find the oil, she found it. She also managed to spare a potato when her daughter needed another lamp for the embroidering.[1]

Day by day the design thrived, and Anna's fingers became more adept as she worked on her handiwork at home, bringing it to school only when the home economics class met. Once, when Anna was babysitting at her aunt Meyndl's after school, Meyndl came home to find her embroidering while the baby slept and asked Anna to let her work on the design for a while. Anna handed it over obediently, but as soon as she could, she wrapped up her embroidery, hurried home, ripped out her aunt's mistakes, and re-worked the design.

Her design unfolded all through the four months of winter. The black thread outlined the rows of stair-stepping squares that formed two large diamonds, while the red thread filled in every other square, leaving the white background in the alternate squares, where a black plus sign was superimposed on a black X. She had stitched the black borders of each square almost as straight as the edge of her school ruler, and she had cen-tered the double diamond perfectly on the linen, just as she had intended.

In March, when melting snow dripped from the roof and from the branches of the tree in the yard, Cousin Zavl, an escapee from the army who had not dared to come out in the daylight for months and months, appeared at their door. Anna went outside with her mother to talk to him. He didn't have to hide anymore, he said, because the tsar had been over-thrown in far-off Petrograd. The revolution that had started far to the north had not yet reached Korsun. Anna continued her embroidering.[2]

Soon after Zavl came out of hiding, the streets dissolved into ankle-deep mud, and Anna carried the traditional Purim holiday gifts of food to neigh-bors and friends. Leya was taking the train to Kiev, as she had been doing since the food shortages brought on by the war and the revolution had pushed her into the black market. Smuggling sugar from Korsun to Kiev, she bartered it there for salt, then traded the scarce salt in Korsun for food to feed her three children, her parents, her sister, and her sister's daughter.

Anna kept embroidering. She completed the last square of the design before the blooming of the Russian Orthodox priest's lilac trees. Now she was ready to crochet the lace edging at each end of the linen, but the nec-essary white thread was nowhere to be found in town, so she had to wait until Leya brought some back from one of her trips to Kiev.

Taking the finished embroidery and the precious thread to class, Anna asked Nina Constantinovna for help in choosing a lace pattern to follow, but the teacher merely told her to go ahead and make anything she wanted. Anna said nothing, but she was angry. It was the teacher's job to help the students. Never having made lace before, Anna expected Nina Con-stantinovna to select a pattern suitable for her skills. Unhappy with the simple lacework pattern she chose, Anna fashioned the trim as best she could, until she was finally ready to sew it in place as the finishing touch to her dresser scarf.

Leya noticed that the linen was now badly soiled from being handled for so long. She took the scarf to the hand laundry, parting with her last few kopecks to have it washed, starched, and ironed. When Anna saw it again, she was amazed. The soiled scarf had become so familiar to her hands and eyes while she was bringing the design to life, one stitch at a time, that she had not truly seen it. Only when it had been out of her hands and out of her sight, and then brought back to her, revived, did it reveal itself to her as a thing of beauty.

Nina Constantinovna was also impressed with Anna's project. She decided to enter it in the statewide contest. She showed off the scarf to the other teachers and to her husband, Luk, the history teacher. The three of them, Anna, Luk, and Nina Constantinovna, stood together between classes, looking at the scarf. Luk agreed that Anna had done a fine job on her embroidery, but he couldn't help mentioning that Anna hadn't made as good a grade in his class as she should have.

Anna said nothing in her own defense, partly because she knew Luk was right—she did spend less time studying history when she was embroidering—and partly because she was unable to speak up to a teacher. Later, though, she wished she could have defended herself. She wished she had explained to him that her tiny oil light was just enough to embroider by, but it was too dim to do any serious reading of her history book. Besides, to make up for spending time embroidering at night, she sometimes got up early to study history in the morning sunlight. But she understood that he was unhappy with her because he had been expecting her to earn the highest grade in his history class. She suspected that he was also a bit annoyed with his wife for encouraging her to spend so much time with the dresser scarf. Although the boys called him *Lukashka* ("puddle of water") behind his back, Anna judged Luk the best teacher at the school. He had high standards. She knew that of all her teachers, he was the one she would remember with the most respect.

Nina Constantinovna sent the embroidery to the contest headquarters in Kiev, and the scarf was almost forgotten. Then one day at the end of May 1917, Nina Constantinovna opened a letter from Kiev, and soon was telling everyone that the school had taken a first prize. Anna's scarf had won.

It was one of the last days of the school year. Anna had gone home earlier in the afternoon. Nina told the students to give her the good news if they saw her, and as soon as school let out, the little sister of Anna's next-door friend ran home, saw her outside the house, and called out, You won! You won! Deciding that it was too late to go back to school, Anna went into the house. She would have to wait until tomorrow to hear the details about the prize.

Anna did not think her prize worth mentioning at home. Compliments were neither given nor expected in her family. But even if she had planned to mention her victory, she had no chance to tell her mother, because the same young messenger spotted Leya coming home and rushed over to let her know that Anna had won. Instead of being elated, Leya went angrily into the house, found Anna there, and scolded her. She had a right to be angry with Anna, she said. Hadn't she gone to all the trouble to find oil for Anna's potato lamps? The least Anna could do was to tell her mother when she won first prize.

Nina Constantinovna made no move to release Anna from her agreement, and when the judges returned the scarf, Nina Constantinovna kept it. Even though Anna had cradled the linen in her lap for months and knew every feature of it as she knew the faces of her sisters, she had understood from the beginning that this was how it would be. She was content. She had a top-grade "five" in home economics, and she could revel in the triumph of winning the competition—only eleven years old, after all, and not even thinking she had a chance. Each clean stitch and each well-placed line in the red and black diamond design existed because of her own determination, care, and skill.

But there was more. The scarf spoke to her of beauty in the same way that the lilac blossoms thrilled her when she saw them trailing over the priest's fence in May. And then, of course, there was the prize. The award was a six-volume set of the poems of Russian poet Mikhail Lermontov. Anna asked to have the books delivered to Nina Constantinovna's. Her own family had already been forced to move twice because Leya had no money for fuel or rent, and Anna didn't know where they would be living when her prize arrived. The same thing was happening to so many families that the post office put up a sign saying they would not deliver the mail anymore; you had to walk to the post office and ask for your letters.

After school closed for the year, Nina and Luk spent the summer in a rented dacha, a typical peasant house with straw-thatched roof and small windows. It was in the open country near a river branch for swimming, a half hour outside of town. Anna walked to the dacha frequently during the summer to ask whether her prize books had arrived. Again and again she approached the clay-walled house where laden fruit trees filled the garden and chickens strutted in the yard. Again and again she stood at the door to ask Nina if her prize had come, and each time the teacher put her off.

Finally, on a day when Anna appeared yet again at the little cottage, Nina Constantinovna angrily held the door against her, preventing her from coming in. Through the nearly closed door Anna saw her prize books, the poems of Lermontov in six volumes, sitting on a shelf.

She stood still for a moment. Then she took herself away from the teacher's house. She went home, she cried, and she never again tried to claim her prize.

Three and a half years later, trying to cross the border into Finland on the way to America, Anna and her family were turned back by Bolshevik soldiers, one of whom took away most of their scanty possessions, including Leya's prayer book and the few school books Anna was carrying. Long afterward, Anna decided it had been just as well that the prize books had ended up in Luk's house. Even if Nina Constantinovna had given the books to her, Anna would have lost them going to America. Luk had been a fine teacher. It was better that he had them.

11

Between Gentile and Jew

Jews and Gentiles in Korsun lived their lives separately because of their different religions, but even before the building of the high school, they had rubbed shoulders daily.[1] They met and talked at the marketplace, buying and selling, bargaining and arguing. They lived with each other as peasant servant girl and Jewish householder, or as peasant apprentice boy and Jewish master shoemaker. They became friends and enemies. Their young people sometimes fell in love with each other, and their older heads helped each other stop them from marrying.[2]

In addition to professing different religions, Christians and Jews spoke different languages and lived mostly in separate neighborhoods. Motivated by mutual self-interest, however, they had turned many barriers into bridges.[3]

Despite tsarist efforts to install Russian as the primary language in the Ukraine, the peasants still spoke their native Ukrainian. The mother tongue of the Jews was Yiddish. To communicate with each other, peasants and Jews learned as much of each other's language as they found necessary or desirable. Ukrainian was the language of the marketplace where peasant women sold fresh food. Like Anna's mother, Leya, many Jews learned enough Ukrainian from the peasants to bargain with them. Ukrainian servant girls in Jewish households, on the other hand, learned Yiddish.

Just as each group might learn the other's language while going about the daily routine, so each group might visit the other's neighborhood in search of profit. Town Jews found business opportunities in the villages of the countryside beyond the town's borders. Jewish "village men," *dorf-mentshen,* walked to the villages and back, buying hog bristles or anything else worth a fee of a few kopecks when they sold it to a merchant or a manufacturer in town. A *dorfmentsh* could sell the hair from a hog's back to brush makers, who used the bristles, bleached white and sterilized, to make toothbrushes and clothes brushes. (Anna's family was too poor to buy toothbrushes. All the women Anna knew were toothless by age thirty-five.)

A few notches higher than the *dorfmentshen* in social stature and in business experience were the Jewish merchants who made the rounds of the villages in their own wagons to buy handmade articles from the peasants. The merchants sent the handcrafted peasant wares, such as wooden spoons, to the big cities for sale.

Town Jews had occasional contacts with the tenant farmers just inside the town borders. In peacetime Anna and her friends would take a Sunday walk near the Jewish cemetery, stopping at the small, outskirt farm of a peasant woman who would sell them milk to drink, fresh from her cow. Leya once sent Anna to buy roses from a tenant farmer in this area. Once in a while, Anna also went to the house of a peasant farmer at the outskirts of Old Town, north of the main street, to buy tomatoes as well as cucumbers, radishes, and new potatoes. The gray dirt road, just wide enough for a wagon, took Anna to the gate in the front fence, where she would stop, fearing the big dog patrolling the garden. She would yell to the house, bringing the woman out at the front door to ask what she wanted. The woman would let Anna into her garden, and a few times even invited her into the house.

The tenant farm families, on their side, had many reasons to visit Jewish neighborhoods. They did the heavy work for the richer families in town. The women whitewashed the walls of rooms or laundered clothes at the river. The men chopped wood or carried water. Their sons, before they were old enough to work in one of the town's factories, could earn money acting as *shabbes goyim*—"Sabbath Gentiles"—for ordinary Jews. For a small fee, a *shabbes goy* lit or blew out candles, turned off the oil lamp that had burned all night, built a new fire in the heating unit, and lit the samovar. Every Jewish household employed such a person to do these tasks, since a Jew was forbidden to work on the Sabbath. Instead of a teenager, the *shabbes goy* might be an older man like the milkman. In peacetime the water carrier did these jobs for Anna's family.

If a family had a live-in peasant maid, she would also serve as a *shabbes goy*. If a family had a "steady" *shabbes goy,* he would come over on Saturday without being called, to attend to any fire that must be started or put out. Usually Anna's house did not get too cold when the fire was allowed to die on Friday night in winter, although the family might wear jackets in the house. If it did get too cold, though, they would call a *shabbes goy,* and if they did not have a regular one, Anna would go outside on Saturday morning to look for a Gentile boy who wanted to earn a few kopecks.

Because fire was essential, the *shabbes goy* was essential. To show how much they needed these helpers, Jews told a joke about a golem, a legendary man-made monster given life by a rabbi. A golem was supposedly created at different times in history to protect Jews from an imminent menace. The notable Prague golem was created—so the legend goes—because Jews in sixteenth-century Prague were commonly accused and assaulted or killed for the so-called "blood libel," the absurd charge that they killed a Christian child in order to use its blood in the making of the Passover *matza*. In Anna's version of the joke, when the Prague golem took vengeance, starting to kill Gentiles, a rabbi quipped, Stop him! Pretty soon we won't have any *shabbes goyim*.

The peasant boys also earned money doing chores for Jews of means. Grandmother Beyla, who kept six goats in her foyer, paid a peasant boy twenty-five cents or so to take the animals to pasture for the day.

The Jewish shoemaker Sholem Alushka employed about ten people. They worked at the shoemaker's benches—chairs with a boxlike working surface attached—in his large foyer. Among them were two peasant apprentices who lived with him. If a Jewish craftsman had helpers or apprentices, they were often either from another town, or peasant boys from surrounding farming villages not near enough to walk home and back every day. It was the custom for a master to let one or two boys sleep in the choice spot in winter by climbing up to the flat top of the eight-feet-wide, six-feet-tall oven, whose bricks radiated welcome warmth all night long.[4] When Mr. Alushka was taken into the army, a handful of the boys remained. No one but the master shoemaker, the *zagotovshchik*—who could even design new models—was capable of making new shoes, but the boys kept the shop open, doing repairs.

The use of the bathhouse, which contained not only the ritual pool of water for immersion (the *mikveh*) but also a public section for water bathing and steam bathing, was not limited to Jews. The primary purpose for the bathhouse, however, was to allow the carrying out of one of the three biblical commandments specific to Orthodox Jewish women, namely to maintain ritual purity of home and person, in this case by bathing in the ritual pool after a menstrual cycle had ended. A shtetl was to be located on a river or at a natural spring because of this commandment, since a bathhouse required a large and reliable source of naturally running water.

In addition, Jewish women in Korsun who were between menstrual periods prepared for the Sabbath by going to the bathhouse on Thursday afternoon or evening. On Friday, Jewish men used the bathhouse. They could bathe, take a steam bath, or ritually immerse in the *mikveh*. In the steam bath, men would wield switches made from green branches, using them to flick their skin invigoratingly, as Scandinavian men have long done in their saunas.

At other times, when the bathhouse was not being used by Jews, it was available to Gentiles. Many Christian landowners brought their families to the bathhouse to bathe. They would send messengers to the bathhouse, which had no telephone, to make a reservation.

Jews had other uses for the bathhouse. On a special occasion such as the Passover holiday, silverware had to be boiled to make it kosher. A poor family had only one set of silver-plated tableware. At Passover, when eating utensils had to be purified of all traces of grain, they were brought to the bathhouse in the morning. Spoons were bundled together with string and placed in a bag with a rope attached. The same was done for forks and for knives. The bags were submerged in the tank of boiling water by their ropes for a short time.

The couple who ran the bathhouse and made sure that the proper rituals were carried out lived in a cottage attached to the bathhouse, in order to be available at all times. The wife attended each woman for the ritual immersion, mixing boiling water in the wooden tub with cold river water to reach a tolerable temperature. Her husband did the same for the men. He also kept the fire burning by adding wood continually to ensure that the water would always be boiling. The job was not a high or well-paid profession. Each bather gave the husband or wife a few pennies for their services. The bathhouse was subsidized by the Jewish community council, so that no poor person would be denied a ritual immersion in the *mikveh*. Poor women who were merely bathing, however, stepped into water already used by someone else.

It was not uncommon for a Jew to have a Gentile living in his house, even though dietary laws prohibited it in theory. If a non-Jew ate from the plates and spoons in an Orthodox Jewish home, the fact that he habitually ate nonkosher food would mean, under the strictest interpretation of the kosher laws, that the utensils would no longer be kosher. For example, the only drinking water in a house was kept in a barrel in the foyer, where a five-cup metal ladle hung on the wall nearby. Anyone who was thirsty dipped the ladle into the barrel. By strictest interpretation, if a Gentile drank from the ladle, it became unkosher. The strictest interpretation was not always followed, however.

Richer Jewish families often hired a live-in peasant maid, a girl who came into the household at age twelve or thirteen, sweeping the floor and rocking the cradle until she was old enough to do the full range of maid's chores. The girl was sometimes an orphan who had no other home than her workplace; or if she had a family, she would be exposed to nonkosher food only when she went home once or twice a year for Easter or Christmas. Although strict observance forbade the maid to drink from a cup or eat with a spoon used by a family member, the importance of strictness faded with time, as the maid ate the family's food day after day, avoided nonkosher food, and became more like one of the family.

Although some of Anna's interactions with Christians arose from her characteristic interest in other people, many came from the fact that she was able to study in Korsun's first public school. This high school allowed numbers of Jewish children to study in company with Gentile schoolmates and Gentile teachers. For Jews and Christians to have daily contact during most of the year was a phenomenon unknown in Korsun until then. Here was a unique opportunity not only for Anna, but also for other Jewish and Christian children to know each other as peers. Such close and sustained contact, if Anna's case is any reflection of the general situation, allowed relationships to develop for the first time among the students and between students and teachers. Two students, for example, had an opportunity to begin to think of each other less as "that Christian" and "that Jew," and more as "my friend Shevchenko" and "my friend Anna."

Jews had reason to fear and hate Christians. Easter was the most dangerous season for the Jews in Russia, since the priests did not often promote friendly relations. More likely at Easter-time they would tell their flocks that the Jews had killed Jesus, inciting the peasants to violent acts against the Jews.

Jewish children, in Anna's experience, were taught to hate and fear Christians, and at the same time developed a hunger for a good word from them. Anna had been cautioned when she was quite young that when she saw a priest, she must hide her hands behind her or he would cut them off. Her own experience taught her otherwise. When she was older, she went inside the Orthodox church many times and often had contact with a priest. Through experiences with her high school classmates and in other situations, she had opportunities to learn about the ways in which people in and around Korsun, especially peasants, practiced Christianity.[5]

To celebrate Christmas, hundreds of peasants came to Korsun from all around, driving their sleighs onto the frozen river, where services were held. Blocks of ice were dragged together on the frozen surface to form a cross. Red beet juice was poured over the cross of ice to represent the blood of Jesus.

The Orthodox Sunday service was brief. Everyone stood, since Korsun's church had no seats. Although Christians were not supposed to buy anything on Sunday, the peasants often stayed in town after the service, some of the women walking down the palace road toward the crossroads to shop at the stores or at the marketplace, some of the men stopping at a tavern to drink whiskey, beer, or mead.

Even if they were not bound for church, each member of a peasant family came to town in their best clothes, and even those who did attend services would spend time in town relaxing. A peasant girl, for example, typically attended no school, working on the farm all week long. Sunday was her day for fun. She went to church in a beautiful white linen blouse, gathered at the neck, its wide sleeves decorated with a conventional Ukrainian design of stylized birds, flowers, or geometric shapes, always in the Ukrainian national colors, red and black. Over the blouse she wore a vest, like a man's, buttoned in front. Her skirt was fronted by a fresh, short apron, usually embroidered with a larger version of the same designs as those on the sleeves.

She wore her braids hanging free, adorned with brightly colored bows and glass beads. On her head was a wreath of flowers like a crown, and from the back of her head, ribbons of all colors, ten or a dozen of them, streamed to her waist. On her neck she wore as many as a dozen strands of beads, the more the better, some handed down from her mother, arranged in graduated sizes from strand to strand, the largest as big as marbles. She carried a small bouquet of flowers to church, the choicest blossoms picked from the family's garden. Usually she was barefoot in spring, summer, and fall. She also wore this Sunday best to festive occasions such as an engagement or a wedding.

Her brother, until he was married at age nineteen or twenty, adopted a more stylish fashion in clothes than his father. For church he wore the same white linen shirt as his father (with the slit from neck to chest placed to the left of the center, and closed by two ties at the neck), except that it had a collar, and it was embroidered at both the collar and the cuffs. He might wear a vest in the chilly weather of spring or fall, not the weekday one made cheaply by a tailor, but the better quality Sunday vest. Leaving aside his everyday belt, he cinched his shirt at the waist with a green or black sash, very much like the *gartl* of the pious Jew, but tied in a half or whole knot at his left side. The shirt partly covered his plain pants, which were cut wide from the waistline and were tucked into his boots.

Anna would see him with his friends coming into town on their way to church, his black boots in shining contrast to his white shirt, the fringe-decorated free ends of his sash swinging as he walked. He wore no undershirt, as Anna discovered one day when she watched two young men take off their white shirts to fight. His leather-visored cloth cap, similar to the one worn by Jewish men, was called, in Ukrainian, a *grechizka*—a "Greek"—and it smartly set off his neatly cut hair.

A schoolmate invited Anna's class to come and see her sister dressed as a bride. The family's ancestors had been serfs, but the higher echelon of serfs, those who worked indoors as nannies or housekeepers rather than outdoors as field laborers. Anna's schoolmate was proud that they were not descended from field hands. Anna and other Jewish girls attending the wedding noticed that the bride's white dress was similar to that of a Jewish bride, while others in the wedding party wore peasant costumes of flowered dresses with beads.

When the elder priest was murdered in his own doorway during the war,

Anna and her schoolmates attended his funeral in the church. His son, also a priest, taught mathematics to Anna's high school class, and it was he who arranged to provide a number of Jewish families with food during the severe food shortage in the spring of 1919 by recruiting Anna and other Jewish students to work in his garden.

But Anna's contact with formal Christianity was not confined to her visits to the church or her dealings with the priest. She had enough contact with peasants to form the opinion that in general they were religiously naive. They believed more in demons than in God, she thought, and they had all kinds of devices to chase out the devil. In a corner of their little house they kept a few icons lit by a lamp, and although some peasants did go to church in Korsun on Sunday, many did not know the meaning of the icons, nor did they know anything of formal religious teachings—the preachings of Jesus, or the Last Supper, or the Resurrection. They did not send their children to a religious school. In Anna's view, the Romanovs and the landowners—many living in Paris, idle except for their card playing—preferred the peasants to remain illiterate and ignorant. On the other hand, the peasants did observe Lent by eating no meat, and they did celebrate Easter and Christmas.

Anna was invited inside the one-room peasant houses often enough to form a good idea of the interior, where a lamp hung on a chain from the ceiling in one corner above the icon. The standard peasant cottage in the Ukraine, as known from the literature, was a rectangle with one short side facing the street, but with the entryway at the short side farther from the street. The house was entered by way of a foyer large enough for storage or for sleeping in the summer. From the center of the foyer one walked toward the street into the one and only room, where the oven took up the nearest half of the right wall. The far left corner of the room, nearest the street, was the icon corner. Benches were fastened to the walls everywhere except at the oven and the icon corner.[6]

In one village house, Anna noticed a pillow on the floor for kneeling in front of the icon. At the home of more prosperous peasants, in a special second room to be used only for guests, she saw the icons and an embroidery-covered kneeling stool, together with a fancy bed and artificial flowers. Though the house still had a thatched roof and a clay floor covered with flat, dried, red-brown grass, the walls were blue-tinted, the sheets were embroidered on the edges like a dust ruffle, and the pillowslips on the square feather pillows were bordered with two inches of white lace. Only the poorest house that she visited lacked an icon.

The lamp above the icon was kept burning with olive oil, which didn't smoke like other oils. With its small wick, the icon lamp gave only a weak light, but the house also had a stronger lamp burning kerosene for general light. Before the revolution of 1917, the peasants crossed themselves each morning in front of their icons. After the revolution, with the Bolshevik ban on religion, they hid them.

Thus, despite the separateness imposed by religion, Jews and Gentiles in the town of Korsun could come into contact that varied from occasional and casual to frequent and close. The images that Jews and Christians formed of each other's lives from such contacts varied in accuracy and in completeness, but the contacts could contribute to a measure of understanding and goodwill.

12
Cousin Zavl

Aunt Khana would rather become a soldier herself than have her son Zavl go into the army. As a mother, she wanted to keep him safe, but there was a second reason for wanting to protect him. As her only son, he was the only person who could perform the religious obligation of saying the prayer for the dead for his parents. When Germany declared war on Russia, Aunt Khana worried even more than usual that her son Zavl would be taken into the tsar's army.

Anna's cousin Zavl was ten years older than she, and he lived in a different town, Tarashcha, so they were never close. Still, because their mothers always stayed in touch, Anna heard about him, and occasionally she saw him. Zavl's mother had decided for some reason not to let him go to Jewish elementary school with the other Jewish boys when he was four years old. She delayed enrolling him until he was six or seven, which meant that he missed some crucial schooling. As a result he could only *dahven*—chant the Hebrew prayers—slowly and haltingly, always falling behind the other boys in the daily readings from the prayer book. Anna considered him an ignoramus about religious matters, but that didn't prevent her from liking him.

Zavl grew to be an engaging young man, not tall, but lean, with brown hair and a ready laugh. Stylish in a suit, shirt, and collar, he was handsome, but not so good looking that he put on airs. He made a joke of everything, and he could make people laugh. Much later, after Anna had seen Eddie Cantor in America, she thought her cousin had been funnier and better looking than the comedian. Everybody loved Zavl.

Aunt Khana was a worrier, but she was also a woman of action. Knowing that police or army agents would probably search the house for her son, she had a secret compartment built—a narrow space within a double wall, entered through a secret door. She hired Jewish masons who would build it little by little, to avoid arousing suspicion. She masked the door, painted white like the rest of the wall, behind a chest of drawers. Zavl would only have to hide there until the agents completed their search of the house from attic to cellar and went on their way.

Despite his mother's efforts, Zavl was eventually taken into the army, but he seems to have spent more time as an escapee than he spent as a soldier on duty. At one point in his underground existence, his mother sent him to Korsun to hide, because he had close family there to help him. He did not stay in one place too long. Occasionally he went back to his hometown, where he could use the secret compartment if necessary, but more often he stayed in Korsun and hid himself at Aunt Feyga's house or at Grandmother Beyla's. The Korsun authorities kept an eye out for hometown boys whom they knew, but they were not so eagerly watchful for draft dodgers and runaway soldiers from out of town.

While Zavl was hiding in Korsun, he worked as an apprentice at the home of a *zagotovshchik*, a master shoemaker. Sometimes Zavl spent most of the morning hiding in a garden behind a fence near Grandma Beyla's house. If he was elsewhere, and he heard that soldiers were looking for him, he would come back and climb over the fence into the garden. Family members took food to him. Anna's aunt gave her a package once, telling her to throw it over the fence as she passed by. Otherwise the children were told to avoid going near the garden, so that they wouldn't be followed, giving away Zavl's hiding place. What Zavl was doing was not unusual. Other young men were hiding from the army in various places in Korsun at the same time.

The authorities would sometimes come to grandmother's house, looking for Zavl or looking for Aunt Meyndl's husband, Yankl, who was also often in hiding from the army. The agents would arrive at one or two o'clock in the morning, search the house, look under the beds, and then go away. If they occasionally caught one of the young men hiding in the house and took him away, he eventually escaped and came back to Korsun. Yankl didn't come back for quite a while, but Zavl would be hiding out again before long.

Zavl's escapades became family legends. Once, when he injured his hand—it might have been accidental, but then again, maybe not—he was taken to an army hospital. His mother found out where he was, and she went there herself, fearing that as soon as his injury had healed, he would be sent to a place where his life would be in danger. After learning that Zavl was allowed to recuperate by taking walks inside a large fenced yard, she would walk along outside the fence. One day, as they walked far from the eyes of the guards, Khana threw a set of men's clothes over the fence.

Zavl took off his hospital uniform, scrambled into the civilian clothes, and climbed over the fence. His mother hurried him into a waiting coach and took him home.

Another time a pair of soldiers was guarding him. They passed a house that had an outhouse in the yard, a rare convenience, and when they agreed to let Zavl use it for a minute, he quickly broke through the boards at the back and escaped.

In a small town such as Korsun, when a woman went to the marketplace for the day's food, she met many people on the way, and when people met, they would gossip and tell stories. The whole town loved the stories about Zavl's escapes. Townspeople especially liked the story about the time he was being escorted by two policemen. He told a little boy who was following them to yell a dirty name at him and then run. Zavl, pretending to be angry, yelled and sprinted after him, leaving the policemen flatfooted, gaping at this innocent chase. The boy's name-calling and Zavl's yelling gave him the head start he needed to elude the police. They finally tired of hunting for him, and went away.

For a long time Zavl had been staying indoors during the day, appearing on the street only at night. In the large cities, in Petrograd and Moscow and Kiev, the streets were lit, and electric lights were no longer a novelty in the home. Small towns like Korsun, though, where no streetlight broke the darkness, and where the kerosene lamps inside the houses threw only a faint light, were ideal for fugitives. Zavl could easily slip around in the dark unnoticed, except on moon-bright nights.

When he suddenly appeared, in the middle of the day, standing outside the house of Oora, the maker of sheepskin coats (Anna's family had moved there from Yenta Koslov's house), Anna and her mother could not imagine what he was doing there. He was usually afraid to be seen. Nobody was supposed to know where Zavl was. The family didn't even talk about him, in case somebody might be listening and might snitch to the authorities. Even among the Jews there were snitchers who would inform the police and collect the reward.

Zavl told Anna and Leya that he didn't have to bother anymore about the agents of the tsar, because the tsar's government was no longer in power. He said all of the men in hiding could come out, because a revolution had begun. The snow was melting and dripping from the roof and from the branches of the tree where Anna was standing just outside the door as Zavl told the startling news from Petrograd. It was March 1917.[1] Zavl stayed in Korsun. He would drop in at his Aunt Feyga's, where the children were closer to his age than those in Anna's house, and sometimes, standing at a window looking into the house of the Budyanska family next door, he saw one or another of their daughters. Their baby and their two young teenagers were only of passing interest, but he also caught glimpses of a blonde young woman.

Sheyndl Budyanska was only a little younger than Zavl. Lovely in both face and figure, she was one of the most beautiful young women in town, a treasure to stir the blood of any young man. He fell in love with her through the window.

Sheyndl had her eyes open, too. She glanced back through her window, and she fell in love with Zavl. They began to spend time together. It was obvious to all that Zavl was courting Sheyndl.

Sheyndl's parents did not approve of Zavl. They did not want their daughter to marry Zavl for three reasons. First, although both families were Hasidic, they followed different *rebbeim*—spiritual leaders of different dynasties of Hasidism—who vigorously disagreed about matters of religious observance. That was true. Second, Zavl's family was not wealthy enough; and third, he was unlearned in religious matters.

Deciding whether Zavl's family was too poor was a little complicated. Sheyndl's father, Shimml Budyanska, owned the larger of the two stores in the marketplace that sold tableware. He did a good business in pots and pans, cups and saucers, dishes, plates, and soup bowls. It was true that Zavl's mother had much less income, but his grandmother was wealthier than the Budyanskas.

The religious shortcomings of Zavl, whose education had started late, and who prayed poorly, were obvious. In contrast, Sheyndl's father was a Hasid, and even though he had adopted a more modern appearance—his beard was neatly trimmed, he had no earlocks, and he wore modern suits—he was more learned in matters religious than Zavl. Furthermore, Sheyndl's uncle was an important and devoted member of the more old-fashioned Hasid community.

Anna had a different view about the religious learning of the two families. The Budyanskas claimed the respect due to a family of long Hasidic lineage, but Sheyndl and the other children were not carrying on the tradition of learning. If Sheyndl's parents criticized Zavl for lack of education, they were the pot to Zavl's kettle. Furthermore, Anna was not fond of Sheyndl and thought the Budyanskas were snobbish, acting like royalty condemned to live among commoners.

To Sheyndl and Zavl, all these opinions did not matter. They were in love. But Anna's grandmother and grandfather fumed, knowing that the Budyanskas looked down on them. The Budyanskas fumed, Anna believed, because their ambition was to have Sheyndl marry into a social circle above their own. Everyone knew that both families were unhappy with the match, and nearly the whole town took sides, discussing and arguing about the burning love story, which began to resemble the story of Romeo and Juliet.

The bitter discussions continued until Sheyndl's family awoke one morning to find that she had disappeared. Zavl's family discovered that he, too, was gone, and soon the whole town knew that the young lovers had eloped. Elopement was a major scandal, as shocking and outrageous in Korsun at that time, the last year of the world war, as living together without being married—living in sin.

When the defiant lovers came back, Anna's grandmother ignored Sheyndl, chagrined to see Zavl married into such a family. Sheyndl's parents also took the marriage hard, seething at their daughter's disregard for social customs and the honor of the family.

Despite the continuing ill will between the two families, the couple rented a house, bought new furniture, and settled down. Zavl took up his trade as a shoe designer, had his own shop, and did well. A handful of shoe designers made a living in Korsun. As a *zagotovshchik,* he was in a higher profession than that of ordinary shoemaker. He not only handcrafted the upper portion of men's and women's shoes, but also designed shoes, adopting the rapidly changing styles as they appeared in the fashionable magazines from the big cities of Europe.

Zavl and Sheyndl were still living in Korsun when Anna eventually left. The two families were still at odds.

13
Leya the Smuggler (1917–1919)

Cousin Zavl had come out of hiding early in March 1917 to announce the overthrow of Tsar Nicholas II. The Bolsheviks had taken power in Petrograd seven months later. Such a momentous change in national government, however, had far less immediate effect on the Russian people than did the scarcity of food.

The distribution of food from farm to city had broken down, partly from wartime disarray and partly from a winter so harsh—temperatures fell to less than forty below zero in January—that for a time twelve hundred locomotives, their frozen pipes burst, stood motionless on the tracks. In the south, in Odessa, people waited two days in line for cooking oil, while in the north, in Petrograd and Moscow during freezing weather, women stood in lines all night waiting for bread.

Leya was a conventional housewife. Her experience outside the home was limited. Like many women who helped their husbands, she had worked at the fair every two weeks, selling Aaron's glass chimneys for kerosene lamps. Once Aaron left for America, though, Leya found no work. She finally took up smuggling so that her family could eat. The spring of 1917 found her taking the train to Kiev whenever she could, to barter on the black market. Once she got the hang of it, she took Anna along occasionally to help.

Leya's smuggling became even more important after August 1917 when Grandmother Beyla lost all of her savings. The Provisional Government in Petrograd declared tsarist money illegal, replacing it with a new currency, which people called "Kerensky money," after the new prime minister, Alexander Kerensky.

The doors of Korsun's only bank were thrown open after it had been stocked with Kerensky money. Every family was obliged to send a representative to the bank (which also served as the post office), where they were asked the number of people in the family, and were given one hundred Kerensky rubles per person. Leya's family of four was given four hundred rubles.

The Kerensky paper money—green twenty-dollar (ruble) bills and yellow fifty-dollar bills, for example—was not unusual, but the small change was laughable. Instead of the tsarist metal coins, the new small change—50, 25, 10, and 5 cent (kopeck) denominations—was not only made of paper, but was only slightly larger than a postage stamp. These little bits of paper were easy to lose; they didn't fit a man's wallet, and a woman couldn't put them in her bosom, because the paper curled up and disintegrated.

Some people seen accepting a tsarist dollar bill were arrested, and some were killed on the spot. Townspeople caught on quickly, and the changeover to Kerensky money was soon completed. People burned tsarist paper rubles, in fear of being found with them. Those who had silver tsarist coins were afraid to use them in the market. Some Korsuners melted them instead and made something of use from the metal. Although the new government had successfully enforced the changeover, it had misjudged the attitude of the peasants, who refused to take the new money, suspicious of its value. Since the farmers refused to sell what few wares they had, the new money was soon worthless.

Because Beyla's savings from her profitable business were in the form of tsarist money in the bank, they were taken from her. She and Avrum were given only their allotted two hundred rubles of the useless Kerensky paper. After having been so secure, a prominent person of wealth, Beyla was suddenly left without savings. Roles were now reversed; Beyla and Avrum were dependent upon Leya, whose smuggling was providing the family's food.

If a commodity was scarce in Kiev but available in Korsun, Leya saw that she could multiply its value enough to pay for food at home. Sugar had always been plentiful in Korsun. The local sugar factory drew on a region noted for its sugar beets. Although the factory was no longer selling sugar, Leya could buy from a few small merchants and other townsmen whose supplies were not yet exhausted. She was able to profit from the black market because sugar was even scarcer in Kiev.

Whenever Leya was able to buy sugar in Korsun, she folded little envelopes of paper, carefully pouring a few teaspoonfuls of sugar into each one. Sliding the envelopes into the small pockets in a vest until she had hidden as many as she could carry unnoticed, she usually set off alone to the train station two miles outside of town. If Anna went along, carrying her own vest-pocket supply of envelopes, they could bring back a larger stock of valuable goods. One time, not long out of her sickbed after passing the crisis of typhus, Anna felt so tired that she kept wanting to sit or lie down. She looked so pale and weak that people asked Leya what was the matter with her daughter. Leya insisted that although Anna had been sick, she would be all right.

Leya was not the only Korsuner who went to a big city to trade on the black market. Anyone who brought goods back from Warsaw or Kharkov or Kiev was sure to have visitors eager to barter for the items they needed. Many people had worn the same clothes until they were almost rags. When a traveler returned from Warsaw, a center for the manufacture of fabrics and clothing, someone would go to them with salt and ask if they had clothes they would trade for the salt—a dress, a shirt, or a child's blouse.

When winter came—first the winter of 1917–1918, with shortages pinching more than in any previous year of the war, and then the "worst winter" of 1918–1919—a person might not have enough warm clothes even to go outside. To own a warm shawl was a great luxury. A good pair of shoes or a wool blanket was a treasure.

During this time Anna was saddened by the sight of a woman wearing a man's shoes to protect her feet when she went out looking for bread to feed her family. Anna was even more distressed to see a man from a nice family named Veeneroff—a bookkeeper who kept the books for small shopkeepers—going about in women's clothing. When she first saw him on the street, she noticed the women's shoes he wore, the lace-holes empty, the tongues standing up awkwardly. She thought he was a woman not only because of the shoes and the lightweight shawl he had draped across his shoulders, but also because he was not wearing his skullcap, a shocking sight that was even more distressing to Anna in a time and place where religious observance was so important. Men might certainly wear shawls. Zyama Rabinovich, the wealthy uncle of the famous writer Sholom Aleichem, used to pass Grandmother Beyla's house every day on his way to swim, even in sixty-degree weather, wearing a light shawl around his shoulders to keep off the chill, but he always wore his skullcap.

A major item such as a pair of shoes or an overcoat suitable for a Korsun winter would bring the owner a piece of gold or silver jewelry. Leya was a poor woman, by now with only a few valuables of her own. She had already sold a ring and a few pieces of silver. Her everyday tableware consisted of four tablespoons, four forks, and a few teaspoons. They were not a set. Nobody had sets. The handles were heavy, not like sterling silver.

Leya's trades were mainly for the food her family needed from day to day. As soon as she returned from a trip, the word flew around town and people came to her house, bringing her whatever they could trade. They gave her half a loaf of bread for a teaspoon of tea. One woman made a cake substitute from pieces of bread dough, slightly sweetened. Baking it quickly, because there was not enough wood for the long process of baking bread, she brought it to trade for Leya's salt.

Most of the time Leya brought back salt, and if she could get a few pounds, it was almost like getting a handful of diamonds. People used to ask Anna if her mother had salt. Anyone in town who needed salt knew that the source was Leya, who sold it by the spoonful.

Anna was sent to trade the salt for whatever the family needed. Not far away lived a husband and wife who made their living by baking kosher bread on Tuesdays. Housewives ordinarily baked their own bread twice a week, white bread on Fridays and the cheaper black bread on Mondays or Tuesdays, after the white bread had been eaten. Now, however, a poor woman who could not spare the wood or ran out of flour might buy bread from the couple. Bread was such a major part of the diet that anyone who had become too poor to buy stale bread knew they were on the brink of starvation.

Anna might be sent to the couple to buy a loaf of week-old bread, which was cheaper than fresh. Although the couple were scrupulously clean in their baking and storing of the bread, their stale bread had a distinctive off-taste. While Anna was buying the bread, the woman might mention that she needed a pair of pants and tell Anna to place an order for Leya's next trip to Kiev.

When Anna went with her mother to the Kiev black market, she could dimly recall a train ride on the same Kiev line before the war. She had been only five years old then, and although she still remembered getting off at Olshanitsa, forty miles from home, and going to her cousin Surka's wedding, she had forgotten the details of the trip.

In Korsun, where many people never traveled more than ten miles from their hometown in their whole life, a train ride was a rare adventure, to be stored in memory for the retelling. In peacetime the tickets had gone on sale thirty minutes or an hour before train time. A warning bell rang fifteen minutes before the train left, then again five minutes before, and for the final time just as the train was starting to pull out of the station. Uniformed policemen, *zhandarmi*, were on duty to prevent any disturbances, and a passenger could enter a complaint in a special book kept at every station.[1]

The blue-painted first-class car had closed compartments, each seating two or four passengers, and each provided with broad upholstered seats. At night the *Provodnik*, the attendant, pushed up the back cushion to form an upper berth. He also gave out the bedding, made the beds, locked each compartment's door to the central corridor when the train stopped at a station, and made himself generally useful, all in the expectation of a generous tip. Both the guard (*Konduktor*), who assigned the seats in the first-class compartments, and the head guard (*Oberkonduktor*), who came to examine the tickets, were uniformed in belted black blouses, baggy pants tucked into boots, and head-hugging caps of fur, but only the head guard could wear shoulder straps and pant stripes of silver and red braid. In those peacetime days, the train even included a separate first-class car for non-smokers and another for women.

In the green third-class car, passengers shed all the hand luggage they had managed to carry and then plopped themselves onto the bare wooden benches flanking the center corridor. Fortunately for the mothers of small children, even the third-class car had a lavatory. Third class in those times was noisy and crowded but companionable, people striking up conversations, sharing food and stories, and sometimes even becoming good friends during a journey.

The world war changed everything. As the conflict plodded into its third year, tickets were no longer issued, and with all the soldiers riding to and from the fighting front, Leya was lucky just to push her way into a car. No longer was she riding in a passenger car, even the third-class car of a passenger train, but instead in one of the boxcars in a freight train.

In the prewar days, the open-topped car behind the engine had held the coal that the fireman shoveled into the furnace to fire the boiler, but after the 1917 revolution, civilians were being forced to dig the coal from the mines, and their diggings went for military use. At the Korsun station, where peacetime trains had taken on coal, now they took on wood cut from the nearby forests. Sometimes the passengers of a train low on fuel were asked to get out, chop down trees, split the logs, and load the firewood into the coal car. For lack of fuel, Leya once spent a few days on a trip to Kiev, which was a train ride of only 128 miles.[2]

When the civil war followed the revolution, whichever army happened to be temporarily in power in the region commandeered the trains, leaving civilians to pile onto any train that came through a town if they were allowed to do so. The trains were so overcrowded on one of Anna's rides to Kiev that she and Leya watched the passengers crawling up to sit on the roofs of overcrowded boxcars. Some travelers might have waited for the next train, but not Leya, who had business in Kiev.[3]

Each freight car had a pair of safety buffers jutting ahead from its front wall like the stems of two mushrooms—one near the left and another near the right edge of the car—the flattened caps of the mushrooms aiming directly at the identical ones that projected backward from the rear of the next car ahead. Leya and Anna laid a board on these steel buffers, which were spring-loaded to absorb the shock if the train jerked and the two mushroom caps smacked together as the cars collided. On the board they spread some rags, and on that makeshift platform they rode, sandwiched between the two cars, balancing there, jolting and swaying, clutching the board, Leya holding on to her daughter.[4]

The first time Anna stepped off the train at Kiev with her mother and walked the several blocks to the marketplace, she saw a vast open square filled with a weaving mass of people. Most of them were either standing about or walking slowly through the crowd. Two people might be talking to each other briefly, then move apart, each of them finding another person for an exchange of a few words.

Only a few scattered vendors had goods on display. Sitting on the ground or on crates, these vendors presented tables and chairs for sale, or displayed boxes piled with skirts or blouses, dresses or shoes, knives or pots. It was a thief's market. As the saying went, "You have to be careful, if you buy pants, that you get two legs."

After spending an hour with her mother in the bazaar, Anna began to understand what all the other people were doing as they stood or walked about. Like other smugglers who made repeated trips to the Kiev black market, Leya had certain preferred customers. Anna saw her walk over to greet someone she had recognized in the crowd. The two women spoke a few words, then exchanged small packets, Leya handing over an envelope of sugar, and in return receiving a packet of tea or a measure of salt. Before long, a woman came quietly near and asked Leya if she had some sugar today. After a few minutes another woman came over, and the process was repeated. Leya approached customers and was herself approached by them until she had bartered all of her sugar. Sometimes, knowing that in half an hour Leya might sell all she had, they asked her if she still had sugar. The same kind of negotiation was being repeated all over the square, one person walking a little closer to another and almost whispering in his ear the name of the item he wanted to buy or sell.

Leya often exchanged her sugar for the kind of salt that was not granulated, but came in rough crystals. Lumpy and too irregular to be measured in a spoon or a measuring cup, it had to be bartered by weight, and it was harder to conceal in Leya's vest for the return trip, but back in Korsun this salt was worth three times the value of sugar. People could do without sugar, but their meager diet was much more difficult to bear without salt.

Whatever was scarce could be had in the square by trading—clothing, medicine, utensils, furniture, food—but Anna never saw any money pass from hand to hand, only the goods being bartered. Money was of no more use in Kiev than it was in Korsun.

Anna learned that the square was called the *zhidovsky bazar* (kike bazaar), but although that name sometimes spewed from the mouths of anti-Semitic Kievans, it was also used by the Jews, who were the majority of the traders there, perhaps in the same way that one African American today will sometimes, in comradeship or affection, call another African American "niggah." It was not an official name, but the name that, as people said, went "from mouth to ear."

Black marketers were flourishing everywhere in Soviet Russia, because city dwellers, townspeople, and peasant farmers alike were suffering from the shortages of food and other necessities. While speculators were hoarding large supplies of grain, many men and women were smuggling, like Leya, not to make huge profits but only to keep their families alive.

Although Anna learned some of the secrets of the bazaar, she did not understand everything she saw. A black marketeer, approaching a prospective customer, would murmur in passing three Russian words sounding to Anna almost like a rhyme. If the prospect was seeking one of the three drugs being named, he would signal by a nod or a word, and the smuggler would stop to negotiate, but if not, the smuggler would pass by, moving on to murmur the three words to another potential customer.

Two of the words she recognized. One was aspirin, which she knew because it was the medicine everyone used in Korsun. The other was opium, which she knew only from reading about long-ago and faraway opium dens in the Orient. Anna heard that the police were well paid to ignore this drug traffic, as well as all the other illegal bartering. She was told that raids occurred once in a while, but when the police did come, the alarm was spread quickly and everybody disappeared.

As she helped her mother, Anna saw a woman take from her bosom a tube that looked like macaroni, guardedly show it to a man, then snip off about an inch and give it to him in return for something he handed her. Inside the tube was a powder, perhaps aspirin, perhaps some other drug. Before long, the woman spat on the customer. He had accused her of mixing her powder with baking soda, but they didn't dare to start a fight for fear of attracting police attention. Because of this fear, Anna decided, the bazaar was the most civil place she had ever seen.

During one of her visits to Kiev, Anna watched an automobile—the first she ever saw and the only one she saw during any of her trips to the big city—bump along the street near the bazaar. The roofless touring car was enameled in blue on the outside, just like a roasting pan, and inside, sitting on the white upholstery, a chauffeur in the front drove the two passengers in the back seat. Although the streets in Kiev were straight and paved, their rough, cobblestoned surfaces were not ideal for the motorcar. Later, Anna wondered if the car belonged to one of the commandants—officials who gained unbridled power during the revolutionary era, and were the only people able to afford an automobile.

On these trips Anna and her mother did not stay long in the bazaar. Leya traded her entire stock quickly, and as soon as the last packet left her hand, she left the bazaar for the poor section of town, where a woman she knew took overnight lodgers. Walking the few miles to the woman's house, she and Anna crossed the whole width of the city to reach Podil, the oldest section of Kiev, cradled by the irregular half-moon bend in the Dnieper River, where Anna saw her first steamboat.

Leya always tried to reach the lodging house in daylight, because Podil, like any poor neighborhood in a large city, was known for its thieves and its crime as well as for its poverty. It was also the section of town where illegal residents found shelter, dodging the tsarist law obliging an out-of towner to get a residence permit. Both the lodger and the poor Podil house-holder to whom they paid rent knew that they risked arrest. Police might raid the house at any time. For a lodger, the punishment could be a walk back to their hometown in the company of a convict gang being sent to do forced labor.[5] Anna and Leya spent the night in their landlady's basement, together with other lodgers, all women and all strangers, as many as could be accommodated on the cots set up there. Early the next morning, they walked back to the main railway station.[6]

Anna saw her mother's appearance change as the trips to the Kiev black market bazaar persisted into the era of the Russian Civil War. Leya, who was only in her early thirties, looked dried up and worn down, but she was the mainstay of the eight people in the extended family. Others in the family had certainly contributed importantly. Anna dragged wood from the forest in winter, sometimes helped by Aunt Meyndl, and she would later shoulder buckets of water from the river. She would earn bread by tilling a garden for the priest's wife in spring, and she would plant a family vegetable garden. For Anna, the choice was clear: she could lie down and die from hunger and cold, or she could struggle to get wood, water, and food.

But it was Leya who had formulated the plan of action and carried it out. It was Leya who had mustered the determination to continue the smuggling as long as necessary to sustain the family. She was working to-ward the time when they would be able to join her husband in America.

The First Pogrom (March 1–8, 1918)

When the first pogrom erupted in Korsun, Anna's family was staying at her grandmother Beyla's house. The weather was still cold, but it was not snowing. A pogrom in the Ukraine in those days did not usually sneak into a town without warning. People had plenty of time to worry. Sometimes the soldiers who started the pogrom were a detachment from the army of the Ukrainian National Republic or that of the Bolsheviks against whom they were fighting early in 1918. The Ukrainian nationalists had declared Ukraine to be a nation independent of Russia and now had to fight to defend it. The Bolsheviks had seized the Russian government in their October 1917 coup and now had to fight to gain control of all the vast lands of the former tsarist empire.

Other times the soldiers who started the pogrom were a body of troops from one of the many different armed forces fighting in the chaotic Russian Civil War in 1918 or 1919. But whoever they were and whatever their allegiance, they would usually grip a town or a region for several days or longer before being driven out by an opposing force or moving on. If a victorious army moved into a town to stay for a longer period, rioting stopped and stability reigned, but during the brief occupations, or in the first days of a longer one, the town was at the mercy of the "*pogromshchiki*," as Anna called both the soldiers and the local peasants who joined them.[1]

A pogrom was usually not a calamity limited to one town, but a raging storm rolling through a region. Refugees walking away from a riot-torn town sought shelter in another community far enough away to be safe, at least for a time, and there they spread the news of the pogrom in their town, recounting its horrors, reciting the names of the people killed, reliving the atrocities. The listeners repeated the stories until everyone had heard the reports and rumors, Jew and Gentile alike. Some of the peasants hearing the news became fearful. Other peasants looked forward to the arrival of the pogrom, knowing that they would be free to plunder the houses of the Jews. For the Jews, the only reaction was fear.

The fear before the first Korsun pogrom began in Anna's family when they heard of a pogrom in Shendervka, a neighboring little town, where Grandfather Avrum had a relative. The family, listening to the report, did not hear of any harm to Avrum's relative, but Cossacks had overrun the town, and one of them saw a Jew named Benyumin walking on the street. The Cossack took out his sword and cut off Benyumin's head. The Cossacks laughed to see the Jew keep on walking for several steps after his head had been cut off.

People knew that a *Kozak*, the wearer of the curved sword of legendary sharpness, was the worst killer in the tsar's army.[2] If the government wanted to devastate a town, they sent in the *Kozaken*. Cossacks had tormented Jews more than once since the middle 1600s, when during their revolt against Polish rule, the Cossacks together with Ukrainian peasants had killed thousands of Jews, destroying their communities, and butchering the many Jews who refused to be baptized. The Cossacks had never lost their virulent anti-Semitism, and Jews had never lost their fear of the Cossacks.[3]

Cossacks were well known to Anna. They had been stationed in Korsun before the war. She had seen them in their numbers, the *kavaleristi* on horseback riding at the head of their unmounted fellow Cossacks, marching into town from the railroad station. She had seen them in a pair when she stood on the palace road watching the royal equipage carrying the tsar's mother, who was touring to raise money for the war. The two Cossacks were serving as mounted bodyguards for the dowager Empress Maria, riding on either side of her four-horse carriage.

The Cossack was instantly recognizable. In contrast to the khaki of the regular soldiers of the tsar's army, the menacing attire of the Cossack was all black. Even so, Anna found his uniform beautiful. His tall fur hat was unmistakable. His overcoat, tied around the waist with a sash, partly covered his loose pants, which were bagged below the knee to disappear inside tall leather riding boots. His saber in its curved scabbard hung from the sash. His spare rifle cartridges, each in its own long slender pocket, marched across his chest.

The *pogromshchiki* walked into Grandmother Beyla's house for the first time early in March 1918. The door was not locked, saving them the trouble of breaking it down. More than a half dozen peasants came in with the few soldiers. Beyla didn't have to ask the soldiers what they wanted. They told her. They said the family's lives were in danger if they didn't bring out their valuables. Beyla said she had no gold or silver or jewelry. She told the soldiers they should go ahead and take anything they wanted. She had buried her few valuables, including the silver candleholders she had been given at her wedding.[4]

The soldiers asked how many men lived in the house. Beyla said there weren't any except for Grandfather Avrum. She knew they weren't looking for old men. The soldiers were clever at finding out how many men lived in a house. They counted the men's hats. If they saw three hats in a house, they knew there must be three men. Besides Beyla and Avrum, there were only women—Aunt Meyndl and her daughter, as well as Leya, Anna, and her two sisters.

Beyla and Avrum had not only buried valuables, but they had also been warned to remove sharp-bladed objects and had removed the knives lying on the kitchen table as well as those hanging on the wall behind it. The soldiers, finding nothing interesting in the kitchen, walked into the dining room and crossed it, walking straight ahead to a door that opened into the formal living room, the parlor. They stopped at the parlor door when the family warned that Aunt Meyndl's six-year-old daughter, Gissie, was in bed with the measles. Standing in the doorway between the two rooms, seeing Gissie's rash, the soldiers decided her illness was real, not a ruse to keep them out of a room where valuables might be hidden.

Anna saw a soldier in a khaki overcoat yank a picture frame off the wall, then rip off the back, looking for money. He was young, maybe nineteen or twenty years old. He threw the whole thing to the floor, breaking the glass, tearing the picture. The torn picture was a drawing of the man known as the Baal Shem Tov, the revered founder of Hasidism, the branch of Judaism to which Anna's grandfather and grandmother belonged. It was the only picture in the house. Beyla and Avrum owned no gold or jewels. Theirs was a religious home, with religious articles that had meaning for them but meant nothing to the soldiers. The soldiers were angry at finding no valuables in such a large, prosperous-looking house.

The family watched from the living room as a small crowd milled around in the dining room—a few soldiers, four or five peasant women, and several teenage peasant boys. The soldiers were ordinary foot soldiers in khaki winter overcoats. They had pistols, and some carried rifles. Still, Anna didn't always know who was a real soldier. After battles, peasants sometimes stripped khaki uniforms from dead soldiers. These men were under the command of Cossacks, but they did not look like Cossacks. Their belts held threatening whips but no sabers. They did not wear the dreaded black uniform with its bullet pockets.

Anna knew some of the peasant women in the dining room by name and knew where they lived. Some of them had worked for Jewish women, so they knew exactly what to take from a house such as Beyla's. In the dining room stood a large chest. Made of good wood attractively finished, it had a curved lid like a steamer trunk and a built-in lock. Grandmother kept her good clothes in the chest. They were old-fashioned clothes that could be folded neatly, not like her daughter Meyndl's more stylish dresses that had to be hung in the wardrobe. On Saturdays, when Beyla opened the chest to dress for shul, Anna would see her grandmother's only jewelry, the chain that her husband had given her when they were married. Anna had never seen her wear the chain.

The peasants went to the chest first. When a rifle-carrying soldier asked for the key, Grandmother Beyla said she couldn't find it. Beyla sometimes took her female grandchildren to the bathhouse on Thursday nights, so Anna knew she wore the key around her neck. Nobody ever talked about it. The soldiers did not notice the thin string around her neck.

Without the key, the peasants could not open the chest. The soldier took an iron club, short and stubby, from his belt and hit the lock once, knocking it open. He opened the chest for the peasants to rob. For himself he wanted only gold—money or chains or watches—so that after looting several homes he would come away with the greatest value in the smallest form, easily carried and safely hidden in his pockets.

Anna and the others were all together in a corner, the whole family. They were expecting to be killed. Later Anna couldn't remember whether she was sitting or lying down, or what she did; she could only remember what she saw. One of the looters pulled Grandfather Avrum's *kapote*, the long black frock coat that he wore on *shabbes*, from the wardrobe where the best clothes were kept. The coat was hung on a hook there to prevent creasing. Only an Orthodox Jewish man would wear such a garment. The looter let it fall.

The looters were pulling drawers open, scattering their contents on the floor. A couple of soldiers were pulling out the drawers of Grandfather Avrum's bed stand when they came across his *tefillin,* the prayer boxes he wore every weekday morning at prayer. Written on parchment inside the two leather cubes were the four biblical paragraphs commanding Jews to bind the words of God to their forehead and arm. Not having any idea what these little cubes were, one of the soldiers suspected they might be hiding places for something valuable. When he succeeded in tearing open one of the cubes, he saw nothing inside except a piece of paper with some odd writing on it. Worthless! He flung it to the floor. Anna shuddered to see him touch the *tefillin.* Even Jewish women were not pure enough to touch *tefillin.*

Avrum had hidden a bottle of ink. He was afraid he wouldn't have anything to write with after the pogrom. The family hid things in such naive places, a child could find them, Anna thought. One of the things that caught her eye during the first day of the pogrom was the puddle of ink on the floor near the open bottle.

One of the peasant looters started to take the clock off the wall. It was Avrum's clock, the one he kept in working order, his pet. As the peasant moved toward his clock, Avrum began to protest, moving toward the peasant. Anna thought the peasant would kill her grandfather, but somebody pulled Avrum away from the looter, and nothing happened.

The *pogromshchiki* were still in the dining room when Anna glanced out the window and saw smoke rising over the single area at the far side of the crossroads where all the wooden buildings of the marketplace were concentrated. No one dared to go outside to have a closer look. First she saw the black smoke, and then the reddish flames and the people running in the streets. She had a good view from the windows of Grandmother Beyla's big house on the hill.

The looters came and went. Usually there would be one or two soldiers, together with some peasant women and teenage boys. This went on as long as there was daylight.

They all left at dark, all the soldiers and peasants. Anna thanked God for the dark. It gave the family a chance to run to the river for water, or to eat a little bread, or to do something besides cower in the corner. The more the night darkened, the more she saw the red fire. She could see it from the attic, where the family had gone to rest or nap. The beauty of the colors surprised her, the gray so lovely a gray, the black so dense a black, and the red varying from rose to pink. During the day she had not noticed the beauty. The family tried to catch naps without taking off their clothes, sleeping only a few hours in the fearsome darkness. The things that happened on the first day shocked Anna. Each new danger, each new insult, each new violation shocked her. After that first day, though, nothing shocked her.

The next day, Anna and her family were cold and without food but afraid to go outside. The looters came in again. One of the intruders pulled Grandfather Avrum's clock from the wall, the clock that had survived the first day. He flung it to the floor and broke it.

Leya's black *chaynikl*—a little teapot—sat on top of the samovar, where it was used to brew concentrated tea. It was worth only a few kopecks, but it meant something to Leya, whose grandmother had bought it as a present when she was born. Seeing it lying broken on the floor, Anna wondered why they had to go and break a little black *chaynikl*.

The looters were not shy. One of the women Anna knew collected all of Beyla's kitchen utensils, but found herself unable to carry everything at once. She left the house carrying one load of utensils, went to her home to deposit them, then came back to get the rest. She even took away the implements whose handles were so long that they were taller than Beyla—the three utensils needed for baking and cooking in the massive oven—the pot lifter, the bread shovel, and the fire poker.

On this second day, Anna happened to be in the kitchen, looking out, when she saw a peasant girl she knew, a girl of about her own age, running with a big bundle. The girl was running toward her house by the river. A Russian man in regular clothes—Anna thought he was probably Gentile— was yelling at the girl, calling her names and shouting that she shouldn't be doing that. Anna hoped that he was a Gentile, because on this second day of the pogrom, Anna was thinking the whole world was against the Jews.

When the rumors of a pogrom had first reached Korsun, Sholem Alushka, the shoemaker let it be known that people could hide their valuables in the ditch he was digging in his foyer. Alushka was still in Korsun because he had been wounded and sent home from the army. Leya wrapped her silver spoons and took them to Alushka's ditch. She had two sterling silver spoons that had been part of her trousseau. She would have had two more, one for Anna and one for Gussie, but her husband, Aaron, unable to afford the customary genuine silver spoon at the birth of each daughter, had bought spoons made of a mixture of metals that looked like silver.

Although Alushka's house and that of a relative were both large, they were attached to each other and they shared a long, barnlike foyer. In Alushka's part of the foyer, he and his employees made shoes. The relative ran a coach service, stabling his horses and coaches in his section of the unpartitioned foyer. The Cossacks who rode into town to make a pogrom, seeing this house with a perfect stable for their horses, made the Alushka building their headquarters.

On the third day of the pogrom, the town was quiet. People chafed to leave their hiding places, wanting to see what was happening outside. Anna and her family were hiding in the cellar. Leya heard no shots, saw no people running about in the streets. Having seen no enemies each time she ventured upstairs to peek out the window, Leya waited through the afternoon before deciding at near dusk that the danger had passed. She told Anna to go to Sholem Alushka's house to bring back her valuables.[5]

Anna went. To keep warm she put on the black broadcloth coat that Leya, who had owned it before she was married, had taken to a tailor a few months earlier to be made over for Anna. The material was still good, and the coat fit her well. She was soon at Alushka's house, but finding the foyer door closed, decided to go to the front door to ask one of the Alushkas if they had dug up her mother's valuables.

She was just grasping the vertical grip of the door handle to open the latch when somebody inside yanked the door open. She saw a man at the door in uniform, and behind him in the room were other men in the same uniform. She knew the uniform. The men were Cossacks.

The Cossack at the door asked Anna where she thought she was going. Then he began to look her over. She understood what he was thinking. She turned and ran.

She knew the town well, knew where the alleys were, and the places where a twelve-year-old girl could hide. She ran across the dirt road into a little alley between the house of Leyzer, the musician, and the stable of a man named Mitzdes. It was an alley seldom used, not wide enough for a wagon, but just wide enough for a person to use as a shortcut. She was acting automatically, plotting her strategy on the run while she kept repeating to herself that if she came out of this, she would go to America.

She saw a pile of manure in the alley, a good place to hide. Mr. Mitzdes dumped the manure from his stable there. Anna ran through the edge of the manure and hid behind the pile. When she peeked out, she saw that the Cossack had followed, and he was looking for her.

She saw that he was looking in all directions except toward her alley. Waiting until she was sure he was looking away from her, she crawled out from the alley and started running. She was running in the wrong direction if she wanted to get home, but that didn't matter, all that mattered was to get away from the Cossack and she would get home somehow, and if she got out of this, she was going to go to America, and in that moment the *Krupnik* pulled her in.

People called him "the *Krupnik*," "the kasha person," because he was the seller of buckwheat groats in Korsun. Anna didn't know his real name. He had a mill in his yard, where his horse, wearing blinders, walked round and round, turning the millstone to grind buckwheat into groats, either coarse or fine, or even more finely into flour. No store sold kasha. If you wanted it, you bought it from the *Krupnik*. His living room looked out on the door of the Mitzdes house. He could see what was going on in that house, as well as in the stable, and in the alley.

While Anna caught her breath, she and the *Krupnik* looked through the cracks and stayed away from the window as they watched the Cossack standing in the road, still looking around for her. It must have been five or six in the afternoon. The day was gloomy, though still with some light. The *Krupnik* made Anna stay in his house until it was completely dark. Then he took her outside, asked if she was warm enough, and told her to be careful not to let anyone see her. She hurried home furtively, hugging houses wherever she could. She saw no one on her way.

When Anna finally opened the door to Grandmother Beyla's house, nobody reacted. Her mother had not even been worried about her. Leya showed neither fear nor love, neither anger nor joy. She showed nothing. Although Anna would puzzle over it time and again, she would never be able to understand what Leya had done that day, sending her daughter out to bring back a few valuables when the Cossacks waited. She would never be able to forgive her mother.[6]

15
The Aftermath (March 1918)

Looking down at the main street from the big house on the hill not long after her escape from the Cossack, Anna saw the Cossack horsemen, the *kavaleristi,* riding away, leading files of their foot soldiers. After they left, it was quiet. For hours, then for a day and more, she saw no soldiers in the street. The Cossacks were fighting a battle somewhere off in the distance. Finally, somebody brave enough to go outside in the morning saw a notice posted by the new occupiers. When Anna's family awoke, people were thanking God that the pogrom was over. The *Kozaken* were gone. The Germans had taken their place.

Word spread, and within a few hours everyone was on the streets, breathing freely for the first time in days. Anna would later find that this sudden outpouring of people, like a gush from the spigot of a samovar, happened each time a friendly army drove out the soldiers who had been making a pogrom.

Anna's family continued to live with Grandmother Beyla for a few weeks after the pogrom, and Aunt Feyga's family moved in, too. Although all three families continued to huddle in two rooms because of the fuel shortage, now they were able to go outside, and they could walk around the town. Eventually, they all moved back, little by little, to where they had been living before the pogrom.

The marketplace fire had little practical effect on life in Korsun. The market had already been nearly deserted for a long time. The peasants had little or nothing to sell, and the trains now rarely brought in goods. People lived by finding something to barter, taking it outside the town to a village, and exchanging it for food.

As townspeople met and spoke of the pogrom, each person told of his or her experiences, and each person absorbed parts of what had happened to others until they had constructed an individual account of the pogrom that was partly personal and partly communal.

After the first night, Grandfather Avrum had said that the cellar would be a safer place for the children to hide and to sleep in case of fire, a sensible suggestion in peacetime, but the family found out that the soldiers often went straight to the cellars to find their victims. In future pogroms people knew they were better off finding hiding places away from their houses.

The soldiers broke windows with the same club they used to knock open Grandmother Beyla's clothes chest. Even though they only broke one windowpane in her house in this first pogrom, the cold came in. The window was the standard kind that had twenty small rectangular panes of glass, and in the top row, as was usual, one of the five panes had been modified into a small door, a *khvortka,* to let the occasional backed-up smoke from the oven out, or fresh air in. The small size of each pane made it easier to replace the glass if one was broken. Anna stuffed rags into the broken pane. When the soldiers left a house, the owner was lucky if they didn't break a window. The sound of shattering glass was their good-bye.

This first pogrom was not like the two that came later; it was like a rehearsal. The thieves did not steal everything, leaving behind many possessions. The peasant women, despite having no experience as looters, knew enough to steal from the better homes. Some women carried bags as big as potato sacks. Others, though, brought their own sheets. They would spread out a sheet, place the stolen goods on it, then tie the four corners together to make a bundle. In this first pogrom the peasants had not yet figured out an efficient procedure for looting, just as the Jews had not figured out the best way to behave as victims of a pogrom. The women could have saved themselves the trouble of carrying sheets from home, since they could steal them from the houses they robbed. In the better homes, where the walls were covered with wallpaper, the looters tore it off. Anna didn't know why they bothered, because the paper money that people hid behind the wallpaper was worth nothing.

Grandmother's candleholders, not the silver ones that she had buried to hide from thieves, but the brass ones that had always been on display every day and had been used every *shabbes,* were just like living things to Anna. They were a tradition, a symbol of stability to Anna, who envisioned them standing in the same place in that same house year after year, even before she was born. After the *pogromshchiki* were gone, somebody came into Beyla's house and warned that the candleholders were a terrible weapon because the soldiers or a peasant could kill with them. Beyla listened. She hid her brass candlesticks.

Not all peasants had taken part in the rioting. Of those who did, some seemed to be angry at Jews. When the looting of houses began, some Jews were brave enough to strike back, killing several peasants. The Cossacks, though, were better at killing. Anna had not herself seen anyone killed, but she learned that the rich people were often the first to be killed, because the soldiers thought they were hiding valuables. She learned that the Cossacks would torture first and then kill. The Cossacks focused on the big houses along the western edge of the fairground. They killed one of the richer men, a next-door neighbor of Zyama Rabinovich. They killed Oodl Slivnik, too, Grandmother Beyla's good friend.

The Cossacks did not ignore the house of the Shapiros, obviously the home of wealthy people. Anna had become friends three years earlier with the Shapiro family. They were modern, assimilationist Jews who spoke only Russian. The father, Mark Shapiro, managed a forest enterprise that logged trees for the lumber mill.

Their spacious grounds, guarded by two imposing dogs, were to be entered through a broad gate, wide enough to accommodate horse-drawn wagons and carriages. In front of the Shapiro house was a garden where flowers bloomed, among them the fragrant white jasmine, and where vegetables grew in such variety that Mrs. Shapiro had no need to buy any in the market.

The first thing the Cossacks did was to shoot the Shapiros' two big dogs. They also shot Mark Shapiro. After the pogrom, his wife was to be seen standing in the marketplace, selling leftover possessions to make money. She and the children eventually abandoned their house.

A few streets away from Beyla's house lived a tailor who was fairly well off. He had several girls working for him. Because he sewed for Christians, he thought the soldiers would treat him differently, would not take away his valuable belongings. He stayed home, not trying to hide. When the *pogromshchiki* wanted to take something from his house, he argued with them, telling them they couldn't do that. When they left, he was dead. When the next pogrom came, people would know that trying to reason with the soldiers would be useless, and that they had better find good hiding places for the younger men.

Later Anna found out that the pogrom had also reached Vinograd, a little town close enough that coachmen from Korsun used to go there before the war, sometimes bringing back gifts to Anna's family from her uncle Meyer. Meyer Spector, the rich man of the family, had been killed in Vinograd. His son Moshke, Anna's first cousin, was also killed.

Anna heard that the family in Korsun living two houses away left a meat cleaver in their kitchen, hanging on the wall over the cutting table. People had told the man that such a sharp blade could be used to kill, but he left it on the wall. A Cossack came into the house, saw the cleaver, grabbed it, and killed the whole family.

Of the picture of the Baal Shem Tov, the picture torn by the young soldier, Anna's family could salvage only the frame. Later, they used the pieces for firewood. At that time Anna didn't know what kind of a picture it was, but years later, remembering its black-and-white tones, and remembering the grain of it, she knew it must have been a woodcut.

Leya never got her valuables back. Sholem Alushka said the soldiers took them.

The Germans Occupy Korsun (1918)

The residents of Korsun, having survived a pogrom shortly before the Germans occupied the town in the spring of 1918, were relieved that a disciplined army had taken power and was trying to restore order. Grandmother Beyla hired a glazier, as did others, to replace broken window glass, presuming that with the Germans in control, the next winter would arrive before the next pogrom. Their optimism was justified. While the Germans controlled the town for the rest of the year, no rioting occurred.

German and Austrian armies numbering eight hundred thousand men had begun arriving in late February 1918, and by early April they had occupied the entire Ukraine. While the Austrians occupied the southern part of the Ukraine, the Germans took over the northern part, capturing the city of Kiev, eighty miles north of Korsun, early in March.

Once they had installed themselves in Korsun, the German occupiers slipped smoothly into the life of the town. Germany issued special occupation money, allowing the Ukrainians to read the words "*eine mark*" printed on the bill valued at one German mark, but in familiar Russian letters.

The language of instruction remained Russian during the high school's spring semester, which had already begun when the Germans took over the town. Anna's class was studying French and German as second languages. Although she liked Olga Alexandrovna, the woman who taught German, Anna realized that the Jews could speak better German than the teacher. While Olga Alexandrovna, a native Russian, was still trying to think of a word, the Jewish children were automatically saying it. The children studying German found their fluency improving as they listened and talked to the German soldiers.

Oddly, the German soldiers and the Jews of Korsun got along with each other very well. The soldiers behaved so well that Anna was surprised many years later to learn how the German people behaved during the Nazi era. Language helped. The Korsun Jews, most of whose mother tongue was Yiddish, a language with strong German roots, could understand what the soldiers said in German, just as the soldiers could make out what the townspeople said in Yiddish. They could talk to each other.[1]

During the first pogrom to strike Korsun, some of the Jews who had watched their own houses being robbed recognized the peasants doing the robbing, just as Anna had. The Germans helped the Jews by sending soldiers to escort a victim of looting to the peasant's house, allowing him not only to search it but also to take back his silver, or his clothes, or whatever the peasant had stolen.

Shortly after the pogrom, a peasant living on the outskirts of town saw a samovar in the house of another peasant in his neighborhood. Since this samovar was obviously too valuable for the neighbor to afford, the first peasant told the owner of the hardware store what he had seen. The owner of the hardware store was a wealthy Jewish man known to keep a number of valuable objects in his house, including an elaborate samovar. When the owner told the German authorities that he knew where his samovar was, they sent two soldiers with him to the peasant's house.

It turned into an event. In Korsun, when something happened, the news flowed as fast as the river during the spring thaw. It was the same with the samovar. Not only did the whole Jewish community know that the samovar had been found, but many of them turned out to see the samovar returned to its owner. On this warm spring day, people ran happily after the soldiers. Anna and others watched the owner walking between the two soldiers in their German uniforms with jacket and belt. On the buckle of each belt was written in German, "God is with us."

The hardware store owner found not only his samovar at the peasant's house, but also his wife's *rotonda*—the word was originally French for a cape, a sleeveless coat that hung down to the floor. Anna's Aunt Meyndl had a similar one. It was lined with luxurious fox fur, and its collar was black sable with its mixture of gray hairs. A *rotonda* was expensive, a mark of distinction, a gift from the parents to a bride.[2]

The German soldiers arrested the peasant. His wife, who may even have been the thief, was unrepentant. She told the hardware store owner to wait until his *zhidovsky* tsar—his "kike's tsar"—left town. Then her kind would take everything back from him.

The occupiers went out of their way to treat the Jews kindly, another reason why they were so well liked. Although the Germans themselves were a major cause of the town's food shortage, they saw to it that the Jews had something to eat. The soldiers made friends with Jewish households, bringing candy for the children, or a loaf of bread. The Germans were slaughtering cattle several times a week to feed the troops. Taking the good meat to feed the soldiers, they donated the parts they did not want—the internal organs such as stomach, intestines, liver and lungs—to the Jews.

The killing of a cow attracted an avid audience. The Jews crowded around, waiting for whatever edible parts the Germans would save for them. On one occasion Anna's family was given a cow's stomach, about two feet long and not very appetizing. Anna could not eat her piece of the smelly thing. The meat was not kosher, because the killing of the cow was done neither in the Jewish slaughterhouse nor according to prescribed ritual, but by then most Jews no longer cared, even those who had been the strictest about the kosher laws. They eagerly sought and accepted any food that would sustain their families for a few more days.

Although the Jews saw the Germans as benevolent occupiers, the peasants had a different view. When they sneeringly referred to the Germans as the "kike's tsar," they likely had good reasons for their bitterness, considering the friendly way the Germans treated the Jews and the harsh way they treated the peasants.

The peasants of Korsun, Ukrainian speakers, could not hold a conversation with the German soldiers. Moreover, the army lived off the land, the same land tilled and harvested by the labor of the peasants. To feed their men, the Germans commandeered animals from the peasants, not only those of the small tenant farms at Korsun's outskirts, but also those of the villages in the countryside, where larger numbers of livestock were raised.

The German soldiers settled down in town for a long stay. They took over the old cement-floored barracks with arched false windows, empty for years since Anna had seen the movie *Moses in Egypt* there before the war. They took over the third floor of Anna's four-story high school building for living quarters, displacing the classes that had been meeting there, but this caused only minor hardship for the students, crowding the second-floor classrooms. Most of the high school teachers, including the principal (the *Inspektor*), were from out of town, and were fortunate to be able to remain in their living quarters on the first floor.

The Germans also took over the entire building of the new boys' gymnasium, a separate high school for the sons of the well-to-do, leaving no room for classes. They set up a hospital for the wounded on one floor, using the rest of the building for living quarters and for other needed functions.

Around the time when the Germans moved into town, Anna's mother, Leya, moved her family into the house of a woman named Esther Devorah, whose husband was in the army, and there they stayed during most of the German occupation. A woman in her early twenties, with one son of toddler age, Esther was in the late stages of pregnancy. Her daughter was born while Anna was living in her house. Anna's family did most of the heavy housework. Esther made some money as a seamstress.

Esther's father was a skilled cabinetmaker who created beds, chests, and all kinds of furniture. Ready-made beds were not available in Korsun. A woman who wanted a bed told the *stolyar* what she needed, and he made it especially for her. Now, however, during the German occupation, since no one could afford to buy new furniture, he could get no work. His family was always hungry, always looking to earn a kopeck to buy bread.

Six years earlier, when Anna's Grandmother Beyla had moved out of her duplex after it caught fire, Esther's father had bought the house. He had brought in his tools and carpenter's table and had partly rehabilitated the burned half, installing wooden floors over the clay and repairing the charred half of the roof before he ran out of money. The walls still showed the water stains where the volunteer fire brigade had put out the fire. He moved into the burned half with his two sons, two of his three daughters, and his wife, paralyzed by a stroke. Esther moved into the other half of the house, helping to care for her bedridden mother.

Esther rented one of the four rooms in her half of the duplex to a woman impoverished because her home, in which she ran the hand laundry catering to wealthy people, had been burned during the first pogrom. By now, few people had money to spend on laundering clothes anyhow. The room was so small that it was tolerable only because it had a window. The laundry woman slept there, together with her daughter and the daughter's boyfriend. Their room was heated by the in-the-wall fireplace that also warmed the larger bedroom on the other side of the wall. In that larger room, Esther slept with her toddler son in one of the two beds made for her by her father. Leya—who stored her own two blackwood beds some-where else—slept in the other one with her three daughters. The heating stove in the wall was kept burning with a wagonload of tree branches from the forest, the gift of the princess to each soldier's wife. In the kitchen and dining room sat the tables and chairs that Esther's father had made for her before the war.

The peasants were bringing some produce to town early in the spring of 1918, but were afraid to take cash for it when the money might suddenly become worthless. Food was scarce. Hearing a rumor that the Germans were handing out seeds and assigning land for vegetable gardens, Anna took Gussie and hurried to the distribution center. To her delight, the authorities marked a plot of land south of the marketplace, near a new settlement, as her garden.

She planted an ambitious garden of vegetables ranging from lettuce and potatoes to a green garlic and Swiss chard. The tomatoes and cabbages were first tended at home in boxes as "set-outs," after which Anna set the young-leaved plants into the ground of her garden. Filling buckets at the hospital's well, a half mile away, she carried them to the garden, where Gussie helped water the plants every day for about a week until they could stand alone.

Gussie and Anna did the planting barefoot. They grew tomatoes without using stakes for support. Breaking up the surface of the ground and laying straw around the stems to keep the soil moist, they thinned the growth until the remaining leaves gave the fruit just enough shade. This prevented too much exposure to the sun, allowing the tomatoes to grow as big as they could before starting to turn red.

The plot of ground promised enough food to nourish the family through the summer and into the coming winter. Before Anna could harvest any except the early vegetables, however—onions, radishes, and lettuce—someone devastated her garden. Hers wasn't the only one; all the gardens were destroyed, but that did not console her. The Germans tried to discover who was responsible, but failed. The hoofprints Anna discovered told her it was a group of mounted soldiers. Since she knew that peasants did not ride around on horses, it must have been raiders from an army.

Anna had planted her vegetables so well that her teacher, the Ukrainian, had told everyone to come and look at them, making her proud that he had singled out her work. She could not understand why someone would ruin her plantings. She mourned the cabbages, lying there, she thought, like the heads of babies, rotting.

The elderly Ukrainian teacher in Korsun's high school became a link to a policy of Ukrainianization carried out under the German occupation of the Ukraine. The Ukrainian National Republic government had successfully supported the use of the Ukrainian language and literature in the previously Russian-dominated schools before the German occupation. The German's puppet Ukrainian government continued the policy.[3] In Korsun, however, no textbooks written in the Ukrainian language were available. Furthermore, only the elderly history teacher, a native Ukrainian, knew the language well enough to teach in it.

He did his best to give the students some knowledge of his mother tongue. Even though he spoke Russian in class, he translated some of his words into Ukrainian. Moreover, in teaching Russian history, he would call students to the front of the room, instructing them to answer in Ukrainian when he asked them to give dates or to describe events such as Napoleon's capture of Moscow.

He also hoped to combine teaching the Ukrainian language and the history of the Ukraine by having the whole class recite or sing nationalistic Ukrainian poems or songs until they had memorized them. The students already knew something about Ukrainian culture. They had often before been taught about the life of Taras Shevchenko, the Ukrainian national poet, because he was not only a writer but also a nationalist hero, as important in the Ukraine as George Washington in America. Anna found the poems and songs an effective way to learn Ukrainian history, but she did not learn to read or write the language. If the Ukrainian nationalists had hoped to turn the Korsun students into Ukrainian-speakers, they were disappointed, for the children continued to converse among themselves in Russian, which remained their language of the street.

When the tsar was executed by the Bolsheviks in July 1918, Anna heard about it within a day or two, as the shocking news was relayed from town to town. Although the tsar was a distant figure, he was not an unfamiliar icon to Anna. Before the revolution, every morning at the start of instruction she and the other students in her first-year high school class had sung a Russian song saying that the tsar was their shepherd and urging God to save the king of a great people.

Anna's family moved in with Grandmother Beyla during part of the German occupation, and two of the walking wounded from the German hospital came to visit Anna's grandfather at the big house on the hill. One was a shoemaker with an interest in books, a Russian Jew, a prisoner of war, Anna thought, but allowed by the Germans to roam the town freely. Grandfather Avrum befriended him, and Anna would see them going down into the cellar at night, carrying several books and a kerosene lamp. They would still be in the cellar, reading and discussing the books, when she fell asleep. The other visitor was the German soldier, also a Jewish boy, who came to see Grandfather Avrum's books about mysticism, Kaballah.

The gymnasium stood on one hill, with Grandmother Beyla's house on the next hill, closer to the Ros River, so peasants crossing the bridge and coming into town along the cobblestoned main street on their way to the marketplace would pass her house just before they reached the gymnasium-turned-hospital. Anna saw peasant women with shoulder yokes carrying buckets of cherries to market. Each woman carried two buckets hanging from short ropes, one at each end of a wooden yoke. The women stopped and gave cherries by the handfuls to the wounded soldiers sitting on the steps of the school.

In the fall, Aunt Meyndl gave birth to a baby girl in the middle of the night. The midwife was the only lay Jewish midwife in town. She had delivered all the children in Anna's family. When Anna awoke in the morning, she had a new cousin called Mahnkela, a name of endearment for a child whose formal name was Mahni. Born with a harelip, Mahnkela could not suckle. A doctor named Pinsker, on furlough from the army, agreed to examine the infant. He said that he might have been able to do something for her if the times were normal and if they were nearer to the modern medical facilities at Kiev.

The family tried to nourish the child, picking sunflowers, collecting the seeds, and chewing them to make a thin paste that they spooned into the baby's mouth, but to no avail. Mahnkela died of starvation. They wrapped her in a sheet and took her to the cemetery. There, with the help of the Jewish man who attended to interments, they buried her. They could not hold a proper ceremony, because their rabbi had been murdered during the first pogrom.

The Bolsheviks had banned all religion in the schools soon after coming into power, but during the German occupation a religion class was taught in the Korsun high school by the *galakh,* the young Orthodox priest. At first, the Jewish students left the room while the priest, his long braid of hair trailing over the back of his long black coat with the pinched-in waist, taught the Gentiles. After a while, the school decided that, to be fair, the Jewish students should also be given a religion class. It turned out to be a class in Jewish literature, not religion, taught for one semester by Yitzkhak (Isaac) Lazarovitch, an educated young Jew from a big city.

Isaac was not sure what to teach in the hour allotted to him each week. He began with Jewish songs. Besides being a socialist (Bundist) and a modern Jew, he had a passion for the emerging Yiddish literature.[4] Not only did Isaac introduce the class to the contemporary Yiddish stories by Sholom Aleichem, but he and his brother wrote a two-act play based on that master's story, *The Bloody Hoax.* The plot concerns two students, one Jewish, one Christian, who exchange lives temporarily. The Christian, who doesn't believe how difficult it is for a Jew to be admitted to a university and to find a place to live in a large city, proposes a test. He will exchange passports with his Jewish friend for one year. By living as a Jew, he will be able to find out firsthand whether or not his Jewish friend is telling the truth. He finds out that his friend was not exaggerating.

The play was presented in the assembly room, with its fine wooden benches, wood-paneled walls, and baby grand piano. Although the class only lasted for a few months, Anna, who had not been exposed to secular Jewish literature and history in her home, appreciated the teacher's enthusiasm for Yiddish poetry and stories.

Winter came, the worst of all the wartime winters, with shortages of food and fuel even worse than those of the year before. On a day so cold that the bread froze too hard for Anna to bite off a piece, Leya was crying, telling her troubles to a Mr. Katsiv, a man she met in the street. Katsiv said, Come with me. I have a room. He took Leya and her three daughters to warm themselves and eat at his house. He knew that people could die from the cold.

Katsiv and his wife, Sosel, who occupied a bedroom and one other room, installed Leya and the girls in a third room, small but warmed by a heating stove in the wall. They slept on the floor, on straw that Sosel spread for them, until Leya arranged to have some of her furniture brought in. Although Leya's feather beds had already been stolen in the first pogrom, she still had one of her two black Chinese beds, and she had a wooden trunk, so big that it took two people to carry it by the handles.

Anna and Gussie slept on the flat top of the trunk, while Mayna slept with Leya in the Chinese bed. Leya no longer had her tall wardrobe or a table, but she still had one chair. Some medicine stood on a wooden box. The room was too small to bring in any other furniture.

Leya meant to stay in the butcher's house only temporarily, but then Mayna got typhus, a disease that typically comes on suddenly with headache, chills, quickly rising fever, and prostration. The headache is severe and does not go away, night and day, and the fever does not come down. Mayna was severely ill with a disease that lasts for an average of two weeks. Finally, Anna saw that her little sister was turning blue.

Anna knew that a new Gentile doctor in town lived in a certain house about a mile away, next door to the high school. She ran to get him. Pushing open the garden gate, she was greeted by a big dog, barking so fiercely that she thought he wanted to kill her. When someone from the house asked her what she wanted, she was able to tell them that her little sister was dying.

The young doctor was at home. Grabbing his coat and satchel, he ran after her. After examining Mayna, he said that she was in the crisis stage, and her fever was now coming down. He left some medicine, telling Anna how to give it. She gave it, and Mayna recovered. Then, probably in the first or second week of December, after Mayna's fever was gone and she was strong enough to go outside instead of using the night pot, Leya became ill with the same disease.

They had to stay on at the butcher's house. All the while, Aunt Meyndl was bringing them food from Grandmother Beyla's house nearby. Anna stayed home from school for a few weeks to take care of her mother. The teachers were used to this, since so many families had typhus.

Leya became delirious, talking out of her head for days. For example, she told Anna she was getting water from a pump in the yard, so Anna knew her mother thought she was in Kiev, where people had pumps in their yards.

Anna brought home buckets of river ice, giving some pieces to Leya to swallow, putting others on her mother's forehead to cool her fever and make her more comfortable. Women washed clothes in the river even in winter by chopping a hole in the ice, and Anna collected pieces they left lying near the hole. When it was too cold and dark to go to the river, she broke icicles from the downspout of the butcher's house, or from a neighbor's.

Once when Anna was on the way to her aunt's house, passing the water carrier's yard, she was happy to see the gleam of icicles hanging from his water wagon in the starlit night. She broke some off and took them in a bucket to her mother, but Leya's delirium would not respond. Because Leya still looked so ill, Anna ran to bring the *feldsher,* the lay healer, who gave her some medicine. In the morning Leya's fever broke, and she started talking normally.

As soon as Leya's fever dropped, Grandmother Beyla sent Anna to the store with money to buy cranberries. The delicatessen on the street of the butchers next to the marketplace sold them out of a big barrel. Before the war this store had sold all kinds of delicacies, besides the ordinary food like the green olives in one barrel, the black olives in another, and the coffee beans bulging the sides of a burlap sack as tall as Anna, its edges rolled down all around. Anna took a pound or so of the red berries to her Aunt Meyndl to cook.

Because Leya was still so weak, Meyndl strained the juice into a narrow-necked bottle, feeding it to her as a tonic two or three times a day. Leya was able to hold a sugar cube in her mouth to take away the tartness, because somebody kindly donated a few sugar cubes to the family. When she had taken all of the juice, they bought more cranberries for the tonic, but having no more sugar, Meyndl added a few apples to the berries, then cooked the mixture on the *trinizhka,* the long-legged trivet, since they didn't have enough wood for the oven. Watching, Anna learned to cook cranberries with apples.

Although Anna knew typhus to be a serious illness, she only knew about it from her experience in her family and in her town. Doctors in Europe were learning about typhus as a disease that stalks populations engulfed by war, famine, and natural disaster. No one in Anna's family died from it, but typhus killed an estimated three million of the thirty million people who caught it in Russia and eastern Poland in the years from 1915 to 1922. Gussie never fell ill. Anna did not catch typhus until the following spring.

During Leya's typhus, when she lay exhausted with high fever, the doctor had sent Anna to fetch some aspirin powder. On the way to the drugstore, the one on the east-west cobblestoned road near the crossroads, she had only reached the region of the five Jewish houses of prayer when she was surprised to see a German soldier running and pushing a loaded wheelbarrow. Abandoning the wheelbarrow in the middle of the street near the houses of worship, the soldier ran toward the railroad station, two miles away.[5]

Anna reasoned that the German troops were retreating from an approaching army—she had no idea which one, although she was familiar with the names of some of the generals in what would later come to be called the Russian Civil War. Anna strained to keep the midwinter wind from blowing her down as it whipped the snow. The hurrying soldier didn't see Anna, and after that day (it must have been in the last half of December) she never saw a German soldier in town again.

Fall and Winter in Prewar Korsun

The beginning of autumn for Anna in peacetime had nothing to do with the official date of September 22, when the sun was poised over the earth's equator. Autumn in Korsun began for Anna on the holiday of *Simkhas Torah* (Rejoice in the Torah). This holiday marked the start of a new annual cycle of reading each day from the Torah, the first five books of the Hebrew Bible. The holiday, falling on the twenty-third day of the month of *Tishri* in the Jewish calendar, a lunar calendar, came anywhere in the Gregorian calendar from the last few days of September to the first three weeks of October.

The weather was gradually getting colder, but not enough for winter clothes. The chill continued after the holiday. Korsun had no Indian summer, saw no sun during the brief autumn. The days were gloomy. On some days it rained. Though the mud was not as deep as in the spring, the wheels of peasant delivery wagons sank into it under the weight of firewood done up in bundles, or a load of potatoes in eighty-pound sacks.

People prepared for winter. In every house, storm windows were put up, and straw-filled burlap-sack windbreaks were hung along the cracks on the outside of the door. Poorer families spread a thin layer of yellow sand at the bottom of the space between the inner and outer windows to block some of the cold air from coming in through the cracks. In Grandmother Beyla's house and in the houses of other families that could afford it, the sand was decorated with small ornaments of the season—a snowman or children's toys—laid on top of a strip of white cotton batting to make a winter scene. During these late October days, although the weather was chilly enough to prevent Anna from going barefoot outside, a poor family would not yet use valuable wood by starting a fire in the heating stove within a hollow wall.

Unlike Korsun's autumn, which didn't begin until after the official starting date, its winter was too impatient to wait for December 22. In late October or in November, not long after the storm windows had been attached, a hard frost marked its arrival. The frost usually slipped in at night. One morning Anna would awaken to find that the muddy road had become a jumble of hardened ruts and ridges, each marking the furrow plowed by a passing wagon wheel, or the imprint stamped by a horse's hoof.

Anna did not like to walk on these unyielding ridges, for fear of twisting her ankle, or worse. The uneven, frozen surface plagued feet, hooves, and wheels for about a week. Then the first snow fell. It was still November. The first snowfall was a signal from nature that the easy part of the year was over. As the snow continued to fall, it filled the ruts and covered the ridges in the roads. Still it fell, often for two or three days, and no one was surprised to see two or three feet of it, or even more, almost as high as the windows in Anna's house.

Everyone changed to felt boots. The snow would harden until the surface was ideal for travel by sleigh. The peasants detached the metal-shod wheels from the chassis of their wagons, setting them aside to wait out the winter. Pulling the long wooden runners down from the rooftops where they had been stored all summer, they attached the runners to the chassis, transforming the wagons into sleighs made entirely of wood. The runners—long, flat strips of wood, their front ends curved upward and then backward—slid easily along on top of the snow.

After the first snow, there would be no more for days or weeks, but then would come a second big snow, and after another interval, a third and a fourth. Each snowfall in turn became packed down, adding a layer to the earlier ones. A snowfall sometimes piled so much weight onto a thatched roof that it broke through a weak spot.

Anna would try to look out through the windows, but they were usually frosted over in hazy designs, unless they began to clear in the afternoon sun. Her house was always cold. The simple heating unit never caught up with the weather. In homes all over town, people filled empty beer bottles with hot water from the samovar, corked them, and wrapped them in rags to use as hand and foot warmers.

On the first day of one big snow, Anna awakened to see a deserted but welcome landscape. The new snow hid the dirt and dilapidation of the town. No children were to be seen, no adults, not even a four-footed animal. A clutch of crows were searching for food on the street. Anna's appreciative eye caught the image of the birds, grubbing about blackly against the mat of quiet whiteness.

Many people remained in their houses on the first day. Women knew they would find little or no fresh food to buy at the market, since few if any peasants from the villages would come into town. People might brush snow away outside their door and next to the house, using a besom or switch broom of bundled tree branches. Ashes scraped from the oven and saved in an iron pot were sprinkled in front of the house to keep people from slipping and falling.

If Anna went out on the first day of a big snow, she waited until there was a path. The pioneers who blazed a trail through the new-fallen snow in the early morning were the men on their way to shul. They went out while it was still dark, well before Anna and other children were awake. After the morning service at shul, the men would walk home to eat breakfast. Then they would go out again to open their stores. Not all men, however, walked from their home to a place of work. Every tailor dedicated a space in his house to his sewing machine and worktables. All of the master shoemakers in Korsun also did their work at home, as did the barrel maker, the seamstresses, and the tinsmith.

A woman who worked in the marketplace during the winter, selling her wares in an open-fronted booth, tried to stay warm by wearing layers of clothes and by using a firepot. During the workday she would warm her hands at the cast iron firepot, in which she would burn coals of wood, but that was not enough to keep the rest of her body warm. Placing the firepot on the floor of the booth, she sat on a chair or stool with her feet resting on the pot. By arranging her shoe-length skirt as an umbrella around and above the firepot, she funneled the warmth toward herself. She warmed herself at the firepot when she was "between customers." Much of her time was spent between customers.

Sleighs slid silently on the snow, but as the horses stepped along, bodies bouncing, the ringing of the harness bells deterred one sleigh from colliding with another at a curve in the road, or from running over an unwary pedestrian.

Although the snow and ice halted the fairs until after the spring thaw, peasants still came into town to buy staples and to sell a few things, even in January, the coldest month. At first they crossed the Ros River on its frozen surface, since the bridge over the river was dismantled every November or December to prevent its destruction by the February–March ice breakup and spring flood. After the ice broke, they used a ferry that ran for four or five weeks.

Not all children had as much chance to play in the snow as the peasant children who went sledding down the hills of Korsun. Most Jewish boys had no time to make snowmen or go sledding. The shortness of the days in winter meant that the boys were in primary school from dark to dark. Anna saw snowmen on the Gentile streets, but only a few on the Jewish streets. The snowmen were very like those in America, having coal eyes and a carrot nose. In Korsun only a few middle-class Gentile girls made snow maidens, clothing them in real skirts.

Ice-skating was a popular sport in Korsun before the 1917 revolution.

The skating took place across the entire width of the Ros River in the section between the bridge and the goat island. Many townspeople stood on the western shore near the bridge to watch, and they would applaud a good skater. To make a figure eight was the great accomplishment. Among both the Gentiles and the Jews, only the boys skated.

On Saturday afternoon the *kheyder* boys stole out of the house and went to the river to skate, even though play was forbidden on Saturday, the Sabbath. Their parents slept after lunch, and this was the only day of the week when the boys had an opportunity to play.

Some people went riding for pleasure in winter. Young couples, or groups of young women who were financially better off would hire a sleigh to take them to the railroad station outside town. They might go to meet someone coming in on a train, but even if they were not expecting anyone, they took a sleigh ride just to watch people come and go at the station.

In February, the slanting sun, still below the equator but moving northward, had gained enough strength to begin to melt the river ice. The breakup of the ice at a given place on a river is usually abrupt, with a large area clearing in only a few hours. The "going of the ice" in Korsun was not to be missed. Peasants and Jews, young and old, went to see it. Except for Mr. Kobek's fireworks, the town could expect to see no other spectacular entertainment in an ordinary year. Anna saw a circus only once and went to only one movie during her fourteen years in Korsun. The first time Anna saw the going of the ice, Leya and Aunt Meyndl held her up so that over the grownups' heads she could see and remember the blue-green mountains of ice riding the river.

The Ros River overflowed each year at the time of the ice breakup, but the town of Korsun did not suffer from the floods. The river had created steep rocky barriers over the millennia as it had cut its course into the granite. The water spread over the sand beach and the adjacent flat land, outflanking the riverbanks in places by a distance of about a city block, but never reaching the telephone exchange, which was the building closest to the river.

When the river ice was going, people would sit around in the evening and talk about stories they had heard from their parents and grandparents about the ice breakups of earlier years. Stories were told about a tree caught in a block of ice, or of a small barn or shed floating past in the river, and even of a live dog stranded on the floating ice going downstream.

18
The Worst Winter (1918–1919)

The memories of peacetime winters, however harsh, became almost nostalgic after the winter of 1918–1919 had done its work. Korsun's high school students had looked forward to classes each fall since the school had opened four years ago, proud of their new, clean building, the first public high school ever built in the town. The first day of each fall semester had been a hopeful occasion when the students met the teachers and sang songs. Going to school was a special joy for students like Anna, thirsting for education. Now, however, with the last battles of the world war still being fought and with the Russian Civil War already almost a year old, the gathering on the first day of school in 1918 was subdued.

Most of the teachers lived in other towns. The principal had held a meeting to tell the parents that the start of school would be delayed because too few teachers had returned. Nina Constantinovna, the home economics teacher, was taking time off to have a baby, but the students did not know why the other teachers were missing. They might have been murdered by robbers or taken into the army. They might have died of typhus, or they might have decided to quit teaching.

Olga Alexandrovna, who taught French and German as well as geography, had tried in vain to recruit a few young women from other towns as teachers. She lived a half block from school and was the only woman among the returning teachers. She came to school with a black patch on her brown skirt. The young Russian Orthodox priest, who had studied at a university, taught mathematics in addition to a religion course for Christian students. He lived a few houses down the street from Anna's grandmother. The third teacher, the Ukrainian, taught history. An older man, perhaps in his sixties, he was not eligible for army service. The fourth returnee was a Czechoslovakian art teacher who had taught drawing at the high school since Anna's first year.

These four teachers for Anna's third-year class taught two subjects each, filling gaps in the curriculum. Classes were improvised. Sometimes the teachers gave lectures, but sometimes the class recited poems or sang songs. With town life so disturbed by the war, the students were happy to be continuing their education in any fashion, happy to have the daily routine of walking to school. Wanting the students to learn the important subjects such as geography and Russian history, the four teachers lectured on those subjects whenever they could. They kept up the spirit of the school, and even though they were not being paid, they were determined to teach. Anna thought them heroic.

In normal times each subject was taught for a one- or two-hour period, the first one from nine to eleven in the morning. Then the next teacher would come into the classroom, and Anna and the other students would take out their books for that class. Anna sometimes brought her lunch and ate at school, but students often went home during the one-hour noon lunch period, coming back for the one o'clock and three o'clock classes. In winter, it was already dark at four when they went home. The schedule was not the same every day of the week. A home economics class met once or twice a week. The last thing on Tuesday afternoon, Anna's class would have an hour of singing in the piano room, and sometimes the whole school assembled there for a lecture or for a student singing recital. The Jewish students, forbidden to write on the Sabbath, attended the half-day session on Saturday morning, taking no notes. A teacher occasionally insisted on a written examination on Saturday. The Jewish students sat idle.

When the school had opened the year before Anna entered, townspeople who favored modern secular education had been proud of its fine new building and excellent teachers. The tuition fees were used to pay the principal, the teachers, and the custodian, as well as to maintain and heat the building. Families with more assets paid higher tuition than those who were poor, and Leya was one of those allowed to pay less. Now, however, the whole atmosphere at school had changed. Many of the parents who had been well off before the war were reduced to poverty. The school's intake of tuition money had fallen. Notebooks, paper, and firewood were all harder to find.

Even though winter began as usual, the worst winter seemed to arrive sooner because of the delayed start of classes. With the onset of cold weather, the supply of firewood dictated the classroom routine. The custodian did everything he could to help. At a nearby property, ownerless since the revolution, he chopped down trees to heat the school for a while. Eventually, on Mondays if it was a very cold day, he heated the rooms just enough to take the chill out. The students sat in their overcoats, and the teacher announced whether or not classes would be held the next day, depending upon the amount of firewood on hand.

Always a good student, Anna was happy if she could attend a full day at school. Once, when classes were cancelled for lack of firewood, a teacher saw her on the street and asked her to gather several students, telling Anna to bring them to her house so that they could go over the lessons together. When classes did not meet, Anna read extra books on her own.

As conditions worsened, the teachers stopped holding school assemblies, and the piano room was kept locked. One day, finding the door open, Anna saw that the fine wooden benches were gone. They had been sawed up and burned to heat the classrooms.

Fewer children came to school. Sometimes about half of the desks were empty. Many of the peasants now had little food and no felt boots to protect their feet as they walked a few miles from outlying villages to school each day. Shortages were not the only difficulties that kept Christians from attending school. One of the girls in Anna's class was Shirina, a good student from a middle-class Christian family. She disappeared. No one inquired why she was always absent, because she was not the first to drop out. One day, seeing her passing Grandmother Beyla's house, Anna stopped Shirina to ask why she was not coming to school. She told Anna that her father had died of typhus, and then her brother. They were both buried in the same coffin. Her mother was sick, and Shirina was the only one left to take care of her. Anna certainly knew that typhus was ravaging the Jewish community—sister Mayna had caught it in November, and then Leya early in December—but she had not known that Christian families were suffering equally from the disease.

The high school teachers tried to hold classes when the spring semester began in January, even though they had no firewood to heat the building. After asking the students to bring anything that would burn, and trying to heat just a single schoolroom, Anna's teacher could only tell the students, sitting in their overcoats, that no more classes would be taught that winter.[1]

The previous winter had been bad, but the winter of 1918–1919 was the worst Anna ever lived through in Korsun. Her mother thought about escaping to America, but saw no chance to do it. The food and fuel situations had become steadily worse after the Germans left. In previous winters and even after the first pogrom, Anna had been optimistic, thinking things would improve, would become more nearly normal, and she had gone back to school expecting that nothing bad would happen again. But as this winter unfolded she did not see how she and her family could survive the hardships any longer. She had no hope.

Anna was hopeless but not feckless. She continued to help the family survive. During the worst winter, she took on the job of keeping the family supplied with water. She was already familiar with the several ways to acquire water. When it rained, a barrel standing under their downspout collected gutter water from the roof, but that water was not used for drinking, and rain didn't fall in winter.

Every family had a teakettle that contained a gallon or two of water. When hot water was needed, someone took the big teakettle to the tea-shop, if there was one nearby. Otherwise, the kettle was taken—often enough by the man of the family, to help his wife—to a suitable section of the river, upstream from the place where horses were washed on Saturdays by coachmen's helpers, but downstream from where people bathed and washed clothes.

Several professional water carriers made a living in Korsun in normal times as well as in the earliest wartime years. Hauling a huge barrel of river water from house to house on a horse-drawn flatbed, a water carrier would pull out a chained plug from the barrel to let the water flow into buckets, then carry the buckets into the foyer. There he would pour the water into a normal-size wooden barrel.

Grandmother Beyla and Leya had never in their lives carried water. Before the war, Beyla's servant did carry a few buckets of water on a Friday if needed, and she would also go to the river when extra water was needed, as when she washed cucumbers before they were put into pickling barrels in the cellar. Leya, like other women in peacetime, had hired one of the *vasserfihrers* to deliver water to her house once a week. The water carrier's wife made weekly rounds of the customers' houses to collect her husband's fees.

Usually the carrier filled both water barrels in the foyer at the beginning of the week, one for washing and one for drinking. On Friday if a barrel was empty, Leya would tell Anna to step out into the street and look for a water bearer, a man who walked around town carrying water in two buckets hung from his wooden shoulder yoke. She could usually find a bearer, a *vassertruger,* easily, because two of them were often in the neighborhood, one a Gentile who carried the yoke over both shoulders—yokes were carved to fit the contours of the shoulders—the other a Jew who liked to support the whole weight of the four- or five-foot yoke on his left shoulder.

During the worst winter, though, no payment could buy the delivery of water. The army had taken the water bearers as well as the water carriers and their horses. Anna realized that she, like every able-bodied person remaining in town, would have to fetch the family's water. She began by carrying a single bucket with both hands, but she found this difficult. She told a peasant girl who was carrying water what a hard time she was having. The girl advised her to get a *koromisl* and urged Anna to try hers.

Anna tried the wooden yoke, with its buckets hung from short lengths of rope, and agreed that it was easier to carry two buckets with a yoke on her shoulder than to carry one bucket by hand. She usually used a yoke from then on, and found it more comfortable to carry on her left shoulder. Not every woman could manage two buckets, as Anna did, and she often saw a woman carrying only one bucket on her yoke.[2]

Anna had made several trips to the Ros River during the first two weeks of her mother's typhus. A nineteen-year-old cousin from Kiev had moved in with the family temporarily to nurse Leya, who was fevered and too ill to get out of bed. One of the first things the cousin did was to change Leya's bedclothes, sending Anna to wash the nightgown and sheet. Anna walked to the river, whose bed was wide, but defined by steep-sided walls of irregular granite blocks. Every so often a series of these rocks led down to the river, forming a shelf here and there. Generations of townspeople going to the river for water had worn footholds in the shelves.

Anna and the other children in town had grown up climbing like goats, jumping from shelf to shelf, sometimes able to jump up to the next foothold only by grabbing a conveniently projecting piece of granite with one hand. The handholds were scarce. Just as it was taken for granted that children in Korsun would learn to swim in the river, so it was assumed that they would become adept at climbing up and down the granite rocks. Anna took pride in her ability as an agile climber.

Now, in early December, Anna carried the wash carefully down the icy rocks to the shore, keeping one hand free for a handhold. She had never washed clothes in the ice-covered river before. Near the place at the shore where women pounded their clothes on the rocks, peasants had already chopped out a *polonka,* a hole in the ice that looked like a small well. The sides were formed by ice three feet thick, but the water, unlike that in an ordinary well, came almost to the top. Anna was afraid of the icy water at first, but as she washed the clothes, the water in the well felt comfortably warm. Having finished the washing, she found that climbing back up was harder than going down, but even though the clothes were now wet, the load was light and she still had a hand free to grab the rock railings. She brought the clean wash safely home.

A few days later the cousin sent Anna to fetch water for Leya's tea. She took just one bucket, and with one hand free, she was able to climb down the slippery rocks to the river. She filled her bucket at a smaller *polonka* made for drawing water. Then, carrying the full bucket in one hand, Anna began to climb back up the treacherous rocks. She was able to make her way for a time, despite slipping and spilling some of the water, but finally she could go no farther. Although she was not far from the top, she was slipping with every step. Anna was afraid she would spill all of the water, or worse, fall and injure herself. After trying again and again to climb higher, she gave up and began to cry in despair.

She was not only stuck, she was also cold. The jacket she wore—her grandmother's—together with the heavy shawl covering her head and shoulders, were the warmest clothes left in the family. The jacket hung on a hook in the kitchen, and whoever went outside—Leya, Aunt Meyndl, Grandmother Beyla, or Anna—put on that jacket and that faded green and yellow Scotch plaid shawl. Two people seldom went out of the house at the same time, since only one could wear the warm clothes. Anna was wearing a dress, but she had no long underwear to keep out the cold. She had no gloves. On her feet, wrapped in rags, she wore a pair of shoes so old and worn that they let the water run in and run back out. She stood still for long minutes until, through her tears, she saw a pair of blue eyes looking down at her, and in the blue eyes she saw tears. She thought at first that she was seeing a vision, but it was a real face, the face of a young man. Although Anna knew most of the people in Korsun, she had never seen this blue-eyed man before.

She was standing on a rock shelf about four feet from the top of the cliff. The young man extended his hand toward her, asked her not to cry, and told her to hand him her bucket. She did as she was told, and he pulled up the bucket. Then he told her to take his hand. Reaching down again, he took her hand and pulled her up. He was kneeling beside the walkway on top of the granite rocks, where houses ranged along a street close to the riverbank. He had been walking on that street, and, hearing someone crying, had bent over the edge to see who it was. He looked like a teenager, with a new beard, blond and curly.

Anna thanked him, picked up her bucket, and made her way home. She was thoroughly chilled and still crying when she put down the partly filled bucket to tell her mother what had happened. As she described her blue-eyed rescuer and told where the incident had happened, her mother said that she had heard of just such a young man, recently arrived to marry a girl from Korsun. Her mother was right. The teenage couple—they both had reddish-blonde hair and could have been mistaken for sister and brother—had moved in with the bride's mother, who lived in the Gentile neighborhood on that riverside street where he had been walking when he heard Anna crying.

Anna did not see her rescuer again until months later, in the summer. He did not recognize her, barefoot now, and not wrapped up against the cold as she had been when he rescued her. Anna recognized him, though. She would not forget the face of the young man of her vision, the face of the tearful blue eyes.

Anna's family moved in with Grandmother Beyla in the second half of December 1918, when Leya was recovering from typhus—able to walk but not yet strong enough to cook. Anna had stayed out of school for two weeks to help her cousin nurse her mother during the illness.

While Leya was recovering, her sister Khana came to Korsun from

Tarashcha, having thought of a plan to help support her family. Khana bought dried fruit, a specialty of Korsun farmers, to sell in a distant city where its scarcity would guarantee her a good profit. She told Leya that she needed Anna's help, and Leya agreed that Anna should go.

Aunt Khana didn't need money for tickets, because tickets were no longer used after the disruptions of wartime. A ride of more than two hundred miles in a boxcar took them to a city somewhere between Kharkov and Ekaterinoslav, where Anna helped her aunt sell the fruit. They started back to Korsun, but the train's route was blocked because of a pogrom down the line. Preferring not to wait, Aunt Khana decided they would detour instead, making their own way to her hometown of Tarashcha. While they rode and rode in a wagon pulled by horses, Anna slept as much as she could. She was exhausted—and hungry as well, because her aunt had nothing for them to eat—but they finally arrived in Tarashcha, where they enjoyed the comforts of Khana's brick house.

After two weeks, when trains were reaching Korsun again, Aunt Khana took Anna on the eight-mile wagon ride to the train station at Olshanitsa, handed her a loaf of bread, and rode off in the same wagon, leaving Anna to wait for the train alone. By the time she arrived home, after forty miles on the train—probably three hours or more in those days—and after the walk from the train station to town, Anna had eaten half of the bread. Gussie and Mayna ate what was left.

Armies were still fighting in the former Russian Empire at the end of 1918, even though the world war had ended on November 11. The Jews of Korsun would soon know the names of some of the commanding generals in the Russian Civil War—Kolchak, Makhnov, Petliura, Denikin—but they were not so much interested in news about large armies. They were concerned about the approach of pogroms. As in the March violence, a pogrom started when a detachment of soldiers fighting for one or another of the many generals in the civil war fought another general's band of soldiers for control of a town. The victorious soldiers, having chased out the losers, would then riot, killing townspeople, especially the Jews, and looting their businesses and homes. News of the pogrom went out to surrounding towns, whose inhabitants were then on notice that they might be next.

At the end of December 1918, Korsuners were hearing this kind of news. Peasants in Korsun heard that a nearby army was promising them free rein to loot and kill Jews as soon as the army had taken the town. A peasant woman, who had heard the army's propaganda, ended a minor dispute with Leya by saying that she would get even with Leya in a week or so.

Hearing the woman talk this way, Leya was now sure that a pogrom would come to Korsun. She insisted that Anna warn Mr. Potashnik, who might know what to do, for he was a *dayan*, the judge of the Jewish community's governing body. Anna found him, told him what the peasant woman had said to Leya, and waited for his answer. He said nothing, merely shrugging his shoulders. She understood the shrug. It meant, We Jews all know there's going to be a pogrom, but what can we do?

Every night Anna and her family had been going to bed in fear of falling asleep. Other people in Korsun, however, believed they could defend themselves. Arranging a meeting in a shul, a young, unmarried tailor who had recently arrived in town succeeded in urging the young men to organize a defense force against the *pogromshchiki*. Several of the older people told the young men to disband, warning them that they would be shot down in the first hour.

Besides forming a defense force, the Jews of Korsun had prepared for this pogrom when it was still in the rumor stage by worshiping in small groups—ten people in one house, ten in another—instead of gathering in a shul. They did this because the Jews of Belaya Tserkov, about sixty miles from Korsun as the army marches, had huddled in their shul for safety during the first pogrom. The *pogromshchiki* had locked the doors, trapping the Jews inside, and set fire to the building.[3]

When the fighting began for control of Korsun, Anna's whole extended family took refuge at Grandmother Beyla's big house on the hill, and for a time they dared not go outside. The water barrel was empty, but they could not go out in daylight, because one detachment of soldiers was on a higher hill, firing rifle shots down into the town, aiming at the enemy soldiers. Anna could see the soldiers hiding in the hilltop crevices of the island in the Ros River where peasants usually grazed their sheep and goats.

After dark, Leya put on felt boots, draped the heavy shawl over her shoulders like a jacket against the cold, and crept out into the night to risk getting water. She was carrying a shoulder yoke with a water bucket for each end. She held the yoke in the usual way, like a soldier marching with a rifle resting on his shoulder, one end sticking up into the air. On her way to the river, she heard a single shot very near, but she kept walking and reached the water safely. She was able to climb back up the rocks in the dark after filling her buckets, but before long she could feel that one of the buckets was so much lighter that it unbalanced the yoke, so she emptied it completely. She reached home safely with one bucket full of river water, and one empty bucket with a pair of holes about a third of the way down from the top, where a bullet had gone in one side and out the other.

Having driven the opposing soldiers from Korsun, the victorious detachment, a band of Ukrainian nationalists, began to loot and to kill townspeople. Some of Korsun's peasant women and children, tattered and wearing rags around their feet, walked into the houses with the soldiers to steal household goods—sheets, pillows, and clothing, especially underwear. The Jews were just as impoverished by the war and the winter as were the peasants, making do with worn-out clothing and bedding, but the Jews happened to have some choice underwear. It was the custom each Passover for a family to give the head of a Jewish household new underwear made from good quality muslin. Since this relatively new underwear was in much better condition than what the peasants had, it was a desirable item to steal from the houses of Jews.

Hearing a noise outside one night during this second pogrom, Anna looked out the window into the yard of one of Grandmother Beyla's neighbors, a water carrier who had been taken into the army. His wife had continued the business in his absence for a while, even after the first pogrom, by hiring a horse for a few hours each day to make her deliveries. Now, in the yard brightly lit by the moon and stars, Anna saw a peasant hammering at one wheel of the water wagon. After he finally knocked it loose and began hammering away at another wheel, Anna realized that he was stealing the wheels.

In the days after the pogrom came to an end, Grandma Beyla's house was merely one of the many Jewish houses showing the tell-tale sign that *pogromshchiki* had paid them a visit—rags stuffed into broken window panes. To Anna, a broken window was not merely a sign of random and senseless violence. She believed that the soldiers wanted the Jews to freeze to death. Grandmother Beyla did not have enough rags to stuff into all the broken windowpanes. The coldest part of the winter was not yet over.

As in the first pogrom, although the violence and looting finally came to an end, it took some time before their echoes stopped reverberating through the town. One of Anna's friends was a girl named Petrushanska. Although Petrushanska was older, they shared a class at the high school, and she sometimes shared her lunch with Anna. When the students were able to go back to school after the second pogrom, she became hysterical one day, between classes, at the sight of a peasant girl wearing a heavy winter shawl that she recognized as her own. A teacher asked Anna's friend if she was sure it was her shawl. Even though she said she was sure, the teacher would not take the shawl from the peasant girl. Petrushanska was doubly angry, arguing that if the girl had her shawl, she must also have other things stolen from the Petrushanska house. This time, though, there were no German soldiers to undo the looting.

Anna had lived through two pogroms without learning which armies had caused them. Even though she knew and feared the names of generals— Petliura, Makhnov, Grigoriev—she could not keep straight in her mind which band of soldiers belonged to which general, or exactly what the fighting was about. In fact, with the armies made up mostly of rural peasant boys still in their teens or slightly older, she believed that many of the soldiers had little idea why they were fighting.

Anna's confusion was to be expected. The second pogrom had been an insignificant incident in the vast Russian Civil War, a chaotic affair in which the fighting was not just between the Reds (the Bolsheviks) and the Whites (their main opponents). In the Ukraine the number of armies was beyond counting, including nationalist forces fighting for an independent Ukraine, an anarchist army fighting to give the peasants self-rule free of any national government, and a multitude of other warlords fighting for their own causes. Armies changed sides during the war. Two of the generals fought sometimes against the Ukrainian nationalists, sometimes against the Bolsheviks, and sometimes for the Bolsheviks.

After the second pogrom, with Ukrainian nationalist forces occupying Korsun, Ukrainian quickly became the official language in the high school, and Ukrainian money became the official currency, replacing the German bills. The peasants would accept neither the older Kerensky bills nor the new Ukrainian paper money, which came in five-, fifteen-, and twenty-dollar denominations. They demanded silver. Leya had no silver coins, and the two sterling silver spoons that she had buried in Mr. Alushka's foyer had disappeared. People had sold almost everything to buy food. Even a sewing needle was worth twenty-five cents.

The police and officials who remained in town did not look any different on the day after the soldiers marched in than on the day before, but they now became agents for the new occupier. The police chief wore his usual uniform decorated with braid, topped by an ornate hat. The lone town policeman, known by everyone, also wore his usual uniform, with his sword hanging at his waist. The several mailmen, privately employed (by a man who owned the coaches and horses that carried passengers and mail expensively from one town to another), had a uniform consisting of military-style khaki coat and pants, knee galoshes, and a sword. People were afraid of anyone who wore a uniform, whether a town uniform or that of an army.

After the trip to Kharkov with Aunt Khana, Anna spent her time bartering the salt her mother brought from Kiev for bread, or searching for food and fuel. The family did not have enough coal oil for lighting, but that was of little importance compared to the need for warmth in Grandmother Beyla's cold house. People were burning their books for heat. Many children were going to the forest several miles out of town, looking for wood.

Walking to the forest two or three times a week, Anna sometimes came upon peasants axing down a tree. She watched them lopping the branches from the felled tree, and then—if they no longer owned either horse or wagon—tying ropes around the trunk, hitching themselves to the ropes, and hauling the trunk away by their own power. If she was lucky, they would feel sorry for her, giving her some of the branches, which she tied around with rope and dragged home. If the pieces were small enough, she carried them home on her back in a burlap sack.

When she met no friendly peasants in the woods, Anna could only chop down a small fruit tree with her "chopping knife"—a meat cleaver—then tie a rope around the trunk and drag it home. She didn't like bringing down trees that provided food, but the family needed firewood, and she had no axe to use on a larger tree. Anna hid her cleaver inside her coat whenever she went to the forest for wood, afraid she might meet a murderer. She knew that one man had been killed in the forest, wrapped up, and brought back not on a sleigh but dragged by horses. Other corpses were found in the woods, and people didn't know whether they had been killed or had just frozen to death.

When Anna brought home a large branch, she sawed it into easily handled pieces on a makeshift sawhorse. The branches were so wet that they took a long time to dry. Sometimes Anna stole outside late at night to chop off a piece of someone's fence, a prime source of dry wood for starting a fire. The wet branches dried out a little if they were placed on top of the burning fence wood. Once, to get dry wood, Anna chopped pieces from a broken telephone pole.

The family had lost the supply of potatoes and cabbages from Anna's vandalized garden. Vegetables were scarce. People were lucky if they had enough wood to heat water for a hot drink, and luckier if they had any tea to flavor it. To make a substitute for tea, Leya grated dried carrots, pouring hot water over the slivers. She had no sugar for the tea, but she was used to making her own molasses, grating white sugar beets on a metal grater and slowly cooking the pulp down to a syrup. When the fire burned out, she kept the pot covered until the next fire was lit. That way the beets were cooked in three or four small fires until done, then strained to remove any beet fragments from the molasses-colored syrup.

At the flourmill, which had burned to the ground because the volunteer fire department no longer had any able-bodied men, people cleared away the top layer of burned debris, uncovering hundreds of sacks of bran that had been spared. Anna went to the mill often, each time fearful of the rats that thought the grain their property, each time carrying bran back to the one remaining storage barrel at her grandmother's house nearby.

The family cooked and tried to keep warm with fires built from pieces of Beyla's furniture and the branches Anna dragged out of the forest. Aunt Meyndl cooked the bran from the burned mill by building a small fire under the long legs of the metal tripod.

Leya no longer had either her Chinese beds or her clothes chest. Anna and her two sisters often lay in bed most of the day to conserve body heat under their grandmother's feather-bed blanket. At night, Leya joined them. Whoever got out of bed put on every piece of clothing and wrapped herself in every cover she could find.

The second pogrom, coming during the worst winter, had been the last straw for Leya. She determined never to spend another winter in Russia. She told her daughters that they would find a way to go to America. It was impossible to go immediately, but as soon as any chance came, they would leave. Now the family had hope. Many in Korsun had given up. Some died during that worst winter, even though they had a little more food than Anna's family, and Anna came to believe that she knew what made the difference. Her family survived that winter because, determined to reach America, they had hope.

Spring and Summer in Prewar Korsun

Before the war, in a simpler time when each season came and went as it had in all the years before, when life in the Jewish community was linked to the seasons by the serene cycle of the holidays, spring was a hopeful time. A Ukrainian rhyme held that March can be so cold that it makes up for a whole winter. Still, the holiday of Purim, which usually fell in March, commonly arrived on a relatively warm day, a day when the ground was muddy but the temperature was sixty or sixty-five degrees, weather for a jacket. It might be warmer or colder from one year to the next, but there was no frost at Purim.

Like autumn, spring was brief. Unlike autumn, spring was eventful. In the warming sun of March, the snow that had stubbornly hidden the ground all winter relaxed enough to become slush. Melting ice and snow dripped steadily from the roofs, pattering onto the watery mixture below. There were no sewers or drainage ditches, so water stood on the ground wherever it had formed or landed. The melting snow and ice took the shape of pools and pockets of water that seeped into the clay soil, mingled with it, and eventually softened it into a gray mud, deep and tenacious.

The spring mud lasted for about four weeks. It was a great nuisance. When a Korsuner walked in it, his foot made an impression in the sopping-wet clay. He had to pull his foot out of the clay before he could take the next step. If the mud was very wet, the footprint would fill up immediately. The impressions from several people's footsteps, however, created a crude path that made walking a little less difficult. People used an expression to describe the improved weather and condition of the mud, saying, It was nice enough to follow the footsteps.

Purim in Korsun was known for its mud. It is the custom on that holiday that a family send a gift to the home of each of its friends and relatives. The usual gift is a plate of food, including such treats as cookies, cake, candy, and fruit. When Anna delivered the gifts, the mud was up to her ankles. She could not afford to waste any food dropped from a plate, so she picked it up, wiped off the mud, and put it back on the plate.

The mud had to be considered in planning how people would go from one place to another, because most of the roads in Korsun were dirt. The mud was deepest and most slippery in the middle of the street, so Anna would walk closer to the houses, where the mud was less of a hindrance.

Once, near her grandmother's old house, she had to hold on to a fence in order to walk straight. Otherwise she was afraid to take a step, not knowing how deep the mud was. It looked to her like a river. Houses in Korsun only seldom had fences, but if she found one, she walked holding on to it. She considered herself lucky not to fall.

The mud gave to travel its old meaning of *travail*, a labor. When the mud became soft enough to retain the impressions of wagon wheels, hooves, and boots, travel became a chore, no matter whether the traveler was a peasant on the road, bringing fresh produce to town in his horse-drawn wagon, or a housewife struggling along the footpaths to the market, to buy the day's supply of food.

The spring mud at its worst could test the driver of a wagon, as well as his two horses. Many times Anna saw a driver, the wheels of his wagon deep in the quagmire, whip his horses, who were already struggling hopelessly on their hind legs. Finally, the driver had to abandon his whip, climb down from his seat, go behind the wagon, and apply his shoulder to it, pushing awkwardly while slipping and sliding in the mud, and all the while urging the straining horses forward.

In the weeks between the holidays of Purim in March and Passover in April, the mud would start to dry, eventually to emerge in the form of gray dirt. Passover meant to Anna that the real spring had begun. In a few weeks, the trees and bushes would blossom. Although there were not many trees in town, Anna had in mind the places where she could see each variety of tree when it came into bloom.

Her grandfather had a small garden with two acacia trees. Anna and her friends were familiar with the sweet-smelling white flowers, arranged in clusters of eight blossoms on a leaf stem. After stripping the petals from a flower to expose a green cup, they sipped from the cup, robbing the birds and bees of the sweet nectar. At about the same time, usually early in May, Anna was also reveling in the sight and scent of the blossoms of the lilac and jasmine bushes.

A little later in the year, on a certain street in Korsun, the blossoms of the chestnut tree opened. The creamy white bunches of blooms standing among the leaves like a bunch of candles were almost regal to Anna. The oak had similar flowers, but for her they were just ordinary compared to those of the chestnut.

Anna passed the homes of peasants and landowners on the way to go swimming in the river. Some of these homes at the outskirts of town had picket fences that she could see through. The homes of the landowners had large grounds, with gardens that sometimes extended all the way to the River Ros. First to bloom in the outskirts were the apple trees, even before their leaves unfolded. Then followed the blossoming of the cherry, plum, and pear trees. When the cherry blossoms fell from the trees, it reminded Anna of a snowfall.

Late May or early June brought the early harvest holiday of *Shavuoth*, which Anna loved because everything was clean and green and in flower. Flowers were as scarce in the Jewish neighborhood as they were common in the gardens of the outskirt peasants. Anna's mother once sent her to the outskirts near the Ros River to buy roses during the Shavuoth holiday.

Summer weather was ideal. With temperatures in the eighties at the hottest, and usually not above the low seventies, the children went swimming every day. Evenings were cool. Not everything was ideal in summer. During the months of dry weather, a top layer of dust formed out of the dried clay of the streets. Behind a passing wagon, clouds of dust billowed in the middle of the road, settling into a haze. Anna's feet would be gray with dust when she came home. Thunderstorms could split the skies and reverberate in the summer air, but the rains were only occasional and mild. Anna didn't mind the summer mud that squished between her toes, even though it was thick enough to hinder her walking. It was soon dried by the sun.

Fruit trees were uncommon inside the town in the Jewish residential districts, but plum trees flourished at the back of the large house of Zyama Rabinovich. Zyama's wife, though wealthy, was a frugal woman. Instead of giving away the plums from her orchard to the needy people in town, she sold them to a man who dried them to make prunes.

Anna discovered the largest stand of fruit trees when she went to the Shapiro house each day for a few minutes of free tutoring by Mr. Yerusalimsky, after he had finished instructing the wealthy Shapiro children. The Shapiro garden was the best Anna ever saw. On one side of the house was a magnificent planting of fruit trees, cared for by a hired man. Anna thrilled at the blossoming of the Shapiros' cherry, apple, plum, and pear trees. Later, she sometimes tasted the ripe fruits. She would never presume to take a delicious pear unbidden, for example, but one of the Shapiro children, or the maid, Khveodora, would ask her if she wanted one.

Bushes in the yard bore the raspberry and the elderberry. A tall mulberry tree was a nuisance to Mrs. Shapiro, who told Anna to take as many of the ground-staining berries as she wanted. Anna could not reach the branches of the mulberry tree, so she picked up the berries from the ground, gathering handfuls in a pail, and taking them home, where she and her mother and sisters ate them on bread.

Other trees were more plentiful at the edges of Korsun than toward the center. Birch, linden, oak, chestnut, and walnut trees ringed the town with a luxurious growth of summer green.

In the waning weeks of summer, housewives of means bought fruits and vegetables in quantity to prepare for winter storage. The peasants earned good money during this August harvest season, selling their fruits and vegetables. Anna would see a wagonload of apples, then a wagonload of cucumbers, and later in the day, a wagonload of mixed carrots, cabbages, and potatoes, all coming into town. Cabbage, for example, was wintered in two ways—either pickled to store as sauerkraut or raw. Anna's grandmother stored twenty or thirty heads of raw cabbage in her cellar to be used later as an ingredient in borscht.

The end of summer did not mean the beginning of a school year for Anna until she reached high school age. Korsun had no public elementary school for anyone, Jew or Gentile. When Anna was ten, the first public high school was under construction, and all of the girls her age were being tutored to prepare them to take the entrance examinations. Anna was tutored for several years, but the tutors were usually second-rate, and the lessons were held only when Leya had enough money to pay for them. Anna did learn arithmetic and some geography. She also learned Russian grammar and how to speak, read, and write Russian—necessary skills since the high school classes were to be conducted in Russian.

The new high school opened in 1915. Anna failed the entrance examination after summer ended that year. Having studied on her own, and having had other tutoring, she took the entrance examination again the next time it was given, and this time, in the fall of 1916, she passed and was admitted at the usual entry age of eleven.

20

Spring and Summer (1919)

In the spring of 1919, Anna missed more than a month of high school because of illness. By the time she caught typhus fever, her mother had sufficiently recovered, during January from her own bout of typhus, to travel again and was on a smuggling trip in Kiev. For a time, Anna lay listlessly on a sofa, her fever high, her head a constant ache. No one in the house was able to go to the river to fetch enough water for her to drink. No one could collect icicles for her, as she had done to soothe her mother's fever. Aunt Meyndl was pregnant and not feeling well. Grandfather Avrum was in bed suffering from his cancer. Only Grandmother Beyla, hampered by arthritis, and ten-year-old sister, Gussie, were fit enough to nurse Anna. Aunt Feyga, who lived next door, was caring for her own three daughters.[1]

The days of prostration and fever dragged on in February until Anna sank into a stupor. She did not know what was happening around her, or how many days had passed, but when she finally opened her eyes, Grandmother Beyla sent Gussie next door to tell Aunt Feyga that Anna had passed the crisis. Aunt Feyga cooked a soup of yellow millet, even though she had neither milk nor salt for it, and brought it over. Anna made herself eat it, but it tasted terrible. She kept it down only until her aunt left the house. Soon, though, she was able to eat well, and later she began to take an interest in the world again. When she looked through the window for the first time, the sight of children going to school made her feel forlorn. Eager as she was for learning, she could not believe she would grow strong enough to return to school that semester.

When Leya came back from Kiev, a peasant woman told her that Anna would recover from her typhus faster if she ate the crude molasses formed during the processing of brown sugar into white sugar—the kind of molasses that people fed their cows to make them produce better milk. Leya fed a whole pot of the bitter syrup to Anna, one tablespoonful at a time. Anna began to recover her strength slowly, whether because of the molasses tonic or in spite of it. She got up from her sickbed as March gave way to April, and on wobbly legs she was able to plant some seeds in her own garden.

Having seen Mayna and Leya regain strength slowly, Anna knew that her own recovery would be a long process. Her legs were still so unsteady when someone brought her a bunch of spinachlike sorrel to eat, that she barely made it down the granite rocks to the river to wash the sand from the leaves. The peasants gave away these sour-tasting leaves (*shchavel* in Ukrainian), because even animals turned up their noses at them. Anna's family called them *shtshav* in Yiddish and ate them.

Anna was strong enough to return to school by mid-April, in time to volunteer to work for the young priest who taught mathematics. Although it was a time of extreme shortages, the Gentiles had some bread after Easter, because even the poorest peasant still had a little flour. The Jews, however, had none, as they had to dispose of all grain, and thus all flour, before the start of the Passover holiday. Each peasant in the priest's church traditionally brought him a gift such as a chicken or a pig at Easter, but now they were so poor that they baked instead, each giving him a loaf of bread. His sizable kitchen table was piled high with loaves. Knowing that the Jews in Korsun were going hungry, and that he had enough to feed only a few families, the priest solved the problem by offering the older Jewish high school students the chance to work in his garden in exchange for bread. Of the ten volunteers, Anna was the first to sign up.

The students tilled and planted the priest's garden each day. Anna's foot pushed her shovel into the earth time after time, turning over the rich black soil teeming with plump white worms. When a day's work was finished, the priest's wife served each child a large piece of bread and a bowl of meatless potato soup or borscht, for she knew that they could not eat nonkosher meat. After they had spooned their bowls dry, she gave each one a large loaf of bread to take home. Anna and the others set plants into the earth for the priest's wife every day until her kitchen table was bare. As long as it lasted, Anna's family feasted on the priest's bread—a slice every morning for breakfast, and another slice every noon for the main meal.

When the children were standing in line, waiting for the loaves to be distributed on the first day, the priest's wife asked each child how many people they had in their family. Anna said four. She could tell that none of the children were adding to the number of people in their families. Then the girl next to her, a girl known to stick up for her rights, also said four. Knowing that there were five in the girl's family, Anna thought the girl had made a mistake. She asked why she had said four. The girl held up four fingers and said that her sister had died. She showed no emotion. Anna stood open-mouthed, unable to believe that the girl felt no sorrow.

While Anna was working in the priest's garden, her mother was again going to Kiev. Leya was speculating in grain, smuggling millet and kasha in small bags suspended from a belt hidden under an ample skirt. Kiev was now the capital not only of its province, but of the potential Ukrainian National Republic, whose nationalist army had been driven from Kiev by Bolshevik forces early in February 1919.[2] In the capital city, which depended for its food upon a surrounding countryside ravaged by civil war, the people were starving. Bartering the five pounds of grain that she was carrying, Leya brought valuables such as needles and thread back home to Grandmother Beyla's big house on the hill.[3] Gussie and Anna took the needles to peasant hamlets three or four miles outside town, bartering them for buckwheat flour or for bread. In the day-to-day struggle to bring in enough food for everyone in the family, Anna had the strongest concern for six-year-old Mayna. Anna took care that her little sister did not go hungry, even going so far as to snatch bread for Mayna from Grandfather Avrum.

As soon as warmer weather had come in March, the students had spontaneously returned to school. By the time Anna had recovered enough to join them, her bald spots from typhus had been made more presentable by a barber who clipped her hair almost down to the scalp. She was ashamed of her baldness and embarrassed at having to walk into the classroom wearing a headscarf to cover her stubs of bristly hair. Just as bad, her scarf had been cut from a cotton tablecloth, her skirt and blouse were made from burlap sacks, and her shoes were torn. The elderly Ukrainian teacher, seeing her embarrassment, came to the door and walked in front of her to shield her from the eyes of the students. As it turned out, she was not the only pupil in makeshift clothing, but the girls did tease her for having hair like a boy's.

In the meantime, the Bolsheviks had again occupied Kiev. Extending their reach to the remote Ukrainian towns, they took power in Korsun without a local battle, and the students there were learning new songs in school, the songs of the revolution. Before the term ended, Anna marched in the parade with all the other schoolchildren, the girls five abreast in their high school's holiday uniforms, each with a ribbon pinned to the shoulder of her white pinafore. No one in Korsun knew the word "Bolshevik" yet, but the ribbon was the color of the revolution—red.

At the head of the town's band marched its leader, Mr. Heifetz, a *klezmer,* or musician (not Jascha Heifetz, already a famous violinist, but his cousin), walking forward playing his flute, then walking backward using it as a baton to conduct the band. The musicians usually played wedding music and dance tunes at weddings in and around Korsun. Today they were playing a different kind of music, while Anna and her classmates were singing the newly memorized words to the Soviet anthem, the Internationale, and the Marseillaise. To Anna, the message was, We'll make a new world. Those who are nothing will be everything.

The organizers, revolutionary young men from the big cities, brought crowds of young peasant women in from all the surrounding villages, and as the rows of peasants marched, the sun highlighted different colored head scarves for each village. Never having seen some of these colors on the peasants before, Anna wondered whether the young women were marching only because the organizers had cleverly given them new scarves. The older people in Korsun, wary of a new regime, did not march.

Anna glimpsed her mother and her two sisters in the crowd that lined the parade route leading from the crossroads at the center of town to the Orthodox church next to the palace. Speakers praised the Communist Party and the revolution to the crowd standing in the church square. They promised the children and young people a new life, no longer a life in fear of the tsar's police.

In some ways things did change after the parade. If someone complained that another townsperson had snubbed them, for example, a party member would give the offender a slap, or a lecture about the Communist slogan— "We are children from one nation." That usually ended the snubbing. In other ways, though, town life went on much as it had before.

The elderly teacher, having noticed Anna's skill when they had tilled adjacent gardens during the German occupation, tried to talk her into staying in Korsun to become an agricultural expert, an *agronom*. Assuring her that she would be a valued member of what he foresaw as a newly independent Ukrainian nation, he told Anna that he and the other Ukrainians would take care of her.

Anna liked him, both because she admired his command of the Ukrainian language and because he had praised her gardening skills when they cultivated their back-to-back garden plots. She was surprised by his offer, especially when he spoke of taking care of her—she knew the extent and depth of anti-Semitism in the Ukraine—and she saw that he was both surprised and disappointed when she told him that she could not accept his offer because she would not be back in school for the next semester. She was going to America! No future in the Ukraine could ever compare with her hopes and dreams about living in that storied land where her father was still waiting for his family after seven years.

At the end of the semester, since the students had attended mainly from March through May, Anna's class was not entitled to credit for a full year's studies. Still, the elderly Ukrainian, who had become her favorite teacher, insisted that she accept a certificate saying that she had completed at least a portion of the third year of high school. He said that it would come in handy.

After the revolution, as families found it harder and harder to make a living, several women realized that they could earn money at the railway station by catering to the many soldiers coming and going on the trains. The women carried to the station any food that they thought a tired and hungry soldier might buy. Some women baked *pirozhki,* small pastries filled with poppy seeds, and Leya once tried this small enterprise. She bought a twenty-pound chunk of poppy seeds, baked a batch of *pirozhki,* and sent Anna off to the railway station with them to wait for the trains. Business was good. Anna needed only about an hour to sell out her supply. She walked home to get more. Back at the station she soon sold a pastry to another soldier, but this one became angry when he took a bite.

The chunk that Leya had bought looked just like poppy seeds, but the soldier, a peasant farmer, was not fooled by the resemblance. He recognized that the pastry was not filled with seeds, but with their black hulls, the by-product after the oil had been pressed out. The cooking oil factory ordinarily squeezed these hulls into large blocks, selling them to farmers who fed them to their cows and pigs, since it filled their stomachs, even though most of the nutrients had already been removed. The only reason Leya had been able to buy it at such a bargain was that the peasants now had so few cows and pigs on their farms that the oil factory in Korsun could sell very little to its usual customers.

Leya was not trying to fool anybody. As a town dweller, she didn't know about the poppy seed hulls, nor did Anna. The farmer-soldier, however, having paid for what he thought were whole poppy seeds, naturally concluded that Anna was trying to cheat him. He was angry enough to attack her, but several of the peasant women selling alongside Anna defended her, explaining to him that she didn't know what she was selling.

Leya tried another way to earn money. She bought some flour, baked about ten loaves of bread, and sent Anna to the railway station with half of them, hoping that if a train came in, she could sell a few slices to the soldiers on the train. Any leftovers would be eaten by the family. Anna took her usual shortcut to the railway station, walking beyond the end of the cobblestoned road at the palace, then heading northwest, cross-country, where no vehicle could travel. Roads did not come this way, only paths near the river, a canal, and a tiny bridge. Sometimes her bare feet were ankle deep in water.

At the railway station, Anna sat on the platform to wait with the others who hoped to sell their wares to the soldiers. When a train came in, hungry soldiers climbed down from the railroad cars, eager to buy food. Anna borrowed a knife from the woman next to her, sliced the round, dark breads, sold the slices, and pocketed the soldiers' green paper Ukrainian money. As the train slowly pulled away from the station, a woman began to laugh at Anna, telling her that the soldiers were getting away and that the money they gave Anna had no value. She told Anna to throw it away.

Anna, crying, ran inside to the stationmaster, asking him to do something. He said that he couldn't do anything about it and that he couldn't help it if the soldiers acted in such a way. She went home, still crying.

The next day, she saw a little peasant boy walking from the Ros River bridge to the marketplace to sell his bundle of wood. Anna stopped him to ask how much he wanted for the bundle. As soon as he told her the price, she bought his wood. She paid him with the green Ukrainian money.

Grandfather Avrum died of stomach cancer early in the summer, leaving Anna to grieve not only for his death, but also for the way she had taken the bread from him at Easter time, the priest's bread she had saved for Mayna.[4] The same summer months also brought new life when Meyndl delivered the last of her three daughters. Because her mother's good friend, Oodl Slivnik, had been killed in the second pogrom while Meyndl was carrying the baby, she named the infant after Oodl. Anna went to the river to wash the diapers for little Oodl.

21
The Third Pogrom
(August 13–26, 1919)

The third pogrom to hit Korsun came rolling in from the southeast in the last weeks of summer. As usual, rumors were flying from mouth to ear, but it became clear that battles were being fought not far from Korsun. It was the custom for a delegation made up of the rabbi and some elders of the town to go to the railway station, where they would meet the victorious general, presenting him with a token offering of bread and salt in the hope that this traditional Ukrainian gesture of welcome would prevent a pogrom. The time for such a delegation had arrived.[1]

Anna was not in Korsun when this pogrom began. She had gone with Leya to Kiev to barter on the black market. Leya was in poor health, and Anna went along to help. They rode the train to Kiev in the company of five other women from Korsun and went to the bazaar, where Leya did her usual bartering. When Anna spotted a woman with a batch of paper from an office that had gone out of business, they made a trade for two tablets, each of about a hundred double-size sheets that she needed for the coming fall term of school. Even though she could not find the books she needed for school, Anna was happy with her paper, the sheets large and lined, just as she wanted. One woman in the group was also happy about her find in Kiev, excited because she had been able to barter for a thimble to protect a sore on her finger.

On the ride back from Kiev, the train was scheduled to stop in a few hours at Belaya Tserkov, the first sizable station, but after about an hour, when they had only reached Vasilikov, they were told the train could not proceed, because the authorities had received a telephone message that bandits had seized control of the railroad somewhere down the line.

Leya, Anna, and the other women from Korsun got off the train. Anna still had her bald spots from the loss of hair that was so common after typhus. The five other women from Korsun were all in their late thirties, but Anna thought they all looked much older, and one woman, a cousin of the artist Alter Koslov, was pregnant. They set out to walk toward Korsun without knowing the way, then took someone's suggestion to walk on the railroad tracks, which would be safe since no trains were running.

Knowing that it was only thirty-two *versti*—about twenty miles—the women set out at six in the morning to walk the tracks from Vasilikov to Belaya Tserkov, stopping once to eat what little food they had carried, and again on the way, at an abandoned garden, where they pulled leaves from a certain plant and ate them. They came to the large station at Belaya Tserkov at six that evening, but fearing an attack by bandits, and wanting to reach home as soon as they could, they decided against stopping to rest. Finally, at a station farther on, they were so tired that they allowed themselves to sit down. No trains came either way while they rested. The woman who was about six months pregnant asked Anna to please give her a drink.

Before Anna could move, Leya yelled at the woman that Anna had walked the same distance, and that the woman should get the drink for herself. Anna wanted to fetch water for the woman but could not, since her mother had spoken, and though she was shocked at her mother's rudeness, she knew that Leya was overburdened with responsibilities and worries and would never behave that way in normal times.

Leaving the station after resting, the women spent the night in a field nearby. In the morning, deciding to forsake the railroad tracks, they set out through the fields, hoping to find any kind of a village, and in the sunshine of summer they walked barefoot, each woman carrying her shoes tied together and slung over her shoulders to avoid wearing them out. Each one also carried the items for which she had bartered in Kiev. Anna had tied her oversized tablets of lined paper with string, stuffing them inside the front of her buttoned jacket. After a time the women saw a *dorf* that a few of them recognized as the village of Shenderevka, about fifteen miles from Korsun, but before they could reach it, two young men stopped them in the middle of a field, grabbing the shoes from around everyone's neck and taking away everything they were carrying from Kiev. One of the robbers held a pistol to Anna's mouth, demanding to see what she was hiding, and when she unbuttoned her jacket, he took the tablets of lined paper, although she couldn't imagine why he wanted them. The two bandits were teenagers and acted a little scared, as if it was their first holdup.

After the bandits left, as the women walked toward the village of Shenderevka, they saw what looked like a funeral procession coming toward them. When they came closer, Anna saw a tableau she had never seen before. She was not surprised that the wagon was rolling along very slowly, but it was packed with people, all sitting inside, no one dangling their feet the way carefree riders liked to do. Trailing behind were about ten more people just keeping pace with the wagon. When Anna's group came up to the wagon, it stopped.[2]

At first, Anna thought they were all Jews, because the first few spoke Yiddish, but it turned out that some of them were peasants, Ukrainian speakers. Anna knew that some peasants were worse off than the Jews. Most of the soldiers killed in the war were their men. The refugees said they just couldn't stand another pogrom. This was the third pogrom in Korsun in less than two years. They had heard that things were better in another province, and that's where they were going. As the two groups talked, the people sitting in the wagon crawled out to walk, and the walkers climbed in to ride. They told Anna's group not to go to Korsun yet, because the *pogromshchiki* were burning houses.

By the time Anna's group reached Shendarevka, they had spent several days walking the seventy miles from Vasilikov. The news that a pogrom was going on in Korsun had reached the agitated villagers, who were fearful that their village would be next. They came running out to greet the women from Korsun, relieved that they were not *pogromshchiki*.

When Leya told how the two young bandits had robbed them, and how she worried about what other outlaws might do to Anna, one woman looked at Anna, bedraggled after the long walk, with bald patches from typhus, and laughed. Leya could stop worrying, the woman said, because no man would touch a girl who looked like that.

The people of Shendarevka put up the Korsun women for the night. One of the villagers turned out to be a relative of Anna's grandfather, so he and his wife took Leya and Anna in, making room on the floor, where Anna slept with her head on her mother's bundle.

Even though the women were anxious about their families—Leya had already convinced herself that Gussie and Mayna were dead, killed in the pogrom—instead of hurrying straight home in the morning, they decided to go slightly out of their way to the little village of Steblev, about seven miles from Korsun, to see what the news was there.

On the road they met a peasant, who asked where they were going. The women said they were on their way to Korsun, where they had left their children and families, and asked the peasant if she knew what was happening there. She said that the pogrom was still going on and advised them to wait for a day or two.

Heedless, they walked on. When they reached Steblev, even though people told them the same thing, they didn't stop. As they approached the tiny settlement of Yablonovka, only about three miles from Korsun, peasants standing in the road told them to keep away from Korsun for a time and to stop instead at their village. Finally, the women agreed to stay overnight. In the morning, as they approached Korsun, they met a peasant family walking away from town. Farther along the road came another, and still farther, another, all refugees from the pogrom, each with a wagon carrying the few possessions they had been able to bring out.[3]

When Anna and Leya finally came into Korsun and turned onto Grandmother Beyla's street, they saw what looked like snow floating in the summer air and whitening the road, but as they came closer they realized they were seeing feathers from the pillows the plunderers had slashed open while searching for hidden valuables. In previous pogroms, looters looking for valuables had ripped open a few pillows, mattresses, and featherbed comforters, scattering the white goose feathers, but such a snow of feathers as this had never been seen before.

Leya and Anna eventually found almost everyone in their extended family. When they were all reunited at Grandmother's big house on the hill, they saw who had come through safely: Aunt Meyndl and her daughter Gissie; Aunt Feyga and her children; Anna's sisters, Gussie and Mayna; and Beyla. They exchanged stories about what had happened during the pogrom. The looting and destruction had been severe. *Pogromshchiki* had forced Uncle Beryl, the honey merchant, to dance as they shot bullets at his feet. Then they murdered him.

Grandmother Beyla was in poor health, but by now she was experienced in dealing with *pogromshchiki*. She told how she had taken ten-year-old Gussie, and Mayna, who was almost seven, across the cobblestoned main street to the clay quarry just beyond her friend Yenta Koslov's house. From this walk-in hollow on the side of a cliff, people dug the yellow clay that gave a clean, fresh covering to their dirt floors each Friday in preparation for the Sabbath. Beyla and the girls hid in the clay cliff side for a few days, the two sisters playing all day in the hollowed chamber, which became their bedroom at night. Then Aunt Feyga had taken her own children, as well as Gussie and Mayna, farther away from the house, all the way to the Jewish cemetery at the southern edge of town, where they tried to hide and sleep, even though they didn't want to close their eyes.

Looking at her two sisters, Anna thought they seemed ill from lack of food. Gussie later told Anna about some things she had seen during the pogrom. She had seen a woman being "robbed of her clothes" in the street. Not until long afterward would she learn the proper word for what she had witnessed and understand what had happened to the woman. Gussie had also seen the row of booths at the marketplace burning. These booths had escaped the fire when the rest of the marketplace structures had been destroyed in the first pogrom. Anna knew the people who worked there. Some of the windows in Grandmother Beyla's house had still been intact when Anna and her mother had left for Kiev. Now, they were all broken.

The anti-Bolshevik soldiers who had taken over the town during this pogrom were "Whites," men of General Anton Denikin's anti-Bolshevik Volunteer Army. They could loot and destroy at will, doing as they liked with the residents. Anna's word for a brutal, murderous man was *khuligan,* a word adopted into Russian from the English "hooligan."[4] Such men would ask a rich Jew where he had hidden his gold and silver, and it did no good if he said that he didn't bury anything, that all of his valuables were there for the taking. They would take everything and kill him anyhow.

Not far from Anna lived a butcher who had returned to Korsun because, he said, he didn't like the food in America. The *khuligani* killed his daughter, and Anna did not like to think about what they did to his wife.

After days of violence—this third pogrom to strike Korsun was the biggest and most disastrous of all—Anna arose one morning to find a quiet town. When she looked outside to see if any *khuligani* were still rampaging or any peasant women were still looting, the streets were clear. People began to come out of hiding, and for a while, parents who had become separated from their children dared to come outside to search.

It looked as though the pogrom was over, but then a few uniformed *pogromshchiki* and some peasants appeared, searching leisurely for any remnants that they and their fellow looters had overlooked. Anna went outside, walking barefoot to her grandmother's house, but stopping two doors short at a house with half a dozen wooden steps leading up to the front door. Mrs. Budyanska, mother-in-law of Anna's cousin Zavl, was sitting on her steps, talking to a small group of women and children.

It was out of character for the wife of a successful businessman, a woman who lived in a fine house built only about ten years before the revolution, to sit on her front steps. Anna had never seen that before. But there sat Mrs. Budyanska, in the middle of a step, facing the group at her right. A soldier in uniform started up the steps, carrying his rifle. Wrapped around his cap, just above the visor, was a white ribbon. He came up the steps on her left, walking casually, as though he were a member of her family. She shifted the least bit, leaning away from him, gathering in her skirt so that he would not step on it, the action of a woman who had nothing more to lose. Behind the uniformed looter walked a peasant woman carrying an empty sack on her shoulder. Mrs. Budyanska did not look around at the soldier or at the woman. Those two walked up the steps, on their way into her house, its windows already stripped of their curtains.

Mrs. Budyanska went right on telling her news to the group, and the women went on asking her for more information. Although she could not read, her husband could, and the Budyanska family was one of those that had received a Kiev newspaper for years. In ordinary times her son was the paperboy who delivered it to subscribers. In most families the man read the paper. He might discuss an item with his wife, and when he spoke at his workplace or his shul to men who had not read a paper, he would pass along whatever news was of interest. The men hearing the news would then come home and tell their wives, most of whom could not read, and when the women in turn met one another going to and from their daily shopping at the marketplace, they would exchange pieces of news heard from their husbands.

The civil war was now nearly two years old, however, and the paper usually did not arrive from Kiev, but if it did, people did not believe much of what they read, knowing that the newspaper was politically controlled. Even so, about once a month somebody smuggled the paper into town for Mr. Budyanska. Sometimes it was a month old, but in any case, it made Mrs. Budyanska a source of news. Her husband might have told her, for example, that a certain border was open, information vital to those people in town who were anxious to know when an escape route to America might open.

As Anna walked over to join the group, the sight of the open front door confirmed what she already knew, that all the doors in the Jewish section were open, for if someone left a door closed, the *pogromshchiki* would batter it open or break it down. Almost nothing remained in Mrs. Budyanska's home. Even though the curtainless windows exposed the emptiness inside, her house was the best one on the block, a magnet for late-coming looters.

Anna stood listening for a few minutes, then walked the short distance to her grandmother's house, where she found the front door also open and the insides as bare as at the Budyanskas'. In this final pogrom, the looters stole everything that had not been taken in the earlier two. It was the pogrom that left in Anna's memory the symbolic image of Mrs. Budyanska sitting on her front steps, shifting her skirt out of the way of the feet of the soldier with the white-ribboned cap and the peasant woman with the empty sack.

Anna saw the soldiers with the white ribbons in their caps only once more. A few weeks later, when the Bolsheviks—the Reds—captured Korsun, they rounded up the white-ribboned soldiers hiding on the island hill in the middle of the Ros River where goats were taken to graze, and in the forest beyond the bridge. From her grandmother's hilltop house, Anna watched the Whites being marched along the main street from the bridge to the center of town. She understood that the Reds had no time for prisoners, and that the Whites were being taken to the Bolshevik headquarters in the old barracks near the marketplace, where they would be shot.

The looting in the third Korsun pogrom was bad enough, robbing the houses of Mrs. Budyanska and Grandmother Beyla and other families of their last food. The murders of Uncle Beryl and the butcher's daughter and the others were bad enough, robbing the innocent families of their loved ones. But the hardest for Anna to think about was what happened to the rabbi at the river.

The story of the rabbi is part of the historical record about towns in the path of General Denikin's White Army. Denikin's army was driving northward on both sides of the Dnieper River, aiming for the Bolshevik capital of Moscow, but the Bolshevik forces were giving battle. To the people of a town, General Denikin's politics did not matter. A former officer in the tsar's army, Denikin did not favor restoring the monarchy, but he led a coalition of anti-Bolshevik officers of varied persuasion, many fighting to restore Romanov rule, many others backing the landowners. What did matter to the townspeople was that he was steadily advancing toward them and that the core of his army was made up of Cossacks, men whom General Denikin did not restrain.[5]

Although the overall northward advance of Denikin's army had not been halted, the fighting in a local region could ebb and flow. A town that had fallen to a detachment of one army might soon be taken by the other side, but then retaken by the original occupier. That is what happened in Korsun.

On August 24 a Bolshevist occupying force pulled out of Korsun, and townspeople learned that a detachment of dismounted Terek Cossacks from Denikin's army of Whites was positioned at a railway station only six miles from town. A deputation of four Christians and three Jews set out to welcome the detachment and invite it to occupy the city.[6]

The next day a small group of Cossacks appeared, and the deputation, with the rabbi at its head, received them amicably. Speeches were delivered at a public meeting, the townspeople pledging that if the conquerors avoided violence, the population would offer no resistance. For the rest of that day and part of the next, calm did prevail. However, when local Bolsheviks again captured Korsun for a few hours on the following day, they murdered Mr. Shonblum and Mr. Slavutsky, members of the Jewish delegation that had welcomed the White Army, for the crime of showing sympathy to the Whites. The third Jewish delegate, the rabbi, wisely hid himself, escaping the Bolsheviks' anger. A detachment of the Cossacks from the White Army returned on the same day. They drove the Bolsheviks from Korsun and began a massacre of the townspeople. It did not help that no one offered any resistance. Only the day before, the rabbi had led the delegation in welcoming the White Army. The Cossacks of that same army now tore him to pieces.[7]

22
How to Tell a Sollop

Any Korsuner who tried to travel from one town to the next by sleigh knew he was taking a risk. He could easily lose his way on the unlighted roads if his sleigh were still out in the countryside at nightfall, and especially if a snowstorm—not a rare occurrence—should overtake the horses. Robbers were not unknown, and everyone knew that ravenous wolf packs were to be feared, but it was the unpredictable snowstorm that always lay in wait.[1]

Anna grew up hearing the story of a young coachman (an *izvozchik*), who became lost in the countryside outside Korsun during a snowstorm. Eventually his two horses could drag the sleigh no farther. It was useless to try to walk through the drifting snow, so he stayed with the sleigh. After a time, another sleigh happened to pass that way, its horses fresher than those in the traces of the stranded one. The driver stopped at the sight of a whitened human figure partly buried in the snow. Helping the *izvozchik* out of the drifts, the rescuer got him into the second sleigh and drove to the palace. The servants of the princess warmed the half-frozen coachman and gave him food and drink. Because they knew he was a Jew, he was not served anything that was not kosher. He was given fish, vegetables, and fruit. He ate herring and he ate cucumbers. He enjoyed strawberries with *smetana* (sour cream).

When he was feeling well enough, he went back home and, of course, told everyone about his good fortune. What a blessing that his rescuer should happen to drive by at just the right time! He was lucky to be alive. And what a luxury to be cared for and fed at the palace! The reaction of his fellow townsmen surprised him. Hearing him say that he had been eating cucumbers at the palace, and—even more outrageous in midwinter— that he had eaten strawberries, they laughed at him. Either he had temporarily lost his mind, they thought, or he was making up a tall tale to impress them. The rescued coachman insisted that he was telling the truth.

In tears, he would plead with people to believe his story, but it was clear to everyone that a man who spoke of winter strawberries could not be trusted. He was branded a liar.

His name was Sollop, a name that entered the language in Korsun. It became the custom that if you did not believe a story someone told, you called the tale "a Sollop." Even the Korsuners who emigrated to America brought with them this expression, "a Sollop," for an outrageously unbelievable story. Sollop lived to a good age, but he no longer had his good name. He lived under the cloud not only of being disbelieved for the rest of his life, but also of having his name used to ridicule a teller of tall tales. Anna grew up long after this incident, in a time when the expression "a Sollop" was in common usage. She knew the expression, but not the story behind it. She had no idea that it was a man's name.

When she was about eleven years old, Anna was sent to the home of a young coachman, not far from Grandmother Beyla's, to hire a wagon. The house was one of the relatively newer houses in Korsun, perhaps fifty years old, its solid tin roof the sign of a family no longer poor. Anna knew both next-door neighbors. On one side was the candy maker, and on the other side lived the family of Mr. Heifetz, who was not only a master shoemaker, but also a musician. When she arrived at the young coachman's house, she saw an old man, presumably the grandfather, sitting outside on the attached board bench that ran the length of the front of the house. He was talking, mumbling to himself.

Anna did not speak to the old man, because she did not know him. Besides, young girls did not speak to their elders. She spoke to the well-dressed young coachman inside, relaying the request that a wagon be sent. Then she walked back home. The young man with whom she had spoken was named Sollop. From this errand, Anna realized that the term "Sollop" came from the name of a man, and that she had seen that very man, sitting on the long bench in front of his grandson's house.

Many years after Sollop's rescue from the snow, but only about a year after Anna had seen him, the Bolshevik Revolution of October 1917 turned the Russian society upside down and triggered the civil war. By the end of 1918, Korsun's elderly princess (Olga Valerianovna Lopukhina-Demidova) had fled Russia for Denmark with her older daughter. Her younger daughter, Vera Nicolaevna Demidova, stayed behind.

Vera Nicolaevna was pregnant and still living in the palace when her estate was overrun by Bolsheviks. She was allowed to remain in the palace, but the estate was in the hands of her enemies. Former servants brought baskets of food and clothes to Vera Nicolaevna, and in the baskets they sent notes written in French, the language cultivated by the upper classes. The Bolsheviks, unable to read French, concluded that Vera Nicolaevna was involved in a conspiracy against them. They had her murdered. She was killed on the bank of the Ros River by a local Bolshevik named Yuri Phesenko, whose motives for the murder were said to be mixed. He was also interested in the princess's treasure, rumored to be buried somewhere near the palace. So far as is known, no treasure was ever found. A shallow grave was dug for Vera Nicolaevna. As the civil war continued through the spring and summer of 1919, one of the White armies, under General Denikin, captured Korsun in August and held it briefly. Discovering the rude gravesite, the Whites arranged a proper funeral service and burial in the cemetery for the young princess. The whole town turned out for the ceremony.

During the occupation of the town and the palace grounds by this anti-Bolshevik army, it was discovered that the estate of the princess included a building unknown to those who had ridiculed Sollop. It was a greenhouse, in which fruits and vegetables such as cucumbers and oranges and strawberries were grown, out of season. Thus it became known that the coachman rescued in the middle of the Ukrainian winter, and cared for in the palace those many years ago, had not told "a Sollop" after all.

23
The Two Korsuns

The way Korsuners treated Mr. Sollop was one of the things that Anna disliked about her hometown. She found many Korsuners to be mean-spirited. They may have been soured by their inability to escape from poverty.

Even men with a craft could have difficulty making a living. The town could not generate enough business for all the tailors and shoemakers. Many of the Jewish men in Korsun, as in any shtetl, were "airmen," *luftmentshen*—so called because, having no trade or profession, they tried to make a living any way they could—"out of the air." They were always on the lookout for a chance to serve as middleman between a buyer and a seller. They kept their ears open for information, which was their stock in trade. Hearing that a certain man wanted to buy a certain item, a *luftmentsh* would hurry to see another man whom he knew wanted to sell that very merchandise. For bringing the buyer and seller together, the *luftmentsh* earned a few kopecks.

Troubled by the petty behavior of some people, Anna tried to balance it with the goodhearted behavior of others. She weighed the "good Korsun" against the "other Korsun." Anna knew that the townsmen and women could be kind and generous. The mother of one of Anna's playmates rented a room to a young couple and their child. The young man was unable to speak. He was known as the mute shoemaker. Although everyone liked him, he was a poor man, a shoemaker in a town with so many others in the business that they had a separate shoemaker's house of worship. His wife was a pretty woman, which usually meant that other women would gossip jealously about her, but because of her husband's affliction, people pitied her and treated her kindly.

One day Anna heard her playmate's mother and a neighbor enthusing about the *khalla* baked by the mute shoemaker's wife. The neighbor said that the excellent white bread owed a lot to the kindness shown to the young wife. First of all, the woman who had sold flour to the young wife felt sorry for her and gave her the best flour. Not only that, but when the young wife stopped at the marketplace on the way home, another vendor felt sorry for her and gave her a present of a few eggs. Of course they were cracked eggs, which the egg lady usually sold at a discount, but they were still usable. Like other poor women, the young wife could not often afford to buy an egg, but on that Friday morning she made her Sabbath *khalla* not only with the usual yeast, salt, and water, but with the luxuries of eggs and the finer grade of flour.

Jews routinely did acts of kindness, both collectively and individually, as part of their religious observance. Every town had a poorhouse to shelter its beggars. One of the individual acts of kindness that Anna admired involved the beggar as guest. If there was a beggar at the Friday night prayer service, one of the married men took her home so that she would have food and a place to stay during the Sabbath. No matter how dirty she was or how shabby she looked, no beggar would be left to spend the Sabbath at the poorhouse. A beggar was not "a guest of the family," but instead was called "a guest of the Sabbath," a name to foster the beggar's self-respect. The guest stayed the night, usually sleeping on top of the oven, a choice spot.

Orthodox Jewish women were responsible for only three good deeds according to Jewish law: to light the Sabbath candles, to bake the Sabbath bread, and to maintain personal and domestic ritual purity. Ordinary women, however, also saw the providing of hospitality for a beggar as their special *mitzveh*, their special good deed, so they were happy when their husband brought a Sabbath guest home. The women fed the guest the fat soup, the best part, with bits of meat, and they liked to give him or her a pair of socks or some other article of clothing. Rich people, in Anna's view, were not so quick to welcome *shabbes* beggars. Some of the well-to-do had peasant servants, orphans or runaway girls from the villages, who slept in the kitchen and worked for almost nothing. Ordinary people joked that a rich man took on a servant so he wouldn't have to take in a beggar on the Sabbath.

Anna had personal experience of more than a few other acts of personal and collective kindness in Korsun. "Blue eyes" rescued her from the ice-covered granite blocks of the riverbank; Krupnik pulled her into his house to save her from the Cossack; Grandmother Beyla gave up her shroud for her friend Oodl; Anna herself collected money to buy eyeglasses for the grandfather of the boy who had stolen her father's merchandise; peasant women protected Anna from the angry soldier at the railway station; peasants pulled her out of the ditch when she was running from Shevchenko; and the young priest and his wife found a way to give bread to hungry Jewish families without damaging their self-respect.

Kindness was not the only thing Anna wanted from her town. As long as she lived in Korsun, Anna was starved for beauty. She did have her grandfather's glass designs, but they were given away as fast as he made them. For other examples of beauty, she looked to nature. If Korsun was an eyesore to Anna during the day, the shabbiness of the town could disappear into the shadows of a scene lit by a midnight moon. In a town with no tall buildings to stand in the way of the heavens at night, and no electric lights to offend the eye, Anna could marvel at the numberless stars.

Also, once a year at *Shavuoth,* the holiday commemorating the giving of the Ten Commandments, the ugliness was partially hidden. The storm windows were taken down, the straw windbreaks were removed from the doors, and the outsides of the houses were freshly painted with whitewash or yellow clay. Inside, the floor was strewn with green-leaved branches of the cane shoots that grew near the river. The holiday came in late May or early June, so mint sprigs could be tied in bunches to be hung on the walls for their fresh scent. The lilac, acacia, and jasmine had already lost their blooms, but if money allowed, a few fresh flowers of the season were added to the decoration.

The Ros River at spring thaw gave Anna the blue-green of its ice floes in their many shapes. A peacetime winter morning brought her the pure image of scavenging crows stepping in silhouette, black against the mat of new-fallen snow. One winter night at age thirteen when she went out searching for ice to ease her mother's typhus fever, she savored the sight and sound of the trees, their ice-wrapped branches sparkling in the moonlight, tinkling in the wind.

Anna enjoyed the garden of Yenta Koslov and the trees and flowers of the Shapiro family. Her own shabby, dirty street offended her sensibilities, but the young priest's house on the corner was well kept, an oasis in a decrepit neighborhood. The scent of lilac blossoms floating down the street in the spring lured her to the row of three bushes just inside the wood fence fronting his house. Standing there, under the flower clusters, she would inhale their sweetness. This was a special double-flowered variety, for instead of the usual four petals, some of the blossoms had eight.

Although Anna could appreciate the individual and communal good deeds in her town, she thought them far overshadowed by the petty approach to life taken by many Korsuners. Perhaps the attitude began with the ungenerous treatment of children. Children in Korsun were afraid of old adults—anyone with a wrinkle or two—because all the old people they knew acted as though they didn't like children. Youngsters were expected to obey adults blindly. Any adult, according to custom, could ask any child to run an errand, and every child was expected to obey. Anna carried many messages for adults who were not members of her family. Often she wanted to say no, but dared not refuse or express her anger.

Children took the place of the telephone, carrying messages all over town. If a tailor wanted to tell a man that his suit was ready to be measured, a boy carried the message, summer or winter. If Anna's mother, Leya, wanted to ask her sister or a friend if they had an item Leya needed, she sent the oldest child in the house—Anna—to ask.[1]

Of course a child could not place an order costing rubles at a large grocery store, and a tailor would not trust a child who ordered a coat or a dress; when real money was involved, the adult had to go in person. Children did the shopping for small items. On Saturday, when it was forbidden to light a fire in the samovar, Anna might be sent to buy a container of hot water for tea. She was also sent by her grandfather to buy a small amount of oil from a store that was the equivalent of ten blocks away. On these errands, she sometimes took along a rubber ball—brought from Kiev by her father—to bounce off the wall of any house on the away. As a seven-year-old, she might stop for a while to watch other children playing.

Leya did not usually have enough money to buy a one-pound box of sugar cubes at a regular grocery store, even though the price per cube was cheaper there. She sent Anna to one of many Jewish housewives whose shops consisted of the shelves they stocked in a cupboard in the foyer or in a small room of their home that could be entered from the street. Anna often went to the house of Leyzer the musician, where his wife, Reyzl (Rosie), poured a nickel's worth of sugar or salt into a funnel she rolled from paper, twisting the pointed bottom and folding the open top to prevent leaks and spills. Anna would bring a bottle if Reyzl needed to pour out a dime's worth of sunflower seed cooking oil or of lamp kerosene. These housewives not only charged more for the small amounts of staples, but they also routinely shortchanged the children running the errands. If the change was seven kopecks, they gave the child five or six. Perhaps the few extra pennies added up to enough to keep food on their tables.

In some situations a child was treated as nonexistent. Leya once took Anna a few streets away to a wedding. A woman offered a tray of strudel to Leya and asked if she wanted a piece for her child. When Anna's mother said, No, Anna cried. As she said later, though, That made a good strudel maker of me. Girls were not invited into the kitchen to learn from their mothers how to cook and bake. Anna made it a point to know the woman hired to do the baking at weddings and other joyous occasions. The bakers liked her, because she made herself useful to them. Anna kept her eyes open. She learned to make good strudel.

The ungenerous attitude was not helped by the curses children heard from the time they were old enough to understand. The men did not swear as often, but Korsun women were known for the way they peppered their everyday speech with curses. They swore at adults and children alike. The curses might be a series of unconnected bad wishes released in an angry tirade, but sometimes they were more creative, using free association, with each new curse springing from words just spoken. For example, if a woman showed you something, but you asked to see it again, she might say, What? You're not blind. You should become blind. The eyes should fall out of your head. I go to the trouble of bringing this out to show you, you should have all the troubles of the world on your head. Your head should be planted in the ground like an onion.[2]

Anna found the social order in Korsun exasperating. The outward sign of the class snobbery and arrogance was the existence of five different houses of worship. The shoemakers (together with non-shoemaker families allied by marriage) had their own building, as did the tailors. At what Korsuners called "the big shul," the town rabbi officiated for other working folk—the butcher, the Friday fish seller, the storekeeper, and the tinsmith. To the fourth building went the members of the *kahal,* the Jewish community's governing body. Anna's Grandfather Avrum attended there, as did most of the more observant Jews. Most were Hasidim, like Avrum, but a few were opponents of Hasidism. The burning enmity of the nineteenth century between the Hasidim (literally, "the pious") and the Mitnagedim ("the opponents" of Hasidism) had cooled, but there were still disagreements between the two. The fifth was the new building, its congregation formed most recently by the modern Jews—those who wore modern clothes and whose men had shaved off their beards and cut off their earlocks. Instead of an old-fashioned women's gallery upstairs, as in all four of the older buildings, the new one had a screen in the middle of the sanctuary, partitioning the women sitting on the right from the view of the men on the left.

Another layer of class-consciousness existed within each congregation. Among the shoemakers, for example, the *zagotovshchik* was on the highest level, since he was able to design shoes as well as to make the difficult part of the shoe, the "uppers." If he catered to the wealthy Gentiles—police chief, judge, lawyer, doctor—he stood above the *zagotovshchik* whose work went to ordinary people. On the lowest rung of the social ladder were the ordinary shoemakers, who were only capable of doing the easier work—making the soles and heels, and doing repairs. Among the lesser workers, the tinsmith was a bit higher on the social scale than the others, because he made tin roofs for the better houses.[3]

Anna despised the class snobbishness among both the Hasidic and the non-Hasidic Jews. Mr. Shmilyosel was one of only two Korsun tailors who dealt directly with the princess. His skill and business connection to royalty put him in the highest social class of all the many tailors in town. His son became a doctor. If a family member was very ill, ordinary people would say it was so serious that they had to call Shmilyosel's son, even though he was the son of a tailor. Also, although the doctor had married a learned young woman, his marriage to a woman of higher social standing was an exception, and no member of the influential *kahal* would have considered him as a son-in-law.

Anna heard a story about the *yikhes*—the pedigree—of a rabbi in another town. Despite being the son of a poor shoemaker, this bright lad was able to pay tuition at the yeshiva, pass all the tests, and be ordained as a rabbi. But no congregation would hire him. Someone advised him to travel to other towns to seek a job as an assistant rabbi to an older man. Then when the elder rabbi retired or died, the assistant could take his place. Discouraged at this advice, he consulted the rabbi of his town, a man in his sixties, already old for a time when a seventy-year-old was remarkable. The young rabbi asked the elder rabbi what to do, saying that he had a wife and needed to make a living. He wanted to know if he should give up being a rabbi, throw it all away and do something else. The older rabbi did not have to think long about his answer. He told the young man that he didn't have anything to throw away. After all, wasn't he just a shoemaker's son?

Anna hated injustice, and although she was not a Communist, the revolution had highlighted for her the idea that men and women could be free to make their own way in the world. She was ashamed and saddened that some Jews continued to embrace the older rabbi's idea of *yikhes*—an attitude that pinned the bright son of a shoemaker forever to his inborn position in the display case of the social order.

A woman named Nekha encountered the ungenerous attitude of Korsuners that Anna so disliked. Nekha had asked Anna to read her the letters sent by her two daughters in America and to write the replies. On one occasion, Nekha was so excited and happy with a photograph from one of her girls that she took the picture to the market to show to her friends and neighbors. The girls had left Korsun as teenagers, but the photograph showed two attractive, slim young women seated side by side. In front of them stood two boys, five or six years old, and behind were their well-dressed, handsome young husbands. The women wore tasteful black silk dresses and well-shined patent leather shoes. Their hair was cut fashionably short. Instead of rejoicing because they remembered those two lovely women as children in Korsun, the neighbors said, Look at the short hair; they must have had it cut because they had typhus with bald spots. And look how thin they are—they must have tuberculosis. Listening to their comments, Nekha cried. Later, she showed the picture to eight-year-old Anna and asked if Anna thought the daughters didn't get enough to eat.

Nekha dictated an answering letter. When Anna had written Nekha's other letters, she had improved the language by omitting or changing many words, but in this one she included every word Nekha dictated, because to Anna every word in this situation was precious. Part of the letter that Nekha dictated said, Please eat enough. I don't want your children to be orphans when they grow up. And gain a little weight. And tell me did you have typhus, or do you have tuberculosis? Nekha wept as she spoke, and Anna had to concentrate hard to keep writing.

Anna knew that the photograph should be dear to the mother's heart, that the daughters were not ill, and that anyone could easily see how much joy the picture must give to a mother were it not for the snide comments. Anna was angry with the mean-spirited neighbors. She knew that by saying hurtful things about the daughters they were not merely trying to ward off the evil eye, as was commonly done when someone achieved a goal or had good fortune. These women were unkind to Nekha purely out of jealousy rooted in their own misery.

Even though her grandmother and grandfather were Hasidim, Anna came to dislike certain things about Hasidism. Anna found that most Hasidim in Korsun not only considered themselves superior but also expected to be given special treatment. Anna worked one summer with a redheaded girl, a classmate, who was a Hasid. The chance to earn money had drawn a crowd of children in their teens and younger to the marketplace. Anna was the first to arrive. An overseer picked workers for the beet fields outside town. Any child strong enough to hold a hoe could share in the back-breaking work of thinning the young beet plants to give those that remained a better chance to thrive.

The children worked the fields in teams. Anna's partner was the redhead. At the end of a week's work, instead of paying each child, the overseer paid each team, and in Anna's case he gave the money to the red-haired girl, telling her to give half to Anna. Anna waited for her share, but the girl never gave her any of the money. She believed that Anna should be happy to work for a Hasid without pay. Not wanting to start an argument, Anna never asked for her money.

Aside from the arrogance of the Hasidim, among the things that troubled Anna about their culture was the custom that Hasidim everywhere would support the grandson of a Hasidic rabbi. He was called an *eynikel* (Yiddish for "grandson"). Anna saw an *eynikel* who came to Korsun before the revolution. He went from town to town every year, visiting only the Hasidic shul in each town, and at each he was given money. The Korsun congregation accepted the custom, but Anna saw it as an example of hereditary special privilege—a well-dressed man supporting himself, his wife, and his children on handouts given him solely because he was the grandson of a *rebbe*.

Korsun for Anna was a slovenly collection of patched roofs and dirty fences; of broken windows putty-mended with half a pane of glass; of dirt streets full of dust except when they turned to mud. The two cobblestoned streets were, by comparison, the beauty of Korsun. Many houses had neither indoor plumbing nor an outhouse, so people used chamber pots and the yard. It was not unusual to walk by a house and see a squatting, bare-bottomed child or two. Older people went to the river. Everyone threw their daily slops into the street or the yard. The only time the streets were not overpowering was in spring, when the scent of blossoms prevailed. When the shutters of a house were pushed open to let the air in, flies and mosquitoes also came in through the unscreened windows. Korsun had no cockroaches, but that was because, as Anna said, the people were so poor that "cockroaches didn't have what to eat."

For Anna, then, just as the good deeds of many Korsuners were overbalanced by their sour behavior, so the few examples of beauty in the town were outweighed by the ugliness, dirt, and dilapidation. According to a Yiddish adage, a tiny worm that crawls into a radish thinks he has the sweetest food in the world. Anna had tasted Korsun. She was about to crawl out into a larger world, where her experience would magnify her understanding of how bitter her radish had been.

24
Moscow (1919–1921)

The Bolsheviks ultimately recaptured Korsun from General Denikin's *pogromshchiki*. Anna brought home the rumor that refugees might be able to cross the Russian border and reach America if they went first to Moscow. Leya gathered her daughters and set out for Moscow.

The weather was still warm and fair, and people were still bathing in the Ros River when they left Korsun in 1919. They hoped to reach Moscow, and from there, America. They wore no shoes and carried no suitcase. Besides the burlap-sack clothes on their backs, they had one blanket of "turned wool," a few books, and some dried bread. They had dug up Aunt Meyndl's *rotonda* and the beautiful comforters they had buried before an earlier pogrom, but had found only rotted pieces. The Bolsheviks were allowing women and children to leave town. It was already the second week of September, and Moscow was eight hundred miles to the north.

Some townspeople, like Yona Rabinovich, thought Leya was foolish to leave. Yona had laughed when Anna told him Leya's plans. He told Anna that she and her family would starve before they could even leave Russia. From the newspaper that occasionally reached town, he knew that people in Moscow were eating their horses. He urged her to warn her mother not to leave. Anna didn't relay the warning. She didn't want to take away her mother's last hope.

The four Spectors said their good-byes to Aunt Meyndl and Aunt Feyga. They said good-bye to Grandmother Beyla, knowing they would probably never see her again.

Leya and her three girls were part of a tattered group of women and children hoping to reach America. One of the other women, Surka, was taking her three children to join her husband, who was already in America. Another, enterprising and energetic Golda—so tall that she was called Golda the Tall—was traveling with her young son, Yosele. A third, Mindl, was escaping Korsun with her two daughters, leaving the ruins of her home, looted and burned by *pogromshchiki*. The group of seven women and their nine children was completed by Anna's cousin Luba—whose husband had escaped to America with Anna's father—and by two other childless women, Khayka and Frimma.

Walking with her family and the others in their group toward the railway station, Anna thought she saw envy on the faces of the townspeople. The group left the onlookers and the town behind and walked the two miles of cobblestones to the station. On one side, people waited beside the tracks for the Kiev-bound trains. On the other side, where Anna's group stood, the train would leave for Moscow. The trains in this time of civil war were crowded with soldiers, black marketeers, would-be emigrants like Anna's group, and refugees from the regions where armies were fighting. Merchandise was so scarce that most of the freight cars were packed not with goods but with people.

Leya had no money for tickets, but it didn't matter. Tickets were no longer used. When the Moscow train steamed in, people struggled to gain a place in a car. Leya and fourteen-year-old Anna shepherded Gussie and little Mayna, burrowing their way inside a car, managing to stay with their group. The train left the station, and they found themselves traveling in a cattle car with livestock droppings and horseflies.

The train stopped for passengers at several small towns, then at Kharkov, the largest city on the route to Moscow, but when the engine pulled out for Moscow, it left the car of surprised emigrants behind. The uncoupled car was shunted onto a side track far from the station. Firemen told everyone to climb down in a hurry and then turned their hoses on the empty, reeking cattle car. Anna did not know whether someone complained, or an official was alerted by the odor, or what. She believed that the authorities had acted from fear that the Korsun group would spread disease if they were allowed to finish the trip to Moscow in that filthy cattle car. The hosed car sat on the siding. Although Anna's group could eat and sleep in the car, they wanted to be in the station as much as possible, hoping to hear that they would be allowed to board an outgoing train to Moscow.

In Korsun, the group had thought they were the only ones trying to emigrate from their region, but in Kharkov they met other people from towns around Korsun, including an elderly couple, the Kohns. Mr. Kohn had been a manufacturer's representative, meeting trains from the cities, hiring wagons, and off-loading merchandise to be sold to stores in the towns. He not only spoke better Russian than others in the group, most of whom could only manage simple sentences in that language, but he was also used to dealing with businesspeople and talking to those in authority. He became the leader of the group and their liaison for the journey to Moscow.

The group had now grown to about thirty people. After they had been stranded in Kharkov for about a week, Surka, one of the original seven women from Korsun, ran into her first cousin, the Korsun-born Alter Koslov. The celebrated artist, who was in the city to attend a meeting, asked what she was doing there. She explained the situation to him. He told her they were crazy to think they could get to America. When she made him realize that they would not be talked out of their plan, he agreed to use his influence to help them on their way. He convinced the authorities to attach an extra freight car to a Moscow train and to see that the group from Korsun was taken on board.

Pausing for passengers at small towns, the Moscow-bound train laid over longer at the cities of Kursk and Orel. At Orel the would-be emigrants tried to leave the car but found that someone had locked them in. Then they heard people yelling, Americans—let us look at you. In Korsun, the group had been known as "the Americans," because they were bound for America, but the people in Orel evidently misunderstood, thinking that the group were Americans who had come to Russia. Finally, the door was opened and the misunderstanding cleared up. The Orel authorities assigned the group the official designation of potential emigrants and allowed them to go on to Moscow.[1]

During the long train trip, Anna's family ate nothing but Grandmother Beyla's unsweetened rusk. Before they had left Korsun, Beyla had found some flour and had baked a few loaves—big, round, black breads, about a foot across, baked on the bare firebrick floor of the oven. She had sliced them, cut each slice into four pieces, and dried them in the oven to make rusk, which she called *sukharey*.

The only change in their diet came when a fellow passenger noticed the crisp, dried bread they were eating. Opening a bag and taking out two fine, yellow apples, he asked eagerly if they would trade some of their bread. They struck a bargain, giving him two pieces of their bread in exchange for his two apples, fresh fruit to break the monotony of eating rusk. When Anna arrived in Moscow, she realized why he had been so eager to trade. In Moscow there was no real bread, only an unappetizing mixture made with bran and spoiled apples.

The farther they went toward the capital, the more like fall the weather became. They finally arrived at Moscow late in September. The eight-hundred-mile trip from Korsun would have taken less than two days in prewar times. It had taken Anna's group more than a week.

The freight car in which the group had been traveling was again uncoupled from the train in Moscow and parked inside the railway station. Even though the officials in Orel had established the identity and status of the emigrants, the Moscow authorities would not be satisfied until they could make their own inquiries. Meanwhile, they didn't know what to do with these people who were bound for America, since the United States continued to withhold recognition of the Bolshevik regime. The authorities seemed to fear that these emigrants might speak out against the Bolshevik government once they had reached their new country. Since the officials could think of nothing to tell the emigrants except to stay where they were, the travelers spread their blankets and continued to make their temporary home in the boxcar.

They were eventually placed in a high school building turned into a camp. Having no separate facilities for Anna's few emigrants, the authorities housed them with people displaced by the world war and the ongoing civil war. Among these were refugees who had been uprooted and displaced by the battles fought in their homelands, which had since become separate nations, newly independent from fledgling Soviet Russia. These refugees from the Baltic nations could not cross the new borders and return to their homes until they could get Soviet passports.

The four-story school building stood on Borodinska Street, a short walk from the Borodinska Bridge, which spanned one of the snake bends of the Moskva River. The first floor was taken up by washrooms and by a kitchen where meals were prepared for the refugees living in the classrooms on all three upper floors. Anna's family lived on the third floor. The school had no elevator. The adults may have had their own ideas about the stairs, but Anna and her sisters, having come from Korsun, where no house had a second floor, thought it great fun to start at ground level and climb all the way up to the top floor.

Although the group hoped that the Moscow refugee camp was the last place they would live in Russia before leaving for America, the Bolshevik government had neither decided to let them leave nor yet set up an official procedure for giving passports to those wanting to emigrate. Anna's group would have to wait. Meanwhile, they had a place to sleep and eat.

Anna had heard before she arrived that people in Moscow were dying in the streets, and although she saw no evidence of that during her time in the city, she soon found how difficult it was to get enough food for the family. Not only was food scarce, but also those who had it would often refuse to sell it for money, preferring to barter. A good coat, for example, might buy a few loaves of bread. Even then, very little bread was for sale, and finding milk was as hard or harder. The shortage of sugar was so bad that a joke went around, saying that when anyone gives a party in Moscow, the hostess hangs one cube of sugar from the ceiling, and each guest licks it before drinking his tea. The inadequate railroad system could not bring to the cities enough of the grains and vegetables that were being harvested in the countryside.

Women from the camp had learned to buy apples at the nearby railroad station from the peasant women who came into the city to sell their farm produce.² The camp women would then walk to the gates of the Kremlin, where they sold or bartered the apples, making enough money to buy extra food. In Korsun, both of the apple varieties that grew in the countryside were merely called apples, but in Moscow Anna found tasty varieties that had names—the Antonevka, resembling a yellow-green Delicious apple, and the Karychneva, small, like a Jonathan, but of brownish-green color. Of the meager food in Moscow, only the fresh apples tasted good to her.

With Moscow enjoying an Indian summer, the first Anna had ever experienced, the weather was still so warm that she went splashing in the Moskva River near the camp. Another day shortly after they arrived, when seven-year-old Mayna took off her clothes to wade and wash herself in the river, a policeman came by. He yelled at her, but let her off with a warning. Moscow was not Korsun, where everyone bathed nude, the women in one part of the river, the men in another, neither within view of the other.

Anna's cousin Luba had begun a bout of typhus on the train to Moscow. Her family could no longer hide the illness when she broke out in a rash so obvious that the officials sent her to a hospital for isolation as soon as they arrived in Moscow. Anna found her way to the hospital, less than a mile from the Kremlin, and visited Luba. On one visit, when Luba was recovering but still in bed, Anna was talking to her when a young doctor came in to see his patient. Luba introduced him to Anna. Although the doctor greeted Anna amiably, he stared at her, astonished, and went away abruptly without the usual polite good-bye. Anna had no idea why he behaved this way until she left the hospital. Reaching the Arbat, the nearby main street, she looked at herself. She was barefoot. Even in these difficult times, Muscovites would never be seen outside their homes with bare feet.³

Anna was noticeable during the first weeks in Moscow not only because of her bare feet, but also because of her attractively curly hair. Back in Korsun, when much of Anna's hair had fallen out after typhus, her mother had taken her to a barber, who clipped off her remaining hair until she was nearly bald. When it grew back in, her hair was so curly and glossy that people in the street stopped to stare at the mass of curls covering her head. She enjoyed them for more than a year until they disappeared as unexpectedly as they had arrived, leaving her with her original plain, straight hair.

Cousin Luba kept the family in food after she recovered from her typhus and through the next summer by selling her gold ring, a small treasure, set all around with emeralds and tiny diamonds. With some of the leftover money, Gussie and Anna went into business for themselves, buying a bushel of apples and taking them to the biggest street near the Kremlin, where the flow of pedestrians supplied likely customers. The two girls set up shop in a garden sheltered by a bridge leading to the Kremlin, hawking their apples to passersby. With the small profit they could buy bread at the market closest to the camp, the Smolensk street market, near well-known Arbat Street. Once, in addition to bread and a few potatoes, they were even able to buy a herring, which they had not enjoyed in several years.

Gradually the family managed to save some money. In the fall of 1919, their first autumn in Moscow, when it was already raining and turning cold, Leya took charge of the apple money and bought a pair of shoes for her barefoot daughter Anna.

Although Muscovites could not openly celebrate religious holidays under the Bolshevik government, the end of the Yuletide season in the first week of January was the traditional time for gift giving. Early in January 1920 a Moscow charity gave the refugees fabrics to make winter clothes. Each child under eighteen was given a piece of pinstriped flannel for pajamas or underwear, as well as a piece of shiny red cotton sateen as dress material. Leya sewed a dress for ten-year-old Gussie, one for seven-year-old Mayna, and a blouse for Anna, all from the red sateen. Red was the color adopted by the Bolshevik revolutionaries, who draped buildings and statues in red cloth to celebrate the success of their revolution. So great was the demand that one factory made only red fabric, a policy that eventually left them with a large surplus of the cloth. This was the red cloth given to the refugees. The pinstriped flannel and the red sateen were welcome, of course, but Anna's group had come to Moscow in the hope of leaving Russia. They needed passports, and the authorities would still not issue any.

The camp building was a confining place for a girl almost fifteen years old. Anna often left camp in search of new experiences and entertainment. She sat in on a Russian language class at a school about two blocks away, but what pleased her most was roaming the great city. Her delight with Moscow had begun as soon as she heard the name Borodinska, the name of both the street on which the camp stood and the bridge nearby. Both were named for the 1812 battle at the village of Borodino, where Napoleon's narrow victory over the Russian armies enabled him to occupy Moscow. Among the verses she had recited in high school was Mikhail Lermontov's poem about the battle. Although she could not share the pleasure with her unschooled mother and sisters, Anna was thrilled to be living among those names carrying echoes of high school and of history.[4]

She became friends with three older students who were also living at the camp, the Weinbergs—brother and sister—and Avraham Shokhet. An ex-soldier in the Russian army, Avraham had been stranded in Moscow at the end of the war, because a new border separated him from his homeland. During the turmoil of the Russian Civil War and the last months of the world war, Latvia had declared its independence from the former Russian Empire in November 1918. Because Latvia had not yet been formally recognized by the Bolshevik government, the border was closed to Avraham. He was required to live at the camp while waiting for the papers that would allow him to return to his hometown of Riga, Latvia's capital. Meanwhile, he was attending the Moscow medical faculty.

Like Avraham, the Weinbergs had been cut off from their homeland by a new border. They were in camp waiting for passports to travel to their small town in another newly independent nation, Lithuania. Like Avraham, the brother had been admitted to the Moscow medical school.

The first thing Anna had noticed about the Weinbergs when they arrived at camp in the winter was that the brother wore two rabbit skins on each foot instead of shoes. Even in Korsun, with its many poor people, Anna had never seen anyone shoeless in the snow. The Weinbergs arrived with only one winter coat and one pair of shoes between them. Fortunately, the brother was only a year older and only a little taller than his sister. Either one could go out, wearing the coat and the shoes, while the other stayed in the building. How famished they were at first was clear from the way they ate at mealtimes, gulping the soup made of horsemeat, cradling the bowl in both hands. They spent the first weeks at the camp regaining their health.

The Weinbergs' father was a teacher of Hebrew in their small town, and the brother and sister had been teaching Hebrew as well. They became friendly with Avraham Shokhet, who wanted to help them find work. Avraham knew that Moscow was a city of many Jewish schools and a rich Jewish culture, and that the remaining wealthy Jews in Moscow often hired the best teachers to tutor their children at home. He quickly found pupils for both the sister and the brother, and before long they each had money enough to buy a suit, a coat, and a pair of shoes. The Weinbergs had not been tutoring long before some of their patrons offered them a place to live, but they could not accept. They would lose their official status as displaced persons if they did not sleep in the camp building.

Knowing his way around Moscow, Avraham became the Weinbergs' tour guide, showing them the most interesting sights. The three of them adopted fourteen-year-old Anna, taking her with them on their excursions. In their company she learned her way around the city, visiting the museums and theaters of Moscow.

They wanted to take her to the illustrious Hebrew National Theater, Habimah, when the renowned Hannah Rovina was appearing. Even though Anna protested that there was no use in her going because she didn't know a word of Hebrew, she went along. She was glad she did. She came away believing that she had understood everything in the play.[5]

Anna also went with the Weinbergs to the Bolshoi Theater, half a mile north of the Kremlin. Knowing only the Hasidic dancing and the music of Korsun (although the local band of klezmorim had played folk melodies adopted by classical composers such as Tchaikovsky, Rimsky-Korsakov, and Mahler), Anna was entranced by the first ballet she had ever seen. Nor had she ever seen such buildings as the Bolshoi, famous for its sculpture of four impressive bronze horses rearing above eight huge white columns.

Anna found Moscow's street plan ideal to prevent anyone from getting lost. She could always get her bearings from Sadova Street, the longer of the two concentric ring streets encircling the Red Square. Its house numbers started at number one and ended after the street had completed the circle, the highest house number right next door to number one.

Her friends introduced her to the Tretiakovskaia Galereia, which she later compared to the Metropolitan Museum of Art in New York. It was the first museum she had ever seen. Her mother had never had a picture in their house, and the only art at Grandmother Beyla's was the woodcut of the Baal Shem Tov. Anna had only found beauty in nature in Korsun, but now she saw the many kinds of beauty that artists could create on canvas. The museum, which did not charge admission, was an easy walk from the camp, through the spacious Arbat Square. After visiting it many times that first winter in Moscow, she held its paintings in memory. To stroll through an art museum, savoring the paintings, would always be one of her greatest pleasures.

She also enjoyed walking to the Imperial University, off Sadova Street near the Kremlin. There, in the shadow of a bronze bust of Mikhail Lomonosov, who was a sort of Russian Benjamin Franklin, "soap box" orators were free to speak.

When it was inconvenient to walk, Anna and her friends, having no money for admission fees or fares, would hold on to the outside of a streetcar, ride to their destination, and jump off as the car was slowing down. Only passengers who moved to the inside of the car paid the fare to the conductor.

Anna's other friends were two girls her age from a small town in Latvia. The three enjoyed leaving the camp behind to see the movies shown in a theater that had suspended its productions of stage plays for the summer, and to explore the famous buildings they had learned about in school. From these excursions with the Weinbergs, Avraham Shokhet, and the two Latvian girls came a substantial part of Anna's education in the liberal arts.

It had been years since the family had had any soap to wash their hair. Leya had made do in Korsun with a certain bitter grass, which she would boil in a big pot of water, cool, and strain before using the liquid. Leya searched for that same grass in Moscow, but the Muscovites she asked had never heard of a grass shampoo.

Residents of the city, though, were struggling with the same shortages as the refugees. The typical Moscow woman in winter was one who pulled a little sleigh sheltering a few precious pieces of firewood. The peculiar combination of clothes she wore was another indicator of the state of the economy—a luxurious Persian lamb coat with everyday winter boots of felt, which was the equivalent of wearing an evening dress with house slippers.[6]

Provisions had dwindled during the winter. By early spring, with even less food in the camp, the authorities began thawing and cooking frozen potatoes to feed the refugees. The apples were already rotten. Since the supply of food in the camp improved only slightly when the spring harvest began, Anna bought vegetables directly from the peasants bringing them in from the countryside.

Even Moscow-area peasants had big-city ways. To these farmers she was the country bumpkin. She kept her money, about twenty cents, in a safe place, as she always had in Korsun, until a peasant told her that in the city it was not nice to keep money in your bosom. Later, Anna went to buy something, stuffing her few coins into the pocket of her little summer jacket. Having decided what to buy, she reached for the coins, only to find that someone had picked her pocket. By taking the peasant's advice, adopting one big-city custom, Anna had made herself vulnerable to another. As she stood there crying, a crowd gathered, asking what was the matter. When she told them that someone had stolen her money, they took up a collection, presenting her with a gift of fifty cents.

Summer came and went. Anna's group had now lived in the Moscow camp for a full year. She had not seen her father for seven years, nor had her mother heard from him. Passports were still not available.

Once, when the fall weather had turned very cold, Anna was selling apples alone not far from the Kremlin. A policeman on patrol noticed her, warned that she was not allowed to stay in that place, and went on his way. Anna stubbornly stayed where she was. When he came back later, to find that she was selling apples in the same spot, he told her that he had given her fair warning, took away her apples, and marched her off to jail. However, when she had a chance to explain that she was living in the camp for displaced people, waiting to go to America, he let her go.

Worried that seven-year-old Mayna might not be getting enough proper food, Anna spent some of her apple-selling money to buy milk from a peasant woman. Taking a container of the milk back to the camp, she poured some for Mayna, happy to be able to nourish her little sister. In a few moments, however, Anna was dismayed to see a residue settle to the bottom. The woman had sold her a mixture of chalk and water.

The food shortage in the city meant that dogs, cats, and horses were dying of starvation. Of the many nobles and other wealthy people who owned chauffeur-driven carriages pulled by teams of horses, a substantial number were killed or exiled in the revolution of 1917. Since those who remained were often impoverished, some of their horses died of hunger, while others were killed for their meat. Horses had become like cows, a source of food, not transportation. Anna did not see any dead horses in the streets, but the story went around that when you saw someone who had meat, you asked two questions: Where did you buy it? and Was that horse killed, or did it starve to death? The few restaurants that were still open served horsemeat. In the last months of 1920, which were also the last months of Anna's stay in Moscow, the food shortage reached famine proportions, especially in the cities. The famine would last for two years.

Before coming to Moscow, Anna had only seen two automobiles in her life—one in Kiev, and the other in Korsun, which had only two paved roads—but in Moscow all the streets were paved, and she saw cars everywhere. Gasoline stations and garages had begun to add themselves to the architecture of the city. Newcomers wondered what the attractive, white, one-story building near the Kremlin was. In this new age it had become a garage for autos. Unable to count on passing a gasoline station, however, the leaders of Russia rode chauffeured cars that carried enough gas to last the whole trip, and the chauffeurs went to school to learn how to take apart and reassemble the machines. Sleighs were rarely seen.

Shawls folded into a triangle were the usual head covering in Korsun, but in Moscow only the peasants wore them. In Korsun, when a woman put on a small head shawl, she pulled the left and right sides (the two long tails of the triangle), down alongside her cheeks, but before tying the ends of the two tails together under her chin, she gave the cheek portion of each tail a half twist. Anna had always done this without thinking, until she became acquainted in the refugee camp with a young woman from Estonia. Anna decided one day that it would be more interesting to leave the cheek portions untwisted. The young woman protested and would not allow Anna to wear the shawl unless she twisted the cheek portions. She explained that only Estonian women should use the untwisted style. From then on, Anna did not wear her shawl the Estonian way when the two of them were together.

Since the family did not pay for its stay in Moscow, Anna assumed that the Bolshevik government was supporting all the emigrants and refugees. At the same time, Americans were giving millions of dollars toward famine relief in Russia. The federally funded American Relief Administration (ARA), directed by Herbert Hoover, sent food and clothes to Russia, as did many private religious and charity organizations in the United States. These supplies were to be given to hungry Russians of all faiths. Anna was skeptical, however, believing that those in the interior of Russia never saw more than a bite of that food or a stitch of those clothes. Many in the small towns died from hunger. People were found frozen, lifeless from hunger and cold.

The American Jewish Joint Distribution Committee was one of the organizations working under the ARA to send food to Russia. Anna believed that the Jews who lived in Moscow were living well, taking advantage of the American food. She heard a rumor that the wife of the man in charge of distributing the relief supplies from America had bought herself a Persian lamb coat on the black market, paying one case of American Eagle Brand milk.

Anna saw no evidence that Moscow's Jews really cared about the Jewish emigrants and refugees. No one among the refugees heard about the food and clothes from America during their early months at the camp. When they did learn of the aid, it was only because, in Anna's view, the Jewish Muscovites were afraid that the refugees who reached America would report that their coreligionists in Moscow had given them no help. By then it was early January 1921, only four or five weeks before Anna and her group left Moscow.

Eleven-year-old Gussie began to sicken on the refugee camp fare of horsemeat, potatoes, and bread made with the meat of rotten apples. No one paid any attention to her condition, even though she was unable to digest her food and she looked swollen. Not until months later would Leya realize that Gussie needed to see a doctor.

Golda the Tall needed food for her son, Yosele. Alert as usual, she learned that food and clothing were being handed out at a shul near the center of the city. Anna was the only one willing and able to go with her. The mothers of the other young women would not let them go, but Anna, attracted by Golda's energy and eager to spread her own wings, refused to let her mother stop her.

They wanted to arrive before the shul opened at 7:00 A.M.. Having no clear directions, they arose in the dark of the small hours and set out by the light of the stars and the sparse streetlights to find it. The streetcar that could have taken them to the shul was not running that early, and they were the only people on the street, little Anna walking alongside Golda the Tall. The shul was only a few blocks away, about a ten-minute walk past the Kremlin, down a hill, but not knowing that part of the city well, they spent three hours finding it. The second time, they found a shorter route by way of Sadova Street's circle around the center of Moscow, but for Anna it was that first walk that defined Moscow. Russians called the city "forty times forty" because it had sixteen hundred churches, and Anna carried with her the memory of Moscow as it had been in the small hours of that winter morning, with the new snow fluttering in white silence, the stained-glass windows dimly seen, and the churches, snow-mantled, looming in the faint light.[7]

Golda and Anna were given cans of Eagle Brand condensed milk at the shul, together with several packs of cocoa and a number of dresses and rough shoes. Much later, in America, Anna learned that the clothes sent to Russia had been made in American factories for women in American prisons. They were ugly, gray clothes made of a material like flannel, one size fits all. The soles and heels of the shoes were of wood, the soles two inches thick. Stapled to the wood on top were pieces of plain, smooth denim cloth on one side and flannel on the other side, with three or four eyelets for the shoelaces. These shoes, which also came in only one size, were too large for Anna's foot, making an embarrassing sound as she walked: *klink, klink, klink, klink*. The shul had no stockings to give away with the shoes.

The American relief organizations had sent no can openers. No one in Anna's group was used to opening a can of food. They knew about tins of sardines and anchovies, but those needed no can opener. When they tried puncturing one end of a can of condensed milk with a nail, they could not make the milk pour out through the single hole. A gypsy at the camp used a rusty hatchet to cut the can open, spilling some of the milk. They finally managed to open all of the cans, and finding the milk sugary, they used it as a spread, smearing it on bread. The family's share of cocoa consisted of a few packets of powder, about half a pound, which they dissolved in water as they had always done in peacetime when cocoa was available in Korsun. No one would have thought of cocoa as a drink to be made with milk.

In the fall of 1920, their second fall in Moscow, the women in Anna's group, with Mr. Kohn as liaison, had begun to go every day to try to arrange their departure from Moscow. The authorities had finally opened a bureau to deal with the displaced people, because, Anna thought, they didn't want to continue to feed them.

A woman named Sonya had joined the group, saying that she and her two children had come all the way from the Black Sea port of Odessa, intending to join her husband in America. She volunteered to handle the customs formalities in Moscow for everyone, freeing the women from their trips to the bureau. To simplify the process she collected all of the identification papers to take to the authorities. On New Year's Day 1921, Sonya gave to each woman the new passport issued by the authorities at the Moscow foreign consulate, giving them the right to leave Russia and enter Finland. Soon after distributing the new passports, Sonya disappeared. Although no one knew why Sonya had left the group, every woman had her own prized new passport, so no one felt the need to pursue the matter.

Sojourning for more than a year in Moscow had meant more to Anna than just waiting for a passport. She had come to know the capital city's streets, squares, and buildings; she had sampled its ballet, theater, and fine art; and she had enjoyed the company of people from other parts of the Russian empire. With her artistic soul newly nourished by the great city, she could look back on her stay there as a time when she had crawled into a delicious pear. With her new passport, she could now look forward to America.

25
Petrograd (1921)

Not long after being handed their new passports, the Korsun emigrants were taken from the camp by truck to a Moscow railway station. They were part of an expanded group of more than fifty people who boarded a train for the Russian border. The thirty-five "Americans" with their newly issued passports now included a handful of people who had boarded the Moscow train at Kursk and Orel. The others were twenty displaced people from the camp, half of them peasants, all wanting to enter one or another of the newly independent Baltic states.

The slow journey of more than four hundred miles brought their bare boxcar to the Russian–Finnish border just beyond Petrograd. A locomotive shunted their car onto a siding near the border, leaving it there. It was mid-winter of 1920–1921. They were still in Russia. They didn't know whether they were being abandoned or were just waiting for another locomotive to deposit them somewhere else.

The boxcar sat on the siding for about a week while the Korsun women and children tried to keep warm and find food in bitter cold weather. Standing in the doorway of the boxcar, Anna looked out across a flat landscape of snow at a distant forest of pines, naming it the Black Forest in her mind because the green needles so far away looked black. At her back, behind the boxcar isolated on the railroad track, lay another expanse of snow, level and bare, with no house, no building, nothing on which the eye could rest.

The women found their first food under their feet. The boxcar was standing at a collection area where large sacks of local fish were brought to the train for shipment to canneries in Petrograd and Moscow. The women only had to bend down next to the boxcar and pick up the fish. The sardine-size morsels, probably spilled from a broken sack, looked like little chips of wood in the snow. Anna and the others brought the fish inside, thawed them, and having no water for cleaning, ate them unwashed.

After the fish had been eaten, the women had no other food. Golda the Tall, always ready to take the initiative, could not rest while her little Yosele had nothing to eat. She took Anna to look for a village where they could beg for food. The day was clear as they walked toward distant smoke, Anna striding through snow halfway up her legs to keep up with Golda, who was twice as tall. The source of the smoke they saw a few miles away turned out to be a border guard barracks. The soldiers who first saw the two, astonished at their tattered appearance, asked where they had come from. Other soldiers, hearing that Golda and Anna had come from Moscow and were going to America, crowded around, eager for a look at the "Americans."

The border guards could not do enough for the "Americans," serving hot tea because the two looked frozen, and bringing out some *sukharey,* like the rusk that Grandmother Beyla had baked when they left Korsun. The soldiers also brought out pieces of sugar tied in little bags, like jewelry, as well as a few potatoes. They gave everything they had to Golda and Anna and told them to come back the next morning. New rations would be arriving then. The soldiers promised to give Golda and Anna whatever rations came.

Golda and Anna were walking back toward the railway, nearing the tracks where their boxcar had been, when they saw instead a long, moving train. Thinking their families were on it, leaving without them, they began to run, Golda yelling, Yosele, Yosele, while Anna shouted, Mama, Mama. Suddenly the last car passed. Anna's mother was standing in the door of their still stationary railroad car, waving to her. The moving train had been blocking the view of Leya and the boxcar on the siding. No other train ever came along the tracks while they languished at the Finnish border.

In the following days, the soldiers escorted Anna and others through the snow to a place where they could get water. From there the emigrants could see a town at the border of Finland. Although they never went into the town, they could see that the houses were round, built, as Anna learned, like igloos to prevent the strong winds from blowing them away. The town, about ten miles from the shore of the Gulf of Finland, was Bela Ostrov, which means "white island," but Anna saw no body of water, only the white of the ice and snow. The women in the village across the border, learning that the emigrants had been abandoned, brought the hungry travelers bread, boiled potatoes, and boiled eggs. They also brought fish roe, fruit, cans of milk, and a thick soup. The food went mostly to the children.

Anna was used to seeing people with slanted eyes and high cheekbones. In Korsun a proverb recognized the fact that intermarriage with the Mongols of Genghis Khan and his successors lay in the ancestry of many peasants. "Scratch a peasant," the proverb said, "and you will find a Tatar." Anna, though, had never seen anyone like the Finnish peasants, who were Eskimos, flat-faced, with the smallest of noses. They were called Samoyed, which Anna understood in Ukrainian to mean, "you go on your own power." The emigrants spent about a week in the boxcar, while the Samoyeds kindly provided not only the food but also water in five-gallon cans. The water was frozen. Anna's group also had an empty five-gallon tin that they used as an oven. The Finns, having no real wood, brought large pancakes of dried animal manure to burn, together with a small jar of coal oil to serve as a fire starter and matches to light the oil. The fuel burned well, bringing the can-stove to a lasting red heat that warmed the car. The women cut up about ten pounds of potatoes donated by the soldiers, arranging the slices around the can to cook.

After a few days, the Bolshevik authorities realized that a freight car sitting on a siding was full of people waiting and wanting to cross into Finland. A soldier—a Jewish woman carrying a gun—stepped into the freight car. Her job was to make sure that no one was taking illegal possessions out of the Soviet Union. One woman in the group had a large collection of wedding candles of pure beeswax. The soldier took the candles. The woman began to cry, saying that the candles were from her wedding. The soldier looked at all the candles and asked sarcastically how many times she had been married.

Anna was carrying a few schoolbooks, those that had not been burned by the family as fuel. The soldier took the schoolbooks. She took away the certificate that Anna's favorite teacher, the Ukrainian, had written to let future teachers know that Anna had finished the first two years and part of the third year of high school. Leya had a Jewish prayer book. The soldier took it. The soldier continued inspecting people until she had taken away the personal possessions of everyone in the car. From then on, watchful Bolshevik soldiers kept the group inside the boxcar. They could go outside to relieve themselves or to stretch their legs, but they were not allowed to wander off.

The border authorities quickly decided that the twenty or so displaced people traveling with the Korsun "Americans" could return to their homes in Finland and other Baltic countries. Avraham Shokhet, the medical student from Riga, was one of those allowed to cross the border. The Weinbergs, their camp papers not yet cleared for Lithuania, had not been able to come along when the group left Moscow.

When the authorities looked at the papers of the Korsun group, however, they found that thirty-five people with identical names on their passports had crossed the border a week earlier. Examining the papers more closely, the officials decided that every passport in the Korsun group was a forgery. Apparently Sonya had kept the genuine passports issued in Moscow, using them as models to have false papers forged. She had given the forgeries to the emigrants in the Korsun group, then disappeared with the genuine passports, presumably intending to sell them to another group.

The border authorities at Bela Ostrov were sympathetic. They seemed persuaded that Anna's group had not done anything illegal—they were carrying forged passports only because they had been duped. Still, without legal passports they could not be allowed to cross the border. Rather than send the emigrants all the way back to Moscow to get new papers, the officials decided to send them to Petrograd, only eighteen miles away.[1]

The trip to Petrograd took only a few hours. The group of emigrants (now all Korsun "Americans") arrived in Petrograd late at night, unwashed, sleepy, and with crying children. Despite the generosity of the Finnish women, they were famished. The train stopped at a station next to a warehouse. The travelers climbed down onto a wooden loading platform and went directly into a kitchen in the warehouse, where a big kettle of kasha was cooking. Anna thought it the best-tasting kasha she ever ate. The emigrants looked so pitiable that the Bolshevik cook started to cry when he saw them.

The Bolsheviks provided hot water for the travelers to wash and warm themselves. They even fired a locomotive to feed steam heat into the big building, where they had prepared individual cots with mattresses, blankets, and cushions. No matter what anyone said about the Bolsheviks, Anna would remember that those at the railroad warehouse in Petrograd had been kind to her group of emigrants.

At the warehouse, the Korsun group met several German war brides, women who had married Russian soldiers in Germany. The soldiers, however, were already married to Russian women and had disappeared as soon as they crossed the border into Russia. These German women had brought supplies of lemons and candy, which they generously shared with Anna's group. All imports into Russia having been halted by the war, Anna had not seen a lemon for years.

Anna and her cousin Luba decided to take their lemons into the city to exchange them for bread. They were still hungry after the kasha. It was snowing so hard that they could barely see where they were going. Finding no road, they walked on the railroad tracks, slogging through deep snow until they came to the modest house of a railroad worker. Opening the door and walking in, they startled a woman, who turned pale when she saw them, afraid that these two human forms covered with a layer of snow must be ghosts. They wore torn jackets without winter linings, the jackets donated by Moscow gypsies who had felt sorry for them. They had no stockings to wear with the makeshift Moscow shoes they had tied onto their feet with rags.

The woman asked hesitantly what they wanted. They assured her that she need not be afraid—they only wanted to exchange lemons for bread. Unable to believe that these ragamuffins had lemons, she asked where they got them. After they explained about the warehouse and the German women, she sat them down to a meal of bread and butter—butter was as unimaginable to them as the lemons were to her—and a glass of tea. The woman, not knowing what to say when she noticed Anna's shoes, could only shake her head in amazement. She was worried about how they would make their way back in the snow, but they assured her they would be able to walk on the railroad tracks, the way they had come.

The Bolsheviks fed and housed the group in the warehouse for about a week in February before moving them five or six blocks away to a clearing-house for refugees in a former seminary building. The travelers took over the rooms once occupied by seminary students. In the center of the grounds stood a large fountain from which the refugees drank. The five-story build-ing was located in a barracks area that had served the tsar's army before the revolution, each street named for a different army company. From the window on the top floor, where she and her family were living, Anna could see a church with onion-bulb spires. A renowned engineering school, the Petrograd Technological Institute, was only a short walk away.

The emigrants were again living with refugees from breakaway nations such as Lithuania. The refugees, like those in the Moscow camp, had been fortunate to escape during the fighting, but now wanted to go back to their homes.

Anna found the Petrograd cold to be dry and not penetrating. The snow on the sidewalks and streets, which no one ever cleared away, never melted during the six months of Petrograd's winter, but instead was pressed into a thin layer, nearly ice. People drove either horse-drawn sleighs or automo-biles with chains on the tires.

Anna went ice-skating on one of the canals not long after arriving, but it turned out to be the only time she ever skated in the city, because while on the ice she broke a bone in her foot. Several weeks later, still in a cast and using a crutch, she stood at a window on the fifth floor of the seminary building, looking down at Leon Trotsky. He was standing on a newly erected scaffold far down the street, in front of the onion-bulb-spired church just across the last street of the barracks area. Trotsky, second only to Lenin in the Bolshevik government, was giving a rousing speech to his soldiers. Although he was too far away for Anna to hear his words, she could see the people on the street applauding.

Anna knew the face of Trotsky well. The walls in the barracks area were covered with copies of a poster showing his face centered between those of the other two icons of the Bolshevik revolution, Marx and Lenin. Looking at the man in the center, Anna thought Trotsky had an ordinary Jewish face, partly covered by his little black beard. Although the picture was unusual in that he was wearing a Roman soldier's helmet, he was easy to recognize. Few people in the government looked like Trotsky.

People crowded at all the windows nearby to watch, and it seemed that half of Petrograd was in the streets on this early March day, eager to see Trotsky. Later she found out that he was urging the troops to crush a rebellion of the thousands of sailors at the Kronstadt naval base, on an island nearby. The Kronstadt rebels accused the Bolshevik government not only of failing to help the starving populations in the cities, but also of mistreating them by imposing unwelcome restrictions and harsh work regulations. Trotsky said the sailors deserved to be attacked because they were threatening the government. When Anna's group heard later what he had said, they agreed with him.

The soldiers, chosen for their loyalty to the Bolshevik government, had been brought from various stations into Petrograd, the closest large city to the rebellious naval base, arriving in time to hear Trotsky's early afternoon speech. They were to stay in the city overnight before going to the ports from which the assaults against Kronstadt would be launched. Throngs of soldiers slept for that one night in the impressive building on 11th Company Street, one of twelve barracks streets. Each street had been named for and long occupied by one of the twelve military companies of the Izmailov Regiment founded by Peter the Great. But the building on 11th Company Street could not hold all the men. Next door was the seminary building that housed the refugees and emigrants. Room was made for a smaller number of the soldiers to spend the night in several offices on the same floor where Anna's family was staying.

Early in the morning, Anna heard footsteps outside her door. The soldiers were leaving for the nearby railway station, to be taken to the jumping-off ports. Anna got up at about seven to find no trace of any soldiers in the seminary or on the streets. Not long after, she heard that the Bolsheviks were winning a big battle.[2]

She stood at the window of the seminary again more than a week later on a bright, warm, spring day, this time watching the ceremony for the soldiers killed at Kronstadt. The funeral procession took an hour to file past. Trotsky did not appear. Little by little Anna found out what had happened in the battle. Most of those soldiers who had stayed in the barracks had died. Anna could not help mourning the young men who had spent the night on her street and in her seminary building, especially one twenty-year-old whose face, briefly seen, she had thought beautiful. She knew, though, that the Kronstadt rebels had been correct in saying that the times were too hard. People were still starving. With no electricity, the streets were dark at night. On the day of the soldiers' funeral, Leya went to a little market near the seminary, hoping to buy as much as a pound of bread. She met a woman hugging something under her coat. Leya told her that she, too, had brought something to barter and asked the woman if she had bread under her coat. In a Russian as strongly Yiddish-accented as Leya's, the woman told her to go to Trotsky and ask him for bread.

After a few months of trying to enroll, Anna realized that she would not be allowed to go to school in Petrograd. She wanted to read, but didn't know where to find books. She found some in the attic of the seminary later, but they were either religious books, which she didn't understand, or books written in Latin, which she could not read. Besides, the electric lights were turned off early at night. Having nothing to do meanwhile, she asked if she could help in the office, and since she was the only one in the group who could read Russian, the staff was happy to have her.

Anna worked in the camp office for some months, sitting at an ancient Russian typewriter, typing with one finger of each hand. The authorities took away all identification from new arrivals, and no camp occupant could leave the compound without a pass signed by the commandant. When someone wanted to go out, Anna took their passport from a file, copied the person's name and number, added a note about their refugee status, inserted her own name, dated the pass to make it usable only on that day, and handed it to the commandant for his signature. For each pass she rolled two pieces of blank paper into the ribbonless typewriter, sandwiching a piece of carbon paper between them. She gave the second page, the carbon copy, to the commandant to sign and then handed it to the person leaving the camp. She discarded the first page, a sheet covered with mere dents made by the bare keys as they struck the paper.

The summer in Petrograd was glorious to Anna, even though the food shortage continued. She went everywhere with her camp friends and learned from them, just as she had learned from her friends in Moscow. The shortage of decent clothing did not prevent them from going to some of the more fashionable places. A Finnish girl in the camp office lent Anna a summer dress to wear to the Malyi, a small but splendid theater, to see Maeterlinck's play *The Blue Bird*. Although the actors were not paid, Anna was impressed by their skill. A few camp people would get together to go to the smaller theaters for concerts or vaudeville, which delighted Anna. Performers still told jokes, even controversial ones mocking the hard times, and despite the wretched conditions, people could still laugh. As one joke said, "Isn't it wonderful that Petrograd is still St. Petersburg, a beautiful city? Now it's a good place to lie down and die."

The city lay close enough to the Arctic Circle to bask in subarctic "white nights"—the three weeks of June when darkness is banished in Petrograd as the sun floats in view near the horizon, sinking out of sight only during the hour or two of daylike night.[3] The brief nights were as bright as a cloudy day for Anna, and she could not tell when they began, but Gussie knew, because the slight dimming of sunlight late in the evening exposed a failing in her eyesight. As soon as the sunlight lost its full brightness, Gussie had to be led like a blind person. Leya finally became frightened when Gussie also developed bleeding gums. The camp officials called a doctor, who said Gussie had night blindness from lack of proper food. He gave her medicine, and he arranged better rations for her—two eggs a week and milk. Anna was given a special ticket, too, entitling her to more food, which she shared, and also to a pair of shoes. She would walk downstairs from the fifth floor to the first floor to get provisions from the cook. Gussie eventually recovered, and her illness never returned.[4]

Only when Anna visited the cities of Europe much later in life did she fully realize what riches she had enjoyed in Petrograd. Florence, like Petrograd, seemed to her an open art museum, and almost as beautiful, but Rome and Paris did not compare. When she saw graceful architecture in Italy, she asked herself where she had seen such structures before. Then she would remember seeing a building in Petrograd that must have been designed by the same architect. Petrograd, for her, was the most beautiful of all.

Although it had nothing like the number in Venice, Petrograd was threaded by several wider canals, each spanned by many bridges. Anna was captivated by the imaginative use of animal sculptures in the design of the long spans. The bridges had names such as The Lion, The Eagle, and The Sphinx. As photographs of the Lion Bridge show, ornamental iron railings flanked the broad, paving-stone walkway, and an impressive lion sculpture sat on a pedestal at either end of each railing. Each of the four lions faced one end of a railing, its forelegs planted just shy of where the railing ended. To Anna, it looked as though the lions were "holding the bridge," because each animal held in its mouth one end of a suspension cable clinging to the side of the bridge, a cable that extended in a sagging arc from one shore to the other. She was proud that Petrograd, built by Peter the Great only a few hundred years earlier, was not only a new city compared to most others in Europe, but a majestic city. Standing at one end of a broad, straight avenue stretching into the distance, she marveled at how far she could see along its carefully planned course.

The two years Anna spent in Moscow and Petrograd were a wondrous gift to her inquiring mind and artistic spirit. Unlike her unschooled sisters, she had read Pushkin's writings describing the buildings, the monuments, and the beautiful streets that she was seeing in person. She could not believe her good luck. She was dirty, she didn't have water to wash her hands or her hair, and yet everything she had read about was now a sight for her own eyes. Having already attended the famous Habima Hebrew National Theater in Moscow, she now saw Shakespeare performed in Petrograd. Musicians and actors, out of work in a city both poverty-stricken and without electricity for nighttime productions, performed in the parks. They presented concerts and plays during the few weeks of nocturnal daylight in the white nights of summer. At the concerts, Anna began to form her taste in classical music. She would later say that great good fortune had come to her only twice in her life—the first time in the form of those two years in the grandest cities of Russia, and the second time in the form of her wonderful children.

In Korsun, one of the finest stores at the marketplace had been Mr. Slivnik's, which sold quality woolen fabrics to be made into clothes for members of the princess's household. Grandson of a revered Hasidic *rebbe,* Slivnik was a tall, bearded man, who, unlike many Hasidim, wore his white socks and long black *kapote* at work. His large clientele testified to his reputation for honesty. Slivnik's son had gone to Moscow to study medicine, and his daughter, having earned a degree in Petrograd, was supervisor of the boy's gymnasium in Korsun. Slivnik's mother Oodl, of course, was a good friend of Grandmother Beyla.

In Korsun, Anna had known Khilya, the daughter of one of Slivnik's clerks. Khilya's father made a good living for his wife and children. Anna saw him from time to time standing with a yardstick in his hand, a bearded Hasid presiding over a display table on the porch in front of the store where neatly folded materials were laid out. One day, Anna had met Khilya walking to school. When they stopped in at the store to deliver a message from Khilya's mother to her father, Anna had a chance to see the yard goods on display inside the store, each costly fabric wound around a long rectangular board.

Mr. Slivnik, having escaped from Korsun and having finally reached Petrograd despite the turmoil of civil war, was now living there with his son. One of the Korsun women, Mindl Knyagansky, took Anna one day to visit the Slivniks. The young Dr. Slivnik and his wife, an engineer, had managed to obtain a permit to live on a main street in a wealthy neighborhood, a wide street where horse-drawn droshkies vied for space with the automobiles. Anna was reunited with her school friend Khilya, who was living temporarily with the Slivnik family. From the Slivniks' luxurious apartment decorated with chandeliers and mirrors, Anna returned to her family's simple room at the camp. Before long Khilya left the Slivniks' apartment, journeying by train to join her father, who had reached Odessa, far to the south.

In the fall, Anna was still working in the camp office. She and several women sat at their typewriters in the open front room of the office, copying documents. The identification papers of the camp's inmates were locked in the back room, to which the commandant had the key. The office workers took turns at *dezhurnaya,* which meant being the woman on duty as the monitor who was responsible for guarding the document room when it was unlocked, and for locking the office at five o'clock in the absence of the commandant.

One day when Anna was the monitor, a stranger wearing a lightweight jacket came into the office and asked for her help. He had a patch over one eye, and on his opposite side he had a wooden leg, an old-fashioned "peg leg," like a mop handle. He was tall and husky, with a voice to match. He told Anna he was an American correspondent, which surprised her because he spoke fluent, unaccented Russian. He said he was looking for the "American women" who were trying to cross the border. Anna understood that he wanted to write a story about her group for an American newspaper.

She locked the office and took him to the living quarters, where each room housed one "American" family. She took him from one room to another, asking each woman how many children she had, the name and age of each child, the age of the husband, and what they planned to do in America. Anna told the correspondent the names of the children in Yiddish, since the mothers gave them to her in that language and they could not be translated into Russian.

He came into the office every day for almost a week. On the last day, he told Anna that his wife was waking in the middle of night because he was talking in his sleep, saying, "Yankele, Shmelkha, Yosele"—the Yiddish names of the children in the "American" families. The correspondent knew he had found a treasure. It was his good fortune that Anna was there to translate from Yiddish into Russian, allowing him to write a story about the long, difficult journey to freedom of the "American" women and children. He left the camp enthusiastic and happy about his project. Anna never found out what he wrote.[5]

Anna and Gussie foraged for food through the fall. As the weather turned colder, they also stopped in at the Hermitage Museum, which was open two or three times a week. They were not much interested in the cultural attractions at those times, but would warm themselves and use the restrooms. Then they would go back to a little market about two blocks from the Hermitage to sell and barter cigarettes and any other goods they could find. Other people were on the street doing the same. If Anna and Gussie were lucky, a woman would tell them she had bread to barter for what they had.

During the months in Petrograd, the goal was always to leave for America. Mr. Kohn went repeatedly to the authorities on behalf of the group, as he had in Moscow, but the situation did not look promising. The United States had still not recognized the Bolshevik regime. Sonya had made off with the genuine passports issued in Moscow, leaving Leya and the others with forgeries. Since all thirty-five of the people in the party from the Korsun region had left home without any identification papers, they would have to begin the process of applying for passports all over again. The authorities, though, were helpful. Knowing that order was beginning to be restored in the Ukraine after the civil war, they telegraphed to Korsun in the hope of verifying that the women had lived there. They were told that *pogromshchiki* had burned the courthouse in which their birth certificates were stored, leaving only ashes.

The authorities eventually decided to issue new passports, relying on the information provided by the emigrants. Anna went to a government office to get papers for the family. She was the only one in the family who could speak and understand enough Russian. She knew her own exact birth date in Russian, the date according to the Christian calendar, because she had needed it when she started high school, and even though she could only tell them the Yiddish birth dates for Gussie and Mayna, dates relating to the Jewish calendar, the officials made passports for all of them.

The group left Petrograd by train late in 1921, bound for the seaport of Bremen in Germany. Although it was not snowing when they left, winter had begun. Anna was now a young woman of sixteen. She was wearing a coat made from a soldier's overcoat. On her head perched a beret she had fashioned from a piece of found material, patterned after one she had seen in a shop window. She had made a new hat for the new life she would make in America. She was ready.

Epilogue

Anna, with her mother and two sisters, traveled by train from Petrograd to the German seaport of Bremen, by way of Minsk in White Russia and Kovno in Lithuania. They landed in America at Ellis Island, New York, on March 6, 1922. From there they took the train to Iowa, joining Anna's father, Aaron, in the small agricultural town of Marshalltown, where he was teaching Hebrew to children and serving in the shul. Anna was now sixteen and had not seen her father since she was seven. The next year they were living about thirty-five miles north of Marshalltown, in the town of Ackley, population about 650.

Anna soon moved to St. Louis, where she met and married Joseph Dien in 1925, the year she turned twenty. They had three children: Albert, who became a professor of Chinese at Stanford; Saul, an architect; and Jane, a fund-raiser for a number of Jewish institutions.

Anna's brother, Abraham, was born in 1923 in Ackley, and by the time he began kindergarten in St. Louis, Anna was already married. Whenever she told her brother a story about her life in Russia, and especially about her experiences in Moscow and Petrograd, he did not believe her. He told Anna's children, when they were small, that she lied about her past. The children didn't know any better until they had grown up.

Anna used her artistic eye in making a career as an interior decorator, first at a St. Louis, Missouri, department store, and later in her own business. She took courses in that field at Washington University in St. Louis.

She and her husband took under their wing a young man named Aaron, who had spent his teen years in a Nazi concentration camp. They located Aaron's uncle in Chicago, but before Aaron could join his uncle, the government needed proof of his identity and birth date to show that the uncle was a legitimate relative. Aaron did not know how old he was, so Anna took him on the streetcar to the St. Louis city hall, where she presented

Figure 3. Anna as a young woman in America, date and place unknown. (Courtesy Anna Dien)

Figure 4. In Iowa, circa 1923. (Courtesy Dien family)

two items sent by the uncle. One was a letter in Yiddish from Aaron's father to the uncle, telling of his firstborn son's arrival, with the date of the birth. The other was a photograph showing the clear resemblance of Aaron to his father. The official at city hall found the evidence sufficient to establish that the uncle was indeed a relative and to allow the issuance of a birth certificate for Aaron. Anna did not lose touch with Aaron. When his son was bar mitzvah in Chicago, she was present.

When Jews were allowed to leave the Soviet Union in the 1970s, Anna became a liaison for those who moved to St. Louis, helping them to find housing and jobs. She made a match between two of the immigrants, and before long she was in charge of the couple's wedding arrangements. Because neither the bride nor the groom was a United States citizen, Anna dealt with endless red tape before the wedding could be held.

When Anna's children were young, she would, as her son Albert recalled, drag her children to the St. Louis Art Museum on Saturdays after working all week. He said she was proud that she had doubted the authenticity of some supposed Rembrandts long before the paintings were deemed suspect by professionals. She kept current with developments in the art world. One of her greatest pleasures was to roam an art museum. The thought of a visit to a museum in New York City made her beam.

She read widely in Yiddish over the years, relishing the works of writers such as the notable trio of Mendele, I. L. Peretz, and Sholom Aleichem. She preferred I. J. Singer to his more famous brother, Isaac Bashevis.

Anna's eyesight had deteriorated in the 1990s. Although she could see well enough to navigate on foot (with help in crossing streets in her immediate neighborhood, the Delmar Loop in the University City suburb of St. Louis), she could no longer read even the largest type. She had been an active participant in the Great Books program of Mortimer Adler for many years. At one period she had belonged to two separate groups, attending them on alternate weeks and reading a different book for each group. When she could no longer read book print, she regularly obtained audiotapes of the books to be discussed from the Wolfner Library for the Blind and Physically Handicapped, a free library service of the State of Missouri, enabling her to continue to participate in Great Books meetings.

Remaining independent in her later years despite her visual impairment, she kept her own small apartment, did her own cooking, and dressed tastefully with an artistic flair. Art works decorated her walls. Her son Saul visited, taking care of the chores Anna's impaired vision made impossible for her. She took a long bus ride each week to visit her sister Gussie, then in a nursing home because of Alzheimer's disease. She habitually struck up conversations with other passengers on the bus.

Friends of long standing visited her often, as did family members, and they gave her valuable help when she was ill. She continued to make new

Figure 5. Anna's ninetieth birthday
party in St. Louis, 1995. (Courtesy
Dien family)

friends. A quartet of younger St. Louisans doted on Anna during her last
several years—Arlene Sandler at first, followed by my wife, Sandy, and me,
and finally by Betsy Ruppa. Anna died in October 1997 at age ninety-two.

If this description has made Anna sound almost saintly, it is only fair to
mention some of her off-putting moments. Her artistic sensitivity was
paired with self-confidence about interior decorating to a degree that convinced her customers about her choices. This helped make her business a
success. Her son Albert tells the family joke about the time a relative asked
her opinion of an interior color scheme that someone else had devised.
Anna replied, Well, you'll get used to it. That illustrates a kind of self-
confidence, which as Al said, was hard to live with at times. When Anna
first came to our home, she paused in the entry hall to look at a large painting while I went into an adjoining room. After a minute I heard her say
something, half to herself. I didn't let on that I had heard her. What she
said was, Well, I don't have to like something just because it's hanging
there.

Appendix A
Shtetl Influences

Anna had little interest in her ancestry. She did not know the names of her great-grandparents or where they had lived. To better understand the conditions in which she lived as a child, however, it is helpful to know where her people had lived, why they came to the Ukraine, and how they had fared there.

Although Jews had earlier lived in the Black Sea region and in Kiev, their concentration in Eastern Europe stemmed from the First Crusade, which gave Jews reason to leave Western Europe, where they had lived since Roman times. In Western Europe, large Jewish communities had existed in Italy, Spain, Gaul (France), and a small strip of future Rhineland Germany (Cologne, Bonn). In the twelfth century, however, some of these Western European Jews in the area of Germany began to emigrate to Poland.[1]

Poland's practice of religious tolerance made it an attractive country to both Jews and non-Jews in the twelfth century.[2] A wave of emigration to Polish cities and towns was set off in small regions of Western Europe when Jewish residents there were murdered in 1096. The murderers were some of the Christians of the First Crusade together with some of the local burghers in the French city of Rouen and in several cities in the German Rhineland. Jews fled to Poland again and, for the same reason but in greater numbers, after the Second Crusade (1147), and after the Third (1189–1192). These Jews came from Germany, Bohemia, and Moravia.[3] Polish kings hired wealthy Jews as "minters, bankers or commercial agents" in the twelfth century.[4]

In the centuries that followed, Jews from Western Europe would often have reason to emigrate to Poland and other Eastern European lands, either in flight for their lives, or in hope for their livelihoods. In the mid-thirteenth century, Poland invited both Jews and Christians as settlers. Poland's population needed replenishment, having been reduced by the

Mongol invasions that began in 1241 under Batu Khan, founder of the Golden Horde, and grandson of Genghis Khan. The immigrants repaid their adopted land, a land of Polish nobles and their serfs, by forming a needed intermediate class of urban traders and craftsmen who enhanced the country's economic development.[5] Boleslav the Pious responded by granting rights to the Jews of Poland in his charter of 1264.

A century later, Jewish refugees escaped to Poland from Western European lands where they were being killed by Christians who falsely accused them of poisoning the wells to cause the Black Death. This plague repeatedly caused devastation in Western Europe from 1348 into the next century.[6]

Conditions thereafter became even more favorable for Jews in Lithuania than in Poland, since Grand Duke Vytautas gave them numerous "privileges (1388–1389), including tax-free concessions for their places of worship and burial, and the right to trade, hold any craft, and own land."[7] After another hundred years, "A number of Jewish physicians" who had been expelled from Spain in 1492 reached Poland, where they "became the attendants of Polish kings and high nobility."[8]

Regarding Ukrainian lands specifically, Jews displaced by the Crusades in the twelfth century formed small settlements in Galicia and Volhynia, regions associated with the origins of the Ukraine.[9] During the fourteenth and fifteenth centuries, these Ukrainian Jewish communities, having become part of Poland and Lithuania, increased in population from new immigration when the murder of Jews in the neighboring countries had become most widespread during the Black Death.[10]

Polish noblemen encouraged Jews to settle on their estates, their latifundia. Many Jews became agents for these landowners. This became especially frequent after Poland assumed control in 1569 over most of the Ukrainian lands, which lay to the east of the long-settled Polish cities and towns. Vast tracts populated sparsely by Ukrainians (Ruthenians) were given by the Crown to Polish nobles, the magnates.[11] The magnates welcomed the help of Jews in organizing and managing their holdings in these undeveloped regions as feudal estates. Eventually these Jews would often lease the land of the estates from the magnates, who preferred to let their holdings be managed while they used the rents to support their luxurious life in the cities.

The Jews who rented from the magnates were known as *arrendators* (lessees).[12] An individual renter would move with his family into one of the small towns and villages that were part of the magnate's holdings, part of his latifundium. A latifundium comprised a number of complexes, each complex consisting of up to ten manors, twenty villages, one or two towns, and the residence of the magnate or his manager. The magnate owned the latifundium outright, including all of its dwelling places, lands, produce, and serfs.[13]

In these private towns that in the sixteenth century were the early shtetls, and in these villages, the Jews enjoyed protection by the magnates, a benefit often lacking for the Jews in the older towns and cities owned by the Crown and influenced by the Catholic Church. Poland did not lack rulers who acted constructively for religious tolerance, but neither did it lack Poles—priests and city-dwelling competitors of the Jews in business—who acted violently against Jews, a situation that would persist for centuries.[14]

The rights to distill and sell liquor in the villages had been preferentially given to Jews. In addition, Jews leased the rights to dairying, logging, milling, salt mining, and other enterprises. They came to control the hide and lumber businesses, both in Poland and internationally. They also collected taxes and tolls from the peasants. In the eyes of the peasants, therefore, the Jews became the hated tax collectors, thereby adding festering social and financial grievances to the peasants' anti-Semitism.[15]

Some cities enacted a law called *"de non tolerandis Judaeis,"* which forbade Jews from living inside the city. Jews were barred from some occupations, and in some towns they were forced to live in prescribed areas. Still, conditions were so much better for Jews in Poland than in Western Europe that Poland from 1580 to 1648 has been called "heaven for the Jews, paradise for the nobles, hell for the serfs."[16] Jews could travel freely in Poland and abroad, could engage in many occupations, and had religious freedom. The Jewish community in an individual town was governed by its own *kahal*, a Jewish self-government, which in turn was subject to the Jewish Council of the Four Lands (the four regions of the Polish-Lithuanian Commonwealth), from about 1580 to 1764.[17]

This heaven, however, descended into a series of catastrophes. The Cossack and peasant uprising led by the Cossack Bohdan Khmelnytsky against Polish rule in 1648 killed tens of thousands of Jews and destroyed a large number of Jewish towns. Then, during the Swedish–Polish War of 1655–1660, Jewish communities in Poland were destroyed by Poles, and those in Lithuania and White Russia were ravaged by invading Russian armies.[18]

Many Polish Jews who had survived these onslaughts of death and destruction yearned for the long-promised deliverer. A Turkish Jew, Shabbetai Tzevi, declared himself the Messiah in 1646, repeating this declaration publicly in his hometown of Smyrna, Turkey, in 1665, only to leave many disillusioned Jewish followers in Eastern Europe when, under threat of torture by the sultan, he converted to Islam in 1666.[19] Some remained faithful, however, forming a new sect, most of whose members followed a second false Messiah, a Ukrainian Jew named Jacob Frank, who eventually converted publicly to Catholicism in 1759, as did many of his followers.[20]

Meanwhile, after the Khmelnytsky massacres of 1648, and in the first half of the eighteenth century, Poland's economy, like the spiritual life of Jews, was in decline. Poland's legislatures imposed progressively larger and more crippling taxes on the Jewish communities in the cities. The number of Jewish men who were both poor and without an occupation was increasing, a situation that led people to coin the term "*luftmentsh*" ("air man"), the man without a trade, who had to make a living "out of the air," by his wits.[21] Many Jews deserted the cities for small towns and villages, where they were physically safer as well as legally and financially better off because the magnates needed their services. The Jews in private towns and villages had reestablished their devastated communities, their relationship with the magnates, and their healthy economies by the beginning of the eighteenth century. In the aftermath of the Khmelnytsky massacres, then, the small market town, the shtetl, became important as an established part of the Polish economy and as an established locus for Jews. The shtetl maintained that importance through the nineteenth century and into the twentieth.[22]

More than half of the 750,000 Jews in the Polish–Lithuanian Commonwealth in 1765 lived in towns and villages of the privately owned latifundia "under the direct jurisdiction of nobility—especially magnate—owners."[23] A significant minority of Jews lived in the villages, and of these, more than three-fourths worked in three occupations. The *arrendators* leased lands and rights, such as taxation of peasants, from the nobles. The *kretshmers* kept village and roadside taverns. Most of the third group, the *shenkers*, worked for the other two.[24]

The killing of Jews recurred during a series of eighteenth-century wars and "virtually continuous" haidamak rebellions (Cossack and peasant uprisings) that expanded into three major revolts, the last one in 1768.[25] As this hundred-year period of Jewish tribulation and disillusionment that had begun with the Cossack massacres of 1648 neared its end, Hasidism, a new branch of Orthodox Judaism was spreading across the Ukraine.[26] It found a welcome among the common people in the small towns and villages. Its founder, the legendary Israel Baal Shem Tov of Podolia, Ukraine, then a Polish province, died in 1760. By 1800, Hasidism was so popular in Russian Poland that it had become the dominant branch of Judaism. The exception was Lithuania, the stronghold of the traditional branch, the *Mitnagedim*. Their leader was a monumental scholar named Elijah ben Solomon Zalman, known as the Vilna Gaon (1720–1797). He denounced Hasidism as heresy and excommunicated its followers.[27]

Coincidentally with the spread of Hasidism, Poland had become so politically weak that Prussia, Austria, and Russia were each able to take control of part of its lands in a series of annexations (the partitions of 1772, 1793, and 1795). Catherine the Great's Russia, through these annexations, had attained control of the Ukraine.[28] The Russian Empire, which had excluded Jews for almost three hundred years, found itself in 1795 to be sovereign over more than half a million Jews in what had become Russian Poland.[29]

Catherine isolated the newly acquired Jewish population by forbidding Jews to leave her "Pale of Settlement," which encompassed all three partitions.[30] Catherine was continuing the anti-Semitic policies of the Romanov tsars and their predecessors. Peter I [the Great, died 1725] "who imported thousands of non-Russian nationals for the sake of modernizing his empire, refused to admit Jews. 'I prefer,' he said, 'to see in our midst nations professing Islam and paganism rather than Jews. . . . It is my endeavor to eradicate evil, not to multiply it." Catherine herself "expressed the same hostility in denying entrance to a group of Jewish tradesmen. 'From the enemies of Christ,' she explained to the mercantilists in her council, 'I desire neither gain nor profit.'" This was in 1762, the same year in which she "permitted all foreigners to travel and settle in Russia . . . except the Jews.'"[31]

In the nineteenth century, three developments impelled most rural Jews to leave the villages. First, when Russia suppressed Polish rebellions in 1830 and 1863, many Polish nobles abandoned estates, forcing their Jewish leaseholders to move to the towns and cities. Second, after Tsar Alexander II freed the Russian serfs in 1861, some of them displaced Jews as moneylenders or businessmen in the villages. Third, the Russian government passed the "May Laws" of 1882, expelling Jews from all villages, prohibiting them from buying land outside the towns, as well as from leasing estates and farmland; and barring them from opening their businesses on Sundays and Christian holidays.[32]

The "May Laws" were not repealed until 1917, but while they were still in effect, it was possible for some people to safely do the things they were designed to prevent. When Anna was born in 1905, "many Jews . . . were still leasing estates, forests and taverns; still marketing nobility and peasant produce in the towns; and still selling finished goods in the countryside." They lived in small towns.[33]

The number of village Jews was now small. The Jews of Eastern Europe lived mainly in the towns and cities.[34] Many, if not most, of the Jewish shtetl-dwellers were poor.[35] Most were struggling shopkeepers, handcraftsmen such as tailors and shoemakers, or they were *luftmentshen,* without a store or a trade. Many Jews in Anna's time had remained religiously observant.[36] They were either Hasidim ("the pious") or the more traditional *Mitnagedim* ("the opponents" of Hasidism). Hasidism taught that God was everywhere and was best worshiped with joy rather than solemnity. Hasidic worship emphasized practices accessible to the common man — heartfelt individual prayer rather than reverential group prayers; singing and dancing over religious learning and Talmudic scholarship. By Anna's time, Hasidism had strayed from its roots, as its spiritual leaders (*rebbeim*) had become charismatic wonder-workers. These *rebbeim* had often assumed the mantle of mediators between God and man, a practice foreign to post-biblical Judaism. The leader of the *Mitnagedim*, Elijah the Vilna Gaon, had judged this to be outside of Jewish belief and akin to idol worship.[37] Moreover, many of the *rebbeim* had acquired their positions by inheritance instead of through religious study and learning. In their luxurious homes they lived in the manner of potentates presiding over personal dynastic courts. This contrasted sharply to the demeanor of rabbis—men qualified by training and study to interpret and teach Jewish Law, and who had been the spiritual leaders of the Jews since their dispersion from Roman Palestine.

Bitter adversaries at first, the two branches of Judaism had found commonality in opposing several late-nineteenth and early twentieth-century social, religious, and political movements that had significantly affected the life in the cities and in the towns like Anna's. The Socialist "Bund" (organized in 1897) agitated and struck for workers' rights in the cities. Emigration beckoned, starting in the 1880s, chiefly to America, known as the "Golden Country." Many who had seen enough poverty, persecution, and pogroms chose to emigrate.[38] Other Jews chose to follow the Enlightenment philosophy born in Western Europe. They discarded many of the traditions of Orthodox Judaism in the hope that to adapt to the modern, non-Jewish culture would be to gain political and social equality. The failure of this hope in the nineteenth century was a significant factor in the growth of the Zionist movement, which held its first international conference in 1897 and which urged emigration to Palestine, where a new nation would form to provide security and political freedom.[39] These four movements—emigration, assimilationism, socialism, and Zionism—together with such factors as economic crises, urbanization, and the extension of the railroad to smaller towns, were features that defined a new age, a modern age that had important destabilizing effects on the shtetl. Although the prevailing opinion has been that the shtetl deteriorated or disintegrated, and did so because of this modernization, that view has recently been challenged.[40]

During the nine hundred years since the First Crusade, then, the experience of the Jews in the Ukraine had been mixed. They had come to a Ukraine ruled by Poland, arriving sometimes when pushed by peril, sometimes when pulled by prospects. Once there, they had been fortunate to enjoy protection and even prosperity under the magnates, but had also been reviled and assaulted under the Crown and the Church. The change from Polish to Russian rule made the experience of the Ukrainian Jews in the nineteenth century even less desirable. The Polish magnates could not be a shield against the centuries-old anti-Semitism of the tsars and the Orthodox Church. The poverty that had been in place in the shtetls under Poland did not abate under Russia. By the time Anna was born in 1905, the *luftmentsh,* the airman, had become a solid symbol of the economy. And by the time Anna emigrated to America in 1922, the shtetl had entered a new phase, that of the interwar years.

Appendix B
The Shtetl Memoir

Much is known about shtetl life.[1] How *Anna's Shtetl* relates to the literature about the shtetl can be assessed by considering materials published in English that describe shtetl life as it existed during two periods. The first period extends from 1900 to 1920, thus encompassing the years of Anna's shtetl childhood from 1905 to 1919. During the earlier period, extending from 1850 to 1900, shtetl life was already beginning to be changed by the major influences that would affect Anna's era.[2]

Primary sources that have contributed to the picture of shtetl life in these two periods are of four kinds: memorial books, literary fiction, sociological studies, and memoirs or descriptive essays.

Memorial Books

Memorial books (*Yizkor Bikher*) have been written about more than twelve hundred shtetls destroyed in the Holocaust.[3] These books gather eyewitness accounts of survivors, materials from the records of community governance, and other memorabilia. New memorial books are still being written. In a related endeavor, two authors, Theo Richmond and Yaffa Eliach, have written books memorializing the town of their roots. They have traveled to Europe and elsewhere, gathering information from survivors and from town records. David Roskies has pointed out the difficulty of relying on information from memorial books, which he finds to be "partisan and partial."[4]

Literary Fiction

The Yiddish stories of Mendele Moykher Seforim and Sholom Aleichem faithfully reproduced the shtetl experience, according to critics in the 1930s to 1950s. The opposite view, taken in the 1990s, holds that the Yiddish masters did not catalog shtetl culture, but instead deliberately misrepresented shtetl life in various ways to fit their aspirations as artists and their ideological agendas as activists committed to the Jewish Enlightenment movement.[5]

How, then, should a modern reader appraise the genuineness of the details of everyday shtetl life in the fiction of the Yiddish masters? A useful point of departure is the observation of Hillel Halkin. After translating nearly thirty of Sholom Aleichem's stories, Halkin commented on their inclusion of seemingly unlikely, but verifiable, details. As a reader so distant in time and place from Sholom Aleichem's Russia, Halkin wondered whether the unlikeliness of the details meant that the author "was deliberately exaggerating for literary or comic purposes."[6] Halkin discerned a half dozen examples of such details. He noted the third-class railroad car in which the passengers are nearly all Jews who tell each other stories, and he also noted a father who "must run endlessly from draft board to draft board because a son who died in infancy still appears in the population registry." He mentioned the Jew named Brodsky, who has become a sugar magnate, and he also mentioned the Jew who "must get a Christian drunk so that he will agree to send his son, at the Jew's expense, to a commercial school together with the Jew's son." He recalled the woman who is a talented "linked-phrase" curser, and he also recalled the apparently normal girl who commits suicide "just because a jilted and possibly pregnant friend has done the same." In each unlikely instance, however, Halkin found historical documentation of such a situation.

While writing this book, I sought information that would confirm or refute Anna's recollections—memories whose apparent authenticity ranged from strongly probable to moderately improbable. In six instances, the writings of Sholom Aleichem include items that are strikingly similar to those recalled by Anna.[7] But if Sholom Aleichem is to be the benchmark against which to judge the authenticity of some of Anna's memories, his own examples must first be independently verified.

In another six instances—in addition to those noted by Halkin—items mentioned by Sholom Aleichem are independently confirmed by the literature. These items concern topics that arose in the writing of *Anna's Shtetl*, as follows: First, shtetl Jews enjoyed Yiddish versions of secular literature, and, specifically, read the tales of *A Thousand and One Nights* (*The Arabian Nights' Entertainment*).[8] The literature confirms that repeated Yiddish editions of romantic, fairy tale, and other secular stories, including *A Thousand and One Nights,* were widely read by Jews. Itinerant book peddlers brought them to the shtetl.[9] Second, a Jewish woman might fall in love with, and marry, a Christian man in a shtetl.[10] In his autobiographical memoir, Joseph Morgenstern mentions that one of his teachers was Reb

Shlomeh, whose only child, a daughter, "fell in love with a son of a peasant neighbor and nothing could be done to save her . . . she was married in the church by the local priest." This happened in the 1880s in Belorussia, in the shtetl Kapulia.[11]

Third, a Christian in Russia might express contempt for a Jew by calling him a "*zhid*" ("dirty Jew," or "kike").[12] The historian W. Bruce Lincoln writes, "[H]e [Tsar Nicholas II] despised Jews, whom he called zhidy (kikes)."[13] Fourth, passengers on a Russian train were warned three times of its impending departure by the ringing of a bell.[14] Baedeker's 1914 Russian travel guide explains that a bell is rung at three fixed times while a Russian train is preparing to leave, the third one at departure.[15]

Fifth, police in Kiev and other Russian cities raided Jewish homes in the middle of the night, rounding up and jailing those who did not have the proper residence permit (*pravozhitelstvo*).[16] From the time of their May 1881 pogrom until the 1917 revolution, Kiev and its police became notorious for "hunt attacks" or "roundups" ("*oblavy*") of Jews lacking the right of residence.[17]

Sixth, a Jew caught without a proper residence permit could be sent back to his hometown, walking in a convoy of transported prisoners.[18] The Yiddish writer Ansky (Solomon Zaynvl Rapoport) has recorded that he was threatened in 1881, in Liozno, Lithuania, with this punishment — being run out of town "with a convoy of prisoners."[19]

These six instances, together with Halkin's six, show that a variety of details of shtetl life in Sholom Aleichem's fiction are accurately portrayed. They suggest that Sholom Aleichem wrote about what he knew to be true. Because Sholom Aleichem has been accurate in every one of a dozen instances of varying improbability, he earns a certain degree of credibility about his putative realities of shtetl life.

The assumption that Sholom Aleichem took care to write factually about realities, and to leave them undistorted by his literary devices, fits well with the following biographical facts. He expressed to his brother a desire to write the Jewish *La Comédie Humaine*. He wrote a letter asking a friend to collect and send him descriptions of factual characters and events observed in several Russian cities. He used facts from contemporary newspaper accounts of the 1913 Beilis trial in his novel *The Bloody Hoax*. He visited the Ukrainian city of Berdichev to collect information by talking to elderly residents about the real violinist who was the model for the violinist Stempenyu in his novel of that name. He recorded words and expressions new to him by writing them in a notebook as soon as he heard them.[20]

This assumption is also consistent with Ken Frieden's comment that Sholom Aleichem favored comic, not satiric, narratives. He did use satire, but it was mainly literary satire, ridiculing not the follies of Jewish life, but the novels that he believed should have been holding those follies up to the light. Sholom Aleichem had to try to balance his "social criticism with literary satire," against his "commitment to realism and the mimetic illusion."[21]

Sociological Studies

Four sociological studies emphasizing group trends have used, as their main source of information, interviews with former shtetl residents living in America.[22] The popularity of one of these—Zborowski and Herzog's *Life Is with People*—is unrivaled in the field, but so too is the amount of adverse criticism it has received. Among the half dozen defects ascribed to it, only one has major significance here; namely, that it contains errors of fact.[23] Unfortunately, the instances of error are frequent enough that they tend to undermine reliance on the rest. Nevertheless, this book, because of its influence on the movie *Fiddler on the Roof,* is the major source of the popular image of shtetl life.[24]

Memoirs or Descriptive Essays

Former residents have written individual essays to describe their towns (e.g., Abraham Ain on Swislocz);[25] they have written essays based on first-hand observation (e.g., Hirsch Abramovicz on rural Jewish occupations in Lithuania);[26] and they have written autobiographical memoirs that include details of their shtetl childhood (many authors).[27]

Many memoirs are told in a series of more or less connected anecdotes about the personal experiences of the author or the author's family. A second type is more structured and more sociologically oriented, dividing the material into chapters about such topics as education, religion, family life, and occupations.[28] In a third variety, a professional writer builds a narrative from the author's manuscript.[29]

We have nineteen autobiographical accounts written by men about their childhood in a shtetl.[30] Of the nineteen childhoods, nine were in the last half of the nineteenth century, and these include the memoirs of four eminent Yiddish writers (Mendele Mocher Seforim, Sholom Aleichem, Isaac Leib Peretz, and Sholem Asch).[31] Eight are from the period 1900–1921.[32] The other two straddle the two periods.[33] In contrast, only eight autobiographical accounts have been written by women.[34] All but one pertain to the period 1900–1920; the sole exception straddles the two periods (Zunser).

Appendix C
How True to Reality Is Anna's Shtetl?

I have tried to judge the truthfulness of this memoir—the degree to which it records what actually happened—on the basis of four criteria: Did Anna have a clinical disorder affecting her memory? Was her memory consistent (reliable)? Was her memory accurate (valid)? Is the present text faithful to her account?[1]

Did Anna Have a Memory Disorder?

It is well known that memory is fallible, even in a healthy young adult. The description of an event observed minutes ago or years ago may be selective, distorted, or false. Memory is affected by illness, medication, fatigue, pain, aging, and psychological factors. Anna was eighty-nine when I first interviewed her, and during the two and a half years of interviews she often both felt and showed the effects of illness or medication. Her physical problems (heart disease, pain in the chest, other pain, insomnia, medication effects) sometimes interfered with her concentration and her ability to recall details. At times they forced her to cut short an interview, as when she was having anginal pain. A "small" stroke on July 12, 1997, caused a partial aphasia, affecting mainly Anna's word-finding ability, but by the end of August she was clearly improving, and by September she was in high spirits and speaking well, although still with some word-finding difficulty. She died in the first week of October 1997.

It is relevant to ask whether Anna's memory could have been impaired by a clinical disorder such as Alzheimer's disease. A critical part of the information necessary for diagnosis would be the assessment of her memory for both recent and remote events unrelated to her childhood in Russia. When she was feeling well, her ability to recall the names of people in her current life and in her seventy-odd years in America was better than average for her age. She lived alone, shopped for herself, cooked, kept appointments, and managed her affairs capably, despite severely impaired vision. (Legally blind, she could not read the newspaper, or even large print. Her son periodically took care of her finances, keeping her checkbook in order.) She was continuing to learn new things. Her recent memory was accurate and detailed.

Anna's demeanor did not suggest a disorder of memory when she was recalling events of her childhood in Korsun, Moscow, and Petrograd (St. Petersburg). She often said, "I don't remember," or "I don't know." For example, she would not hesitate to say that she did not know what season or month or year it was when a certain event occurred. Often in such a situation she would then recall some detail that shed light on the chronology. In one instance, she did not know, at first, when certain events had occurred in Petrograd. However, she was then able to recall that a girl from Finland had lent her a dress at that time, and that it was a summer dress. Based on that memory, Anna concluded that the weather at that time had been warm.

She often apologized for her inability to recall the name of a person or a place, but almost invariably the name came back to her during the conversation, or not long afterward—a typical memory feature of normal aging. She apologized, too, when she could not think of the English word for a utensil or an object. She was re-creating a mode of existence not only removed in time and space, but also based on a culture that has largely disappeared. Many of the things she was describing have long ago gone out of fashion, out of use, and out of production. All the while, however, she had a clear picture in her mind of the object's shape, size, construction, and use, as well as its name in Yiddish, Russian, or Ukrainian. She said on several occasions that when she was reminiscing about Korsun, she thought in Russian.

In April 1996, having been concerned about whether she could correctly recall details from her childhood (in this instance, the colors of certain scarves), she took a memory test given on television to illustrate the fact that many suspects are falsely imprisoned because of faulty identification by witnesses. She said she was incorrect about the suspect's age, and that she had always had trouble judging age, but that she correctly answered every other question asked, including what he wore, the color of his shirt, the color of his hair, and so on.

I conclude that Anna did not have a clinical disorder affecting her memory.

The Consistency (Reliability) of Anna's Memories

Anna's memory was sometimes unreliable, in that occasionally something she told me in one interview was apparently different from what she told me in a later interview. However, her memory was reliable more often than not. Her reliability was supported by the manner in which she retold incidents; by a single instance in which she told an incident to one person, and then told the same incident to another person ten years later; and by her ability to satisfactorily explain errors made in a first interview when an apparent contradiction arose in a second interview.

She might tell the same story on two different occasions. The story might be used to illustrate one point in one context, but another point in a different context. She was consistent in the major points of the story as well as in some of the minor details, but she did not tell a story in the same way twice, and in the second telling she would recall one or more details not mentioned in the first telling.

One of her friends gave me a tape recording of an interview she had done with Anna ten years before I met Anna. This offered a unique chance to compare Anna's memory of an event in her childhood, as expressed during two of the interviews with me, with her memory of the same event as she had expressed it ten years earlier, when she was in better health, and of course, younger. The event was the priest's beneficent project of distributing bread to Jewish children in Anna's town of Korsun in return for garden work. Each time Anna told the story, she mentioned the same details with the exception that in the 1985 tape she said the priest's wife had served the children potato soup for lunch, whereas in the March 1995 interview she said it was borscht; and six months later, in September 1995, she said she couldn't recall whether it was soup or borscht, but she was sure it was liquid because she recalled eating it with a spoon. The minor variation in detail in these three interviews falls within the normal range of memory function, and also illustrates the kind of variation in memory expected of a trustworthy source.

On a number of occasions, Anna told me something that contradicted a statement she had made during an earlier interview. When I would ask her to discuss that event again, she would think out loud and arrive at the reason for her error, meanwhile clarifying the event by her discussion in a way that left little or no doubt as to the correct version.

I conclude that Anna's memory was, in the majority of instances, consistent.

The Accuracy (Validity) of Anna's Memories

I constructed a chronology, and, wherever possible, checked Anna's recollection against the accounts of historians and contemporary writers. In most instances, the accounts corroborated her recollections. For example, she recalled arriving in Petrograd in February 1921.[2] She also recalled that a few weeks after the Kronstadt rebellion, she saw the funeral in Petrograd of the many soldiers who had been killed in the battle. When I looked up the Kronstadt rebellion, I found that it occurred in "March 1921." It was "the first major internal uprising against Soviet rule in Russia after the Civil War (1918–1920), conducted by sailors from the Kronstadt naval base. . . . The sailors [were] located at the Kronstadt fortress in the Gulf of Finland overlooking Petrograd [Leningrad]" (*Encyclopedia Britannica* qv Kronstadt Rebellion).

A second instance of agreement involves the date of the third Korsun pogrom, after which Anna's family left Korsun for Moscow. My estimate of the date was August 1919, because Anna said she left Korsun for Moscow in late August or early September. Later, I found a historical account of that pogrom, which assigned the start of the pogrom to August 13, 1919.

In a third instance, Anna said that the tsar's mother had visited Korsun to raise money during the war. Anna described the royal parade in detail. Later I received a letter from Klaudia Kolesnikova, a resident of Korsun, and an employee at the Korsun-Shevchenkovsky historical cultural preservation park, saying she had found that Maria Fyodorovna, mother of Nicholas II, had visited Korsun in 1916, and had planted a ginkgo tree near the palace, a tree that was still growing there.[3]

A fourth instance of agreement involves the difficulty of surviving during several winters. The winter of 1916–1917 was hard, and Anna described the winter of 1917–1918 as bad, but that of 1918–1919 as the worst winter in Korsun. In *Doctor Zhivago*, Boris Pasternak says, "Winter came, just the kind of winter that had been foretold. It was not as terrifying as the two winters that followed it, but it was already of the same sort, dark, hungry, and cold . . . [with] inhuman efforts to cling to life as it slipped out of your grasp. There were three of them, one after the other, three such terrible winters, and not all that now seems to have happened in 1917 and 1918 really happened then—some of it may have been later. These three successive winters have merged into one and it is difficult to tell them apart."[4]

Agreement with contemporary writing also supported Anna's description of conditions in Moscow in the winter of 1919–1920. Paraphrased, her description is as follows: Not only was food scarce, but often those who had it would refuse to sell it for money, preferring to barter. A good coat, for example, might buy a few loaves of bread. Even then, very little bread was for sale, and finding milk was as hard or harder. The shortage of sugar was so bad that a joke went around, saying that when anyone has a party in Moscow, the hostess hangs one cube of sugar from the ceiling, and each guest licks it before drinking his tea.

For comparison, the diary of I. V. Got'e, a forty-four-year-old history professor in Moscow, describes the food situation in Moscow at that time: "28 [September] [1919] The whole morning was occupied with exchange: a felt jacket for potatoes, shoes for butter; we sold a lady's cloak for money and with the money bought flour. A pair of shoes is priced at 1,500 rubles!" And later, "13 [November][1919] The problem of food supplies overshadows everything else except the problem of heating. . . . Traffic is coming to a standstill even on the railroads. As a result of that we are sitting here without firewood."[5]

In a fifth instance of agreement, Anna described a total eclipse of the sun, and knew the house at which she was living when the eclipse occurred. She also knew the approximate ages of her sisters, judging from their motor skills at that time. If a total eclipse had indeed occurred during that period, this would support her account. A solar eclipse occurred on August 21, 1914. The eclipse was total in Victoria Island, Canada, Greenland, Scandinavia, Ukraine, Persia, and India. No other total solar eclipse occurred in the Ukraine in the years during and surrounding the war, or from 1898 to 1914.[6]

A sixth instance of agreement of Anna's recollection with the historical record concerns an injury to her foot, and the military barracks in which her family was housed at the time of the Kronstadt rebellion. Anna was still wearing a cast, she said, while watching a speech (to the Bolshevik soldiers imported to crush the Kronstadt rebellion) from the window of her refugee camp building in Petrograd. She had broken her foot while ice skating on a Petrograd canal, probably in February (she had arrived in Petrograd in February, she said), and the fact that she was still in the cast at the time of the March 8 Bolshevik attack on Kronstadt placed her at the window at roughly the right time. (A broken foot bone would have taken, say, six weeks to heal well.) The Kronstadt rebellion actually occurred from March 8 to March 17, 1921. Also, the building from which she watched, she said, was on a street called "Eleventh *Rota*." A 1914 map of St. Petersburg (whose name was changed to Petrograd in that year) shows a street called "Odinnadtsataya Rota," the Russian phrase for "Eleventh *Rota*" ("11th Military Company"). The street is in the military barracks area, and is one of twelve streets named for the military companies stationed there since the time of Peter the Great. (The name of the street has since been changed to "11 Krasnoarmeiskaia" ["11th Red Army"].)

Finally, I have cited Anton Chekhov in support of Anna's view of peasant religious observance in Korsun. Chekhov has been commended for telling the truth about the Russian peasant, for "describing what he saw — not what he thought he ought to see," in contrast to the more usual romanticized descriptions by Russian novelists.[7] This speaks to the accuracy of Anna's reporting in this one instance.[8]

In a few instances, Anna remembered dates incorrectly. She repeatedly said that World War I had begun in 1913. She said she had arrived in America on February 22, 1922. The correct date was March 6, 1922. (She had sailed from Bremen, Germany on February 21, 1922.)[9]

I conclude that Anna's memory was, in the main, accurate.

The Fidelity of This Book to Anna's Account

In trying to ensure the fidelity of *Anna's Shtetl* to Anna's account, I have adopted Mark Kramer's "breakable rules" for literary journalism. Notable among these rules are: "no composite scenes," "no misstated chronology," "no falsification of the discernible drift or proportion of events," "no invention of quotes," and "no attribution of thoughts to sources unless the sources have said they'd had those very thoughts."[10]

Nothing has been changed or added to what Anna told me, with the following three exceptions:

(a) quasi-quotations, in which conversation that took place in Russia is presented without quotation marks, as explained below;

(b) inferences about Anna's (or others') behavior, thought, or emotion; and

(c) information from sources other than Anna.

Quasi-Quotations

A major issue in deciding how to write Anna's story was the rendering of conversation that had occurred during Anna's childhood. I have severely limited the use of dialogue as recalled by Anna. Only eighteen such items are included in the text. There are at least five reasons why dialogue that occurred long ago in Russia is usually impossible to reconstruct precisely.

First, the conversations took place about eighty years before Anna related them, and it would be rare for anyone to recall the exact words spoken so long before.

Second, Anna was reporting the words to me in English, whereas the conversations took place in Yiddish, Ukrainian, or Russian.

Third, Anna sometimes related the same event in more than one interview, using different words or adding other pieces of conversation, making it awkward to splice together a complete discourse. Similarly, her recollections in one interview sometimes required clarification by questions in other interviews.

Fourth, although twenty-four of the interviews with Anna were tape-recorded verbatim, I typed the majority of the rest into my computer while speaking to her over the telephone. In some of the telephone interviews, I was able to transcribe certain passages verbatim, and so mark them, but in the vast majority I did not capture every word.

Fifth, just as I have not tried to create speech that evokes the shtetl of Anna's childhood, so I have not tried to create her adult speech with its rich Yiddish accent and occasional Yiddish word order. Her English vocabulary was good to excellent, and she usually used grammatical English.

Given these barriers to precise reconstruction of dialogue, and given the fact that the function of quotation marks is to indicate that the words enclosed are verbatim as the original speaker said them, I have used what may be called quasi-quotations. The eleven quasi-quotations omit quotation marks, and include all statements made by people other than Anna during her childhood, as well as all nonverbatim statements made by Anna as an adult.

Quasi-quotations are to be distinguished from true quotations. The seven true quotations include quotation marks, and include Anna's words verbatim when she is speaking for herself, as if in Korsun, describing what she heard or knew; or when she is speaking in St. Louis, for herself, describing what she said eighty years after an experience in Korsun.

I have constructed quasi-quotations in either of the following two ways, depending upon the form of Anna's original words. Sometimes I have combined the words she spoke at different times into a composite, either because the ideas in a quotation were stated by Anna in more than one interview, or because in a single interview she digressed from the subject, then returned to it. At other times I have deleted parts of her quotation, or added a word or words, or changed the word order, to achieve a sentence that is shorter or clearer.

For example I constructed a quasi-quotation of the words of Domakho, the peasant who gave Anna milk, to read: Come over and bring your pan on Sunday, and I'll have some milk for you. Anna's actual words were: "She said, Come over, come over this weekend, Sunday. I'll give you something. . . . And bring along that pan. . . . So I knew what she meant, that she'll [sic] give me some milk."

No quasi-quotation is entirely invented. Each is based upon a statement by Anna. I have retained her words wherever possible.

Inferences about Behavior, Thought, or Emotion

Inferences of behavior, thought, or emotion occur in three instances.

1. I infer that Anna was "heartsick," based on her description of her discomfort about lying and about opposing her mother in court. [On the appointed day, heartsick at being told to lie but unable to defy her mother openly, Anna got ready for the trip to court.]

2. I infer that older women's faces look younger when they laugh. [The old faces . . . become younger in their laughter.]

3. I infer that she had the three symptoms—headache, listlessness, and fever—based on the classical course of typhus. [For a time she lay listlessly on a sofa, her fever high, her head a constant ache.]

4. I infer that she would have thanked "blue-eyes," and that her bucket by then was half empty. [Anna thanked him, picked up her bucket, and made her way home. . . . she put down the half empty bucket.]

I conclude that the present text of Anna's experiences is faithful to her account.

Appendix D
Material from Sources Other Than Anna

Readers who want to make specific use of Anna's recollections of shtetl life
will want to distinguish those recollections from the following list
of material that I have added from sources other then Anna.

Chapter 2

Korsun was a . . . market town/as . . . there.//
the palace road//

Chapter 3

thirty-six miles//
pen . . . masters/in 1827/at age twelve/Many . . . survivors./Russian
    law . . . twelve./Only . . . army//
Seven . . . 1856,//
prayer buildings/Jewish . . . prayer/ much . . . Korsun./Beyla was . . .
    others.//
those . . . Scheherezade./by . . . downstairs/in a women's Torah volume.//

Chapter 4

Yikhes meant . . . "good" family.//
his small . . . free school./another . . . community./eight . . . old//
thirteen . . . Talmud//
a title . . . law./it was . . . water./The Hasidic branch . . . melody//
copied . . . noblemen./or "ear," . . . bootstraps."//
(a "righteous . . . Hasidism,/(like a yarmulke) //
Every . . . the community./a metal . . . writing.//
the nib,//
a general . . . Jews.//

They were . . . miracles.//
(One ruble . . . cents.)//

Chapter 5

thirty-four . . . Korsun/crown . . . trials//
twenty miles away/Over . . . Kiev.//
The First . . . Turkey.//
the disastrous . . . year./twenty-seven . . . away.//
it was . . . rabbi.//

Chapter 7

Anna's . . . events.//
(One kopeck . . . penny.)//

Chapter 8

Olga . . . Peter I)//
Dowager . . . Fyodorovna//
Although the serfs . . . commoners.//

Chapter 9

The work was tedious . . . oil lamp. /and the old . . . laughter.//
Oora's anger . . . lambskins//

Chapter 11

Motivated . . . bridges.//A golem . . . matza//
Although . . . against the Jews."//
The standard. . . . corner.//

Chapter 12

In the large . . . home.//
acting . . . commoners.//

Chapter 13

The Bolsheviks . . . bread//
In peacetime . . . journey./In the prewar . . . use.//
When the civil . . . do so./Each freight . . . ahead./ which were spring- . . .
        collided./balancing . . . swaying //
perhaps . . . "niggah."/Black . . . alive.//
she and Anna . . . River/For a lodger . . . labor//

Chapter 14

The *kavaleristi*//
A pogrom . . . fear//

Cossacks had tormented . . . fear of the Cossacks./
the *Kavaleristi*//His overcoat . . . March 1918.//
he wore . . . and arm.//

Chapter 15

the *kavaleristi,*/like a gush . . . samouar//
modern, assimilationist//

Chapter 16

German . . . March.//
the word . . . cape//
and not very appetizing//
the elderly . . . policy/a disease . . . weeks//
Doctors . . . 1922.//
(it must . . . December) //

Chapter 17

the official . . . equator./came . . . October.//
the official . . . December 22.//
the slanting . . . northward,/The breakup . . . few hours.//

Chapter 18

The memories . . . work.//

—probably three . . . those days— //
Armies were . . . November 11/As in the March . . . be next.//
The second pogrom . . . for the Bolsheviks //

Chapter 19

Before the war . . . hopeful time.
The mud gave . . . labor.

Chapter 20

her head . . . ache //
as March . . . April,//
Kiev was now . . . starving//

Chapter 21

It was the custom . . . arrived.//
about twenty miles//
tiny . . . from Korsun,//

The story . . . pieces.//

Chapter 22

What a blessing . . . palace.//
(By the end . . . found.//

Chapter 23

They may have . . . poverty
She weighed . . . Other Korsun."//
an attitude . . . order//

Chapter 24

The trains . . . fighting.//
The eight . . . times.//
less . . . Kremlin//
the end . . . gift-giving.//
where Napoleon's . . . Moscow.//
During . . . 1918.//
half . . . Kremlin.//
famous . . . columns./the longer . . . Square.//
By taking . . . another.//
a famine . . . years.//
At the same . . . faiths./The American Jewish . . . Russia.//
the sparse streetlights//
Anna carried . . . light.//
She had come . . . pear.//

Chapter 25

The slow . . . miles //
The Kronstadt . . . regulations./The soldiers, . . . Great//
The city . . . daylike night.//
As photographs . . . other.
She had . . . ready.//

Notes

Map Caption

1. The 1897 census lists three towns named "Yablonovka." I have chosen this one, even though it is said to be in Vasilikov district, because it is the only one of the three whose population is less than 1,000, thus conforming to Anna's description of a town so close to Korsun. The one "Yablonovka," said to be in Cherkassy district, and thus closer to Korsun, has a population of 3,102, too large to fit. There is no independent evidence, however, to confirm the possibility that an error was made in listing the districts in the census.

Preface

1. Anna gave more than three hundred interviews. More than fifty of these were in person, of which twenty-four were recorded on tape, the others in handwritten notes. The rest were typed into a word processor program during phone conversations, or, infrequently, within a day or so of a conversation. The duration of an interview ranged from a few minutes to several hours, depending on Anna's schedule, her health, and the nature of the interview. I sometimes telephoned her—or she, me—for a few minutes to clarify a single point. At other times we spent up to several hours talking about a number of topics. Other details about the methodology used are given in appendix C.

2. For many Americans, shtetl life is typified by *Fiddler on the Roof*, the 1964 stage play and 1971 movie. The movie is set in 1905 (Anna's birth year), when the cocoon of shtetl life was unraveling under the influence of social, economic, and political changes. Tevye the dairyman is the main character. Despite poverty and problems, he lives in a romanticized world of comfortable Jewish "tradition." He protests his lot by having ironically humorous monologues with God. His world is far removed from the disheartening realities described by the men and women

who have written about their shtetl childhoods. Anna's memories of her shtetl suggest that Tevye may have been looking to the heavens so often because of the unpleasantness he saw when he looked in any other direction. (For another view see Heszel Klepfisz, *The Inexhaustible Wellspring*, pp. 37–45.)

3. To many readers, Anna's portrait of existence in Korsun will be unfamiliar, even unsettling. Life in her shtetl was not *Fiddler on the Roof*. She does not romanticize it. She gives us a shtetl as seen through the eyes of a girl of inquiring mind, artistic sensibility, and intolerance for injustice. The common vision of shtetl life is an understandably sentimental one, held by many who properly mourn the shtetl as the irretrievably lost home of their forebears. In that vision, the benefits and pleasures of shtetl life tend to be remembered well, but the difficulties and unpleasantnesses tend to fade, or to be treated as interesting curiosities. Certain customary behaviors have had little or no attention, at least in the English literature on the shtetl. Anna was angry about the habitual use by adults of other people's children to run errands. She noted the routine shortchanging of children by the many women who sold a nickel's worth of sugar or a dime's worth of cooking oil out of a cupboard or a small room in their home. She described a kind of mean-spiritedness that she found too often among Korsun's adults.

Chapter 1

1. Klavdia Kolesnikova found the name "Shpector" in the State Archives of the Cherkassy Region, under the heading, "The register of studying the students of the first class of the Korsun high school (1917–1919)." This confirms Anna's recollection that she was known officially throughout her high school career as "Shpector," not as her real name of "Spector," because her Czechoslovakian teacher could not pronounce her name correctly in Russian, and wrote it as "Shpector." Ms. Kolesnikova also found listed for the same era the name "Yakha Petrushanskaya," who is almost certainly the Yakha Petrushanska whom Anna mentioned as a friend. (Letter of August 10, 1998, from Klavdia Kolesnikova, Korsun-Shevchenkovsky historical cultural preservation park.)

2. Anna used the Russian phrase *smutnoe vremya*, which is usually translated as "time of troubles." It meant originally the chaotic period 1605–1613 in Russia (from the death of Boris Godunov to the election of Michael Romanov, founder of the Romanov dynasty of tsars), but the term has also been used by Russian authors to designate other eras of fighting and confusion. (Marcus Wheeler, *Oxford Russian-English Dictionary*, qv *smutnyi*, *vremya*; *Encyclopedia Britannica* qv Romanov; Iurii Vladimirovich Got'e, *Time of Troubles, The Diary of Iurii Vladimirovich Got'e: Moscow, July 8, 1917, to July 23, 1922*, pp. 3–24; p. 16; Lars T. Lih, *Bread and Authority in Russia, 1914–1921*, p. 2).

3. Anna appears to be grossly wrong here in placing the Bolshevik capture of Kiev in the summer, because the Bolsheviks took Kiev on February 5, 1919, and held it until General Anton Denikin's Volunteer White Army took it on August 31, 1919. It is still possible, however, that the Bolsheviks, despite holding Kiev from February 5 onward, did not control the Korsun area until summer.

Chapter 2

1. In the Russian language, Korsun was neither a village (*derevnya* or *celo*) nor a *gorod* (both city and town), but a *mestechko,* meaning a small place, a small town. Anna thought of Korsun as a *mestechko* (in Yiddish, a *kleynshtetl,* meaning a small *shtetl*); namely, a population center of a size somewhere between a village and a small town. As part of the answer to the question "How Jewish Was the Shtetl?" Ben-Cion Pinchuk presents quantitative data showing that Jews formed a majority of the population in 462 small towns (in Russian, "mestechki") in the entire Pale of Settlement in 1897; and that they made up more than 80 percent of the population in 25 percent of those 462 towns. (Pinchuk, "The Shtetl: An Ethnic Town in the Russian Empire"; "How Jewish Was the Shtetl?"; and "The East European Shtetl and Its Place in Jewish History.") Pinchuk finds that "Although not all of the shtetls were included in this official category [*mestechki*], those included do represent the bulk of the shtetls in the region" ("How Jewish Was the Shtetl?" p. 112). Missing, however, is the total number of small towns, a number that would be needed in order to calculate the percentage of small towns that have a Jewish majority (Pinchuk's apparent working definition of a shtetl is a small town with a Jewish majority). Also missing is the total number of *shtetlekh,* which would be needed in order to calculate the percentage of *shtetlekh* that have a Jewish majority. Still, it is fair to conclude from this helpful study that not only were there hundreds of small towns in the Pale of Settlement in which Jews were in the majority, but also that there were more than one hundred such towns in which more than eight out of every ten inhabitants were Jewish. Although the term *shtetl* cannot be precisely defined in terms of population size or other features (John D. Klier, "What Exactly Was a Shtetl?" pp. 17–18), the word has entered the English language as "A small Jewish town or village formerly found throughout Eastern Europe" (*American Heritage Dictionary of the English Language,* 4th ed.). However, this definition should omit the word "village," since the typical village, whose inhabitants were almost all peasants, lacked the community of Jews, and their buildings, that gave the shtetl its identity.

2. The Korsun palace was built from 1785 to 1789 by the last king of Poland (ruled 1764–1795), Stanislaw Poniatowski, a former lover of Catherine the Great. In 1799 Tsar Paul I gave Poniatowski's Korsun estate to Prince Petr Vasilievich Lopukhin, its first Russian owner, in recognition of the fact that the tsar had recently selected the prince's nineteen-year-old daughter as his next official mistress. (*Encyclopedia Britannica,* qv Stanislaw II Augustus Poniatowski; Klavdia Kolesnikova, personal communication; *Encyclopedia of Ukraine,* qv Korsun; qv Stanislau II Augustus Poniatowski; Max L. Margolis and Alexander Marks, *A History of the Jewish People,* p. 585.)

Chapter 3

1. Louis Greenberg, *The Jews in Russia,* pp. 48–52; Margolis and Marks, *History of the Jewish People,* pp. 313–15; Diane K. Roskies and David G. Roskies, *The*

Shtetl Book, p. 102; Isaac Levitats, *The Jewish Community in Russia, 1844–1917,* p. 37. The military conscription of Jewish children into cantons was abolished by Tsar Alexander II on August 26, 1856. Jews were to be treated the same as Christians in military conscription from then on. However, a rider decreed that those Jewish children who had converted to Christianity in the cantons were not allowed to return to their homes if their parents persisted in being Jews, and instead were to be placed in Christian homes (Simon M. Dubnow, *History of the Jews in Russia and Poland: From the Earliest Times until the Present Day,* vol. 2, pp. 155–56).

2. However, Milton Meltzer quotes Morris Cohen's 1949 description of an old man, a *Nikolai soldat* (Nicholas soldier) whose regiment "participated" in the Crimean War [of 1853–1856]. He returned to the town of Neshwies, married, became a water carrier, and brought up two adopted children (Meltzer, *World of Our Fathers,* pp. 51–52).

3. That women expected simply to serve as footstools for their husbands is mentioned in the following: Ruth Adler, *Women of the Shtetl—Through the Eyes of Y. L. Peretz,* p. 28; Isaac Bashevis Singer, *In My Father's Court,* p. 5; Isaac Bashevis Singer, "Big and Little," p. 65.

4. Anna did not know that novels and other books such as *The Thousand and One Nights* were made widely available in the shtetls by traveling booksellers when Beyla was young. The following accounts, among others, attest to their availability: Sholem Aleykhem, *Ale Verk Fun Sholom Aleykhem,* vol. 5, p. 190; Cecil Roth and Geoffrey Wigoder, eds., *The New Standard Jewish Encyclopedia,* qv chapbooks; Mark Zborowski and Elizabeth Herzog, *Life Is with People: The Jewish Little Town of Eastern Europe,* pp. 126–27; and David G. Roskies, *The Jewish Search for a Usable Past,* p. 5.

Chapter 4

1. Roth and Wigoder, qv Hasidism; David Bridger, ed., *The New Jewish Encyclopedia,* qv Hasidism.

2. Tsar Nicholas I began censoring and destroying Jewish books in 1836. Kaballah books were censored at first. Rabbinic books were added to the list in 1841 (Simon M. Dubnow, *History of the Jews,* vol. 5, pp. 165–66; Chaim Aronson, *A Jewish Life under the Tsars: The Autobiography of Chaim Aronson, 1825–1888,* pp. 55, 294; Israel Cohen, *Vilna,* p. 270).

3. Despite the freezing of the clothes, they did eventually dry and thaw. Singer also mentions this (Singer, *In My Father's Court,* p. 30).

Chapter 5

1. Hirsch Abramowicz, "Rural Jewish Occupations in Lithuania," pp. 117, 292–93.

2. Leya was twenty years old in 1905 when Anna was born, and thus had been born in 1885. Anna was born on June 26, 1905 (new style), and Gussie about De-

cember 24, 1908. Mayna was born on August 28, 1912. Anna was born while Russia was still using the Julian (old style) calendar, which was thirteen days behind the Gregorian (new style) calendar. On February 1, 1918 (old style), the Bolsheviks changed the date to February 14 (new style), and Russia has used the Gregorian (new style) ever since, like the rest of the world.

3. The railroads in the Ukraine were built largely in two periods: the trunk lines in the 1860s and 1870s, and the "mainly branch lines, secondary tracks, and the various local spurs" from 1893 to 1905 (J. Metzer, "Railroad Development and Market Integration: The Case of Tsarist Russia," pp. 529–50, 535; *Encyclopedia of Ukraine* qv Railroad transportation).

4. Although I have not been able to confirm that Germany bought beet seeds before World War I began, I believe Anna's account. A possible motive for Germany's eagerness to buy beet seeds (if that is what happened) can be seen in Napoleon's subsidization of the rapid development of a sugar beet industry in France when the British blockade cut off France's importation of cane sugar from the Caribbean islands. I am indebted to agronomists Stephen Kaffka and Roger Roslund for suggesting this historical precedent.

5. Among the events leading to World War I, a prominent role was played by those in Africa and the Balkans in the late 1800s, and by the Serbo-Bulgarian War of 1886. The two Balkan Wars that immediately preceded World War I, beginning in 1912, did not resolve the tensions in that part of Europe, and only strengthened the widespread belief that a general war loomed (*Encyclopedia Britannica*, qv World Wars; qv Balkan Wars; Samuel R. Williamson Jr., "The Origins of the War," pp. 9–25). The First Balkan War began in October 1912 and ended in May 1913. The Second Balkan War began twenty-nine days after the peace treaty had been signed, in June 1913, and ended in August 1913 (W. Bruce Lincoln, *In War's Dark Shadow: The Russians before the Great War*, pp. 403–19).

6. "Incidentally, it wasn't the usual thing to drive through the city. Why should anyone know where you were going, and on what sort of business?" (Isaac Leib Peretz, "My Memoirs," pp. 263–359, 284.)

7. Aaron left Korsun for America early in January 1913. Mayna was then four months old (born August 28, 1912) and Leya was still nursing her. The photo was presumably taken in March, April, or May of 1913, because Anna says it was taken that spring. Because Mayna looks at least a year old in the photo, I am arbitrarily choosing May, which makes her about nine months old.

Chapter 6

1. Beyond doubt, Anna lived with Yenta Koslov within the first month of the war, because she saw a total solar eclipse while living there, and the eclipse occurred on August 21, 1914. The eclipse came between 2:20 and 2:32 P.M. local time, and lasted two minutes and about thirteen seconds. No other total solar eclipse occurred in the Ukraine in the years during and surrounding the war, nor in fact from 1898 to 1914 (Jean Meeus, Carl C. Grosjean, and Willy Vanderleen, *Canon of So-*

lar Eclipses, pp. 1–5, 335). That Leya and Yenta didn't seem at all disturbed about the eclipse raises the possibility that they had heard it was coming, or that they had seen an eclipse before. (Details about total solar eclipses are discussed by Fred Espenak, *Maps of "Total and Annular Solar Eclipse Paths"*; Espenak, personal communication; Pierre Guillermier and Serge Koutchmy, *Total Eclipses: Science, Observations, Myths, and Legends*, pp. 146–47, 149–50; Mark Littman, Ken Willcox, and Fred Espenak, *Total Eclipses: Science, Observations, Myths, and Legends*, pp. 52–53, 116–17; Duncan Steel, *Eclipse*, pp. 23–25, 333–34, 423–24.)

Chapter 7

1. When the public high school was built in 1915, it gave the children of Christians and Jews an important opportunity: for the first time they had continuing and close contact. The Christian townspeople also bought farm produce from the Christian peasants; or from the large grocery and general store; or from the delicatessens, which bought wholesale from the farmers. Another partnership was in simultaneous operation, this one between the princess and her entourage, and those townspeople who supplied the needs of the palace. Beyla, for example, had supplied the palace with foodstuffs that she also bought wholesale from the farmers. That interaction is further considered in chapter 8 (but only briefly, since Anna knew little about it), as well as in chapter 6, in a discussion of Beyla's selling of provisions to the palace. The fine stores selling clothes and textiles are mentioned later in the present chapter.

2. Before the first frost came, a housewife would arrange to have vegetables delivered by wagon in preparation for winter. Anna's grandmother bought potatoes, eighty pounds to a burlap sack. She bought carrots, beets, and cabbages in quantity, and she bought cucumbers, which she put up as pickles. People who had enough money, as Beyla did before the revolution, bought apples to make *kvas*. All of these were stored in the rude dugout "rooms" of the earthen cellar. Onions and garlic would have sprouted in the damp cellar, so they were strung in garlands and hung to dry wherever there was a nail, usually in the kitchen, warmed by the oven. In the tightly closed house during the winter, the odor of the garlic and the onions mingled with the smell of camphor, which was usually used in cold medicines. In peacetime, peasants split logs, bundled them for firewood, and brought the bundles to town by the wagonload. A family that could afford it paid a peasant to stack enough wood to last the whole winter against one wall of the foyer.

Chapter 8

1. That Olga Valerianovna would have actually "owned" the town is in doubt (Paul Robert Magocsi, personal communication; Magocsi, *A History of the Ukraine*, pp. 141–42, 183, 334–37, 391).

2. "On November 23 [1917] . . . in Petrograd . . . the Soviet Council of People's Commissars met under Lenin's chairmanship, and a fantastic stream of decrees . . .

uprooted every institution and tradition in Russian life. . . . Men and women were declared equal in law . . . All titles were submerged into the universal "Citizen" or "Comrade" (Alan Moorehead, *The Russian Revolution,* pp. 260–61. See also Evan Mawdsley, *The Russian Civil War,* p. 32).

Chapter 9

1. Although death from cancer was usual, it was not universal in the Korsun area. Anna's aunt Khana Rukhl (Grandmother Beyla's oldest daughter) had a hemi-mastectomy for cancer as a young woman, before 1900, and survived. The operation was done in Kiev, where doctors practiced who had studied in the best hospitals in Germany and France. Anna saw that her aunt had had only half of one breast removed.

Chapter 10

1. "[W]e used scooped-out potato halves filled with oil for Chanukah. . . . The wicks in the potatoes, our Chanukah candles, smoked and sputtered" (Sholom Aleichem, "Benny's Luck," pp. 17–44, 39–40).

2. The first of the two phases of the 1917 revolution began with worker demonstrations in Petrograd on February 23, and ended with Tsar Nicholas II's abdication on March 2, 1917 (old style; March 8–March 15, new style). The demonstrations became violent on February 25 and were fired on by the tsar's order on the twenty-sixth. Most of Petrograd was held by mutinous soldiers on the twenty-seventh. On March 3, Grand Duke Michael refused the crown, and the Provisional Government took power (Orlando Figes, *A People's Tragedy: The Russian Revolution, 1891–1924,* pp. 308, 344; Richard Pipes, *The Russian Revolution,* pp. 850–51). The Bolsheviks took power in the second phase, a nearly bloodless coup starting on October 25, 1917 (old style) (Figes, *People's Tragedy,* pp. 480–81, 484, 493; Pipes, *Russian Revolution,* p. 493, 853).

Chapter 11

1. A subject not well covered previously is the personal relationships of Jews with Christians in the shtetl. It has commonly been held that the two communities lived separate existences, coming into contact mainly in the marketplace, and that neither one knew or understood the life of the other. That was not Anna's experience. Miron points out that it served the purposes of prominent authors of the Jewish Enlightenment to depart from reality by making their literary shtetls virtually devoid of Christians, as in the Yiddish stories of Mendele Mocher Seforim (commonly known as Mendele) and Sholom Aleichem, and also in some works of Isaac Leib Peretz and Shmuel Yosef Agnon (Dan Miron, *The Image of the Shtetl and Other Studies of Modern Jewish Literary Imagination,* pp. 2–4).

In the memoirs in English about shtetl life during the period 1850–1919, it is typical for peasants or other Christians to appear in peaceful numbers at the marketplace during market days and fairs. Otherwise, they may only be seen in a group assaulting Jews during a pogrom, or even in ordinary daily life. Christians as individuals may appear once or twice in a book, usually because they have rescued a Jew from danger or hardship, or occasionally because they have become a friend of the author. Mendele describes the relationship in his hometown of Kapulie in Minsk province as pure friendship (Mendele, "Of Bygone Days," 355–56).

In Korsun, Anna's interactions with individual Christians were more numerous and more varied. The situations in these interactions are widely different from one another, as are the attitudes and actions of Anna and the other person involved in each encounter. The large number and variety of personal interactions that Anna had with Christians in Korsun has no parallel in English memoirs of shtetl life during Anna's era and in the half century before.

2. One of Morgenstern's teachers in the 1880s in the shtetl Kapulie was Reb Shlomeh, whose only child, a daughter, "fell in love with a son of a peasant neighbor and nothing could be done to save her . . . she was married in the church by the local priest" (Joseph Morgenstern, *I Have Considered My Days*, p. 59). A better-known example is Sholom Aleichem's Chava, daughter of Tevye the dairyman, who marries a village peasant (Sholom Aleichem, *Tevye the Dairyman and the Railroad Stories*, pp. 69–82).

3. Published material in English dealing with the relationships between Jew and Gentile in the shtetl of 1850–1919 was scant until the 1952 appearance of *Life Is with People* (Zborowski and Herzog, pp. 152–58). With the notable exception of Annamaria Orla-Bukowska's excellent 1994 paper, which concerns interwar Galicia (Orla-Bukowska, "Shtetl Communities: Another Image"), little has been added since. (See Jacob Katz, *Exclusiveness and Tolerance: Studies in Jewish-Gentile Relations in Medieval and Modern Times*; Roskies and Roskies, *Shtetl Book*; George J. Lerski and Halina T. Lerski, *Jewish-Polish Coexistence, 1772–1939: A Topical Bibliography*; Murray J. Rosman, *The Lords' Jews: Magnate-Jewish Relations in the Polish-Lithuanian Commonwealth during the Eighteenth Century*, p. 209–10; Barbara Kirshenblatt-Gimblett, "Introduction" to *Life Is with People*; Gennady Estraikh and Mikhail Krutikov, Preface to "Shtetl Image and Reality"; Klier, "What Exactly Was a Shtetl?" p. 30; Max Gross, "Traveling Back to a Place of the Past"; Rosa Lehmann, "Jewish Patrons and Polish Clients: Patronage in a Small Galician Town"; Kate Brown, *A Biography of No Place*, pp. 72, 74. However, continuing interest in this area of research is shown in the collection of papers on "The Shtetl: Myth and Reality" (Polonsky).

4. Korsun had a brick factory, and Anna was aware of several brick buildings in town, namely the hardware store and some butcher shops at the marketplace; Mr. Mai's pharmacy building of yellow brick; the gymnasium; government buildings; and the two-story building housing the fancy delicatessen and the dentist.

5. Views of peasant religion that are much the same as Anna's are those of Anton Chekhov, *The Oxford Chekhov*, vol. 8: *Stories 1895–1897*, pp. 1, 3–5, 308; Lincoln, *In War's Dark Shadow*, p. 62; Richard Pipes, *Russia under the Old Regime*, pp. 160–61. Because Anna said that the great Russian writers express the

same view of peasant religion, it may be that some or all of her ideas on the subject were influenced by what she read, whether in high school or in later years.

6. Mary Matossian, "The Peasant Way of Life," pp. 1–40.

Chapter 12

1. Zavl appeared in March 1917 (old style), as attested by the dripping snow. This is in accord with the fact that Tsar Nicholas II abdicated on March 2, 1917 (old style), in the first phase of the revolution.

Chapter 13

1. The details of railway travel included in this and following paragraphs are those described in Karl Baedeker, *Baedeker's Russia,* pp. xx–xxiv; Moscow map I. Sholom Aleichem mentions the third bell of the train (Sholom Aleichem, "Cnards," p. 425). The paragraph on life in the third-class car is based upon the description by Sholom Aleichem in his short story "Third Class" (Sholom Aleichem, "Third Class," pp. 292–97). Chekhov corroborates certain of these details in his short story "The Jailer Jailed," mentioning the "stink," the crowding, a man overloaded with baggage, baggage theft, and the third bell (Chekhov, *Anton Chekhov: Selected Stories,* pp. 56–60). In another of his stories, "On the Train," Chekhov tells of a non-first-class car, passengers sleeping under the benches, eating, and playing cards by the light of their cigarettes; of the theft of the narrator's suitcase by a pickpocket who had earlier found his pocket empty; and, in a first-class car, of the theft of a passenger's shoes and socks while he sleeps (Chekhov, "On the Train," pp. 9–18).

2. [In April 1920] "[w]hen they rode the train, it would stop at each station, and Israel and other passengers would go into the woods to fetch wood for fuel" (Bettyanne Gray, *Manya's Story,* p. 105).

3. The absence of tickets and the crowding on trains are mentioned in Rosalie Sogolow, *Memories from a Russian Kitchen: From Shtetl to Golden Land,* pp. 100–01.

4. On European trains, two adjacent cars were prevented from crashing into each other by a set of four spring-loaded "spring buffer[s]" (John H. Armstrong, *The Railroad, What It Is, What It Does: The Introduction to Railroading,* p. 87). Buffers are seen in photographs of a French "Travelling Post Office" from the "early 1870s" (Cuthbert Hamilton Ellis, *The Pictorial Encyclopedia of Railways,* fig. 311, fig. 327), and of a Russian passenger car from the 1890s (J. N. Westwood, *Geschichte Der Russischen Eisenbahnen,* absent figure and page numbers). The front buffers are well shown in a 1911 color photo of a locomotive in the Urals (Library of Congress, "Transportation: The Empire That Was Russia"). Alexander Berkman saw Russians riding the roofs and bumpers of crowded trains during famine in 1920, and Walter Duranty saw them in 1921 (Berkman, *The Bolshevik Myth: Diary 1920–1922,* p. 158; Duranty, *Duranty Reports Russia,* pp. 15–18).

5. In "Sticks and Stones May Break My Bones," Sholom Aleichem talks about staying in Yehupetz (his Kiev) without a residence permit, and about a raid by the authorities, who sent the guilty man walking back to his home town together with

a party of "transported convicts" ("Sticks and Stones," pp. 145, 147). In "Millions" he describes a lodging house raid for illegal residents in Kiev ("Millions," p. 113). From the May 1881 pogrom until 1917, the Kiev police were notorious for their rough, middle-of-the-night roundups of Jews lacking residence permits (*Encyclopedia Judaica* qv Kiev). *Oblava* in Russian is a raid or a "beating up" (Wheeler, *Oxford Russian-English Dictionary*, qv *oblava*). For more details on the Kiev *oblavy*, see Lucien Wolf, *The Legal Suffering of the Jews in Russia: A Survey of Their Present Situation, and a Summary of Laws*, pp. 44, 46; Michael F. Hamm, *Kiev: A Portrait, 1800–1917*, pp. 131, 197; and Dubnow, *History of the Jews in Russia and Poland*, vol. 3, pp. 19–20). On the Pale of Settlement, to which Jews were restricted, see *Encyclopedia of Ukraine*, qv Jews, pp. 386–87). For a fuller picture of what the roundups meant to an individual Jew who lacked a residence permit, see pp. 36–46 in Sholem Aleichem's novel, *The Bloody Hoax*. These raids in Kiev were widely known to Jews at the time (*Encyclopedia Judaica* qv Kiev; Dubnow, *History of the Jews in Russia and Poland*, vol. II, p. 346).

6. Isaac Babel, in "The Road," describes conditions at the Kiev train station early in 1918 as follows: "I arrived in Kiev the day before Muravyov began shelling the city. . . . In all the world there is no more cheerless sight than the Kiev train station. For many years makeshift wooden barracks have defaced the town outskirts. Lice crackled on wet planks. Deserters, smugglers, and gypsies were all crowded together in the station. Old Galician women urinated standing on the platform. . . . Three days went by before the first train left" (Babel, "The Road," p. 423).

Chapter 14

1. Taras Hunczak concludes that the earliest pogroms of the Russian Civil War erupted near the end of 1917. They were different from those that occurred in the spring of 1918 and continued through 1919. The early pogroms were made by Russian soldiers who had deserted and who were demoralized and hungry. The later ones were often made by units from organized armies fighting in the Civil War (Hunzak, *Symon Petliura and the Jews: A Reappraisal*, p. 12).

2. "Cossack" is *Kozak* in Ukrainian (C. H. Andrusyshen and J. N. Krett, *Ukrainian-English Dictionary*; M. L. Podvesko, ed., *Ukrainian-English Dictionary*); and also in Yiddish (Uriel Weinreich, *Modern English-Yiddish, Yiddish-English Dictionary*; Alexander Harkavy, *Yiddish-English and English-Yiddish Dictionary*). It is *kazak* in Russian (Wheeler, *Oxford Russian-English Dictionary*).

3. Magocsi has recently evaluated accounts of the massacres during the revolt led by the Cossack Bohdan Khmelnytsky, as follows: "The number of Jewish victims during the period from 1648 to 1652 has been estimated at from tens to hundreds of thousands, and no exact number is ever likely to be known. . . . Almost without exception, today's specialists on the period reject what they describe as the grossly exaggerated figures in the chronicles. The Israeli scholars Shmuel Ettinger and Bernard D. Weinryb speak instead of the 'annihilation of tens of thousands of Jewish lives,' and the Ukrainian-American historian Jaroslaw Pelenski narrows the number of Jewish deaths to between 6,000 and 14,000" (Magocsi, *History of the*

Ukraine, pp. 200–02). For a recent attempt to estimate the casualties, see Shaul Stampfer, "What Actually Happened to the Jews of Ukraine in 1648?" 207–27.

4. The historical dates of this first Korsun pogrom are March 1–8, 1918. A Ukrainian military detachment of *haidamaks* under Kiritshenko arrived in Korsun on March 1, 1918, staying at least through March 8 (A. Tsherikover, *Antisemitizm un pogromen in Ukrayne, 1917–1918,* pp. 121, 267–68). The haidamaks were bands of "runaway peasants, manorial servants, or craftsmen" who waged "virtually continuous" guerilla war by specifically attacking the estates of Polish landowners early in the eighteenth century. These attacks became uprisings when the haidamaks and the peasants joined forces against the Polish government and nobility, as in the revolts of 1734, 1750, and 1768. The haidamaks killed Jews as well as Poles. The name haidamak was resurrected and applied to certain of the Ukrainian nationalist forces during the Russian Civil War of 1917–1921 (Magocsi, *History of the Ukraine,* p. 295. See *Encyclopedia of Ukraine,* qv Poland; Haidamaka Uprisings; Dubnow, *History of the Jews in Russia and Poland,* vol. 1, p. 182–86; Rosman, *Lords' Jews,* p. 4; Mikhail Bulgakov, *The White Guard,* pp. 249, 290). On the same day that Korsun was taken by Kiritshenko's haidamaks, Kiev was taken by German and Ukrainian nationalist (UNR) troops, the latter under Generals Petliura and Prisovsky (*Encyclopedia of Ukraine,* qv Kiev, p. 508; qv Ukrainian-Soviet War, p. 462; Volodymyr Kubijovyc, ed., *Ukraine: A Concise Encyclopaedia,* vol. 1, p. 744; Peter Arshinov, *History of the Makhnovist Movement, 1918–1921,* p. 65).

5. The events that I have arbitrarily attributed to "the third day" indicate my best understanding of the sequence of events.

6. The first Korsun pogrom is discussed in the following two excerpts from Tsherikover, 1923:

> In the shtetl Korsun, Kaniev district, Kiev province, on March 1, a group of Haidamaks with a government commissar, V. Kiritshenko at its head, demanded that the Jewish population bring within a half hour 2000 rubles and 6 pair of boots. This demand was immediately fulfilled. Also, next day the head of the militia, Kopatshevky himself called upon the chairman of Korsun's [middle class?] board, M. Ziskin, with the following letter, number 366: "I received a verbal decree from the commissar of the central RADA, B. Kiritshenko, that the Jewish population should today prepare 100 pair of good boots, 300 caps, 30 military overcoats, 100 shirts, 100 pair of drawers, 100 pair of [cloth wrappings for soldiers' legs under knee boots?], and 7 fur caps with red cover [for the crown of the head].
>
> Even though this demand is illegitimate, there was no way for people to fulfill it. On March 8, Kiritshenko demanded 3,000 rubles from the Jewish population—and they were received. Presently both of them—Kopatshevsky and Kiritshenko—terrorized the entire local population. [Tsherikover, 1923, p. 268 and last paragraph on p. 267.]
>
> The pogrom wave that had arisen with the return of the Ukraine military and that had made its greatest impact in Kiev, had in March–April

captured a line chiefly in the Kiev area. On March 1st, a Ukrainian military detachment arrived in Korsuń, led by one Kiritshenko. Kiritshenko had dubbed himself "Commissar of the Central RADA." He had disarmed the shtetl's volunteer defense force, threatened "to slaughter every kike" and demanded tribute from the Jewish population." [Here footnote 2 reads: "Archive of Jewish ministers, registry number 1165 of April 9th, 1918, information about the events in Korsun from the Jewish members of the zemstvo (district elective council)."] [Tsherikover, *Antisemitizm un pogromen in Ukrayne*, p. 121, L.A.C.'s translation].

Chapter 16

1. The Jews of Korsun did not always get along so well with the German occupation force (Tsherikover, *Antisemitizm un pogromen in Ukrayne*, p. 174, my translation). For German occupiers' attitudes toward Jews in other places, see John D. Klier and Shlomo Lambrosa, *Pogroms: Anti-Jewish Violence in Modern Russian History*, p. 294–95.

2. In Russian, *rotonda* is "lady's cloak" (Wheeler, *Oxford Russian-English Dictionary*). In French, *rotonde* is: (a) "long sleeveless cloak" (*Cassel's French Dictionary)*; and (b) "Manteau taillé en ronde et retombant à grand plis"; i.e., a cloak or mantle cut in a circle and hanging in great folds (Gillon Augé, ed., *Petit Larousse*).

3. The process of Ukrainianization was begun by the Ukrainian National Republic (UNR), which had declared its independence from Russia on January 25, 1918, and continued by the Hetmanate, the Germany-backed replacement for the UNR. Germany's major immediate goal in occupying the Ukraine had been to feed its own population, hungry after nearly four years of world war. After less than two months of poor cooperation from the UNR, Germany backed a coup to install the puppet Hetmanate, so called because its nominal head, the former tsarist general Pavlo Skoropadskyi, took the title of *hetman,* a title worn by his Cossack ancestor in the early 1700s under Peter the Great (Magocsi, *History of the Ukraine*, pp. 245, 488–91).

4. Anna said that she didn't become a socialist (Bundist) or Zionist for several reasons. She was too young, no one in her family read books or newspapers, and no one in her sphere encouraged her to learn about socialism or Zionism. About Zionists she knew only that they got together to sing. She recalled no workers' strikes.

5. Details about typhus are to be found in T. R. Harrison, et al., eds., *Principles of Internal Medicine*, pp. 1034–36; *Cecil Textbook of Medicine*, pp. 1672–79; A. B. Baker and L. H. Baker, *Clinical Neurology*, vol. 2, chap. 27, pp. 2–4.

Chapter 18

1. I presume that the spring semester did not start until after Epiphany (Three Kings Day), which fell on January 6 (or on January 19 if the old Julian calendar of

the Orthodox church was still in effect in January 1919). Thus, school would have been abandoned in the second week of January at the earliest, and perhaps not until the third week in January.

2. Pasternak also mentioned the one-shoulder carry (Boris Pasternak, *Dr. Zhivago*, chap. 9, p. 245).

3. "No region of the Russian Empire witnessed more violence, more destruction, and more unvarnished cruelty of man to man during Russia's Civil War than the Ukraine. . . . 'These were convulsive, violent times,' wrote Konstantin Paustovskii in his recollections of the months he spent in Kiev during 1918 and 1919. 'It was impossible to grasp what was going on'" (W. Bruce Lincoln, *Red Victory: A History of the Russian Civil War, 1918–1921*, pp. 302–03).

Chapter 20

1. Although Anna did not mention it, headache is such a typical symptom of typhus that I have inferred it here.

2. Bolshevik forces had driven the nationalists of the Ukrainian National Republic (UNR) from Kiev on February 5, 1919. The Bolsheviks held the city until August 30–31, 1919. The UNR had been fighting three different armies: the Bolsheviks, the anti-Bolshevik Whites (the White Guard), and the German army's puppet Ukrainian (*Hetman*) government (Leslie Milne, *Mikhail Bulgakov: A Critical Biography*, pp. 12–13).

3. I am placing Leya's trips to Kiev in late April or early May.

4. Avrum probably died in June or early July.

Chapter 21

1. The third pogrom occurred from August 13 through August 26, 1919 (N. Shtif, *Pogromy na Ukraine: Period Dobrovolcheskoi Armiy*, p. 42; Nahum Stiff, *Pogromen in Ukraine: Di Tsayt Fun der Frayviliger Armey*, p. 56).

2. I did not ask Anna to explain the significance of sitting inside the cart with no one dangling their feet, but the following two translations of a single passage from Chekhov seem to indicate that dangling the feet outside a cart was a sign of a casual or merry ride: "A cart would drive by. . . . then a cow was led along by the horns . . . then a cart again, and in it drunken peasants swinging their legs" (Chekhov, "In the Ravine," in Avrahm Yarmolinsky, *The Portable Chekhov*, p. 486); "a cart, bearing drunken peasants who were hanging their legs over the side" (Chekhov, "The Hollow," in Robert N. Linscott, ed., *The Stories of Anton Chekhov*, p. 279 ["The Hollow" in Linscott is the same story as "In the Ravine" in Yarmolinsky].) Anna had earlier said that she had seen peasant youngsters ride into town in wagons with their feet dangling, yelling and singing.

3. Although Anna did not name it, the *dorf* at which they stayed is probably Yablonovka, about three miles directly west of Korsun (U.S. Army Map Service, *Belaya-Tserkov, USSR Section*).

4. Sholem Aleichem uses the word *khuligan*. (Sholem Aleichem, *The Bloody*

Hoax trans. Aliza Shevrin. Bloomington: Indiana University Press, 1991. pp. 42, 95, 118, etc.)

5. Confirmation that Mai-Maievskii's Volunteer Army was not merely advancing north toward Moscow but was also sending units northwest toward Kiev, and thus would have been passing through the Korsun area, is the following: "On July 3 [1919] . . . Denikin . . . announced: *'Today I have ordered our armed forces to advance against Moscow.'* Mai-Maievskii's Volunteer Army [was to] attack Kursk, Orel, and Tula, after sending units against Kiev to protect his exposed western flank, before launching assaults against Moscow from the southwest." (Lincoln, *Red Victory,* pp. 217–18).

6. The Terek Cossacks were one of eleven Cossack groups or "hosts" (*voiska*) (*Encyclopedia Britannica,* qv Cossack). Discussing "the Cossacks fighting in the Ukraine" in 1919, Peter Kenez says of the Terek, "Above all, however, the Terek Cossacks had the most bloodthirsty reputation" (Kenez, "Pogroms and White Ideology in the Russian Civil War," p. 303).

7. The fate of the Korsun delegation at the start of a pogrom was apparently typical, for immediately following the passage about Korsun, Stiff describes how the delegations in the three towns of Kaharlik (Kiev province), Kobistshe (Tshernigov province), and Makarov (Kiev province) were assaulted or butchered by Denikin's army (Stiff, *Pogromen in Ukraine,* p. 29).

Chapter 22

1. Sleigh rides in Russian blizzards are described in detail by Bulgakov and Pushkin (Mikhail Bulgakov, *Diaboliad, and Other Stories,* p. xix). Bulgakov's short story, set in 1916–1917, vividly describes both a snowstorm (the poor visibility, the cold, and the ease of losing the way, even on a road well known to the driver), and a pursuit by wolves (at night in the depths of rural Russia not far from Moscow). Pushkin's story also vividly describes these, omitting a pursuit by wolves (Bulgakov, "The Blizzard," pp. 81–93; Alexander Pushkin, *The Collected Stories,* pp. 86–99).

Chapter 23

1. The other method of contacting another person was to meet them by chance at the marketplace. The telephone exchange near the Ros River was only for the wealthy, or for communication with other towns or cities.

2. Maurice Samuel gives the names "linked phrase," or "apposite," or "apropos" cursing to this free association cursing (Samuel, *World of Sholom Aleichem,* p. 205). "The eyes should fall out of your head" is taken from Sholom Aleichem, *Tevye the Dairyman and the Railroad Stories,* p. 142. "You're not blind. You should become blind" is Anna's example. "Your head should be planted in the ground like an onion," a version of a prototypical Yiddish curse found in various stories ("May you grow like an onion with your head in the ground") is listed by James A. Matusoff, *Blessings, Curses, Hopes, and Fears: Psycho-ostensive Expressions in Yiddish,* pp. 84, 98.

3. In each of Korsun's five houses of prayer, members included not only *Hasidim,* but also smaller numbers of their opponents, the *Mitnagedim.*

Chapter 24

1. Anna's group, reaching Orel in mid-September, had outrun Denikin's army, which, in its threat to Moscow, did not capture Orel until October 11–14 and was then pushed by the Reds progressively farther from the capital, never to recover its winning ways (Got'e, *Time of Troubles,* p. xviii).

2. The Bryansk railway station is only about a quarter of a mile from the western edge of the Borodinski Bridge; this is presumably the station where Anna bought apples as well as the one at which her group arrived in the city (Karl Baedeker, *Baedeker's Russia,* Moscow map I, after p. 280. A modern map shows the Kiev Rail Station in the same place [*Fodor's 91 Soviet Union,* map, page 130]).

3. As Anna later found out, Muscovites wore old galoshes or anything they could find to cover their feet. The doctor had apparently noticed her bare feet and then jumped to the conclusion that her lack of shoes was a sign of poor breeding. Not all Moscow residents were aware that the city was sheltering Anna's small group of emigrants as well as a larger number of ill-clad war refugees.

4. Anna apparently misspoke when she said that Pushkin wrote the Borodino poem. It was Michail Lermontov (1814–1841) who wrote "Borodino" in 1837 (Anatoly Liberman, *Michail Lermontov: Major Poetical Works,* pp. 101–05).

5. Anna said that she understood everything, but she did not say that her friends helped her. Perhaps the action of the performance helped her to understand. Her knowledge of Yiddish would have helped some, but probably not enough by itself, because although Yiddish contains Hebrew "loan words," they make up less than 25 percent of everyday speech (Philologos, "Fusion without Confusion," p. 13; William F. Weigel, *Yiddish*).

6. Arthur Ransome noticed a similar mismatch of clothing in Petrograd in early 1919: "The second noticeable thing [in Petrograd] . . . is the general lack of new clothes. . . . I saw one young woman in a well-preserved, obviously costly fur coat, and beneath it straw shoes with linen wrappings" (Ransome, *Six Weeks in Russia in 1919,* p. 10).

7. Anna said religious people called Moscow "forty times forty" because it had sixteen hundred churches. "And in Moscow . . . there are many, many churches, forty times forty, dearie" (Chekhov, "Peasants," in *Anton Chekhov: Selected Stories,* part 1, p. 246).

Chapter 25

1. Anna gives four different durations of the stay near Bela Ostrov, namely "ten days," "one week," "four or five days," and "one or two days." I have arbitrarily chosen the one-week value.

2. Two railway stations, the Baltic and the Warsaw, were very close to Anna's camp, and both served trains to and from the west along the southern shore of the

Gulf of Finland. "At about the same time [October 24, 1917, about 8:00 P.M.] troops of the Izmailovsky Guards regiment, the first major garrison unit to come to the government's aid in July, took control of the Baltic Station, rail terminus for loyalist reinforcements arriving from the seaboard along the Gulf of Finland and points west" (Alexander Rabinowitch, *The Bolsheviks Come to Power: The Revolutions of 1917 in Petrograd,* p. 262; Karl Baedeker, *Baedeker's Handbook for Travellers,* St. Petersburg map).

3. "White Nights [occur] around the summer solstice (June 11 to July 2). During this period there is only about three-quarters of an hour of twilight, with daylight for the rest of the day" (Karl Baedeker, *St. Petersburg,* pp. 8–9). For a particularly evocative description of the white nights in Petrograd during World War I, see Arthur Ruhl, *White Nights and Other Russian Impressions,* pp. 33–34.

4. Gussie's swelling, bleeding gums and night blindness probably indicate a multiple vitamin deficiency involving vitamins A, B1, and C. Although Anna did not mention the legs—saying only that Gussie was swollen—I infer that her legs were swollen, since her three symptoms were typical of "wet scurvy" seen in sailors returning from long voyages before the discovery that citrus fruit prevented scurvy. (For details, see Kenneth J. Carpenter, *The History of Scurvy and Vitamin C,* pp. 221–23; J. Christopher Bauernfeind, *Vitamin A Deficiency and Its Control,* pp. 177, 185.)

5. The identity of Anna's American correspondent in Petrograd is a mystery. Also, I have not been able to find any articles written about Anna's "Americans." Although the prime candidate for the correspondent is Walter Duranty of the *New York Times,* because he had a wooden leg, he cannot be the correspondent Anna helped. He fits neither Anna's description of the correspondent nor the time when Anna was in Petrograd. Of the half dozen items that do not fit, the most obvious is that although Duranty had a wooden leg on the left, he did not acquire it until 1924, two years after Anna had arrived in America. I have considered and discarded a number of American correspondents, including Sam Spewack and Henry Alsberg as well as John Reed and Alexander Berkman. Others, such as Kenneth Durant, I have not yet been able to investigate thoroughly.

Appendix A

1. H. H. Ben-Sasson, *A History of the Jewish People,* map, p. 365; Dubnow, *History of the Jews in Russia and Poland,* vol. 1, pp. 13–38; Margolis and Marx, *History of the Jewish People,* pp. 525–31.

2. Rosman, *Lords' Jews,* pp. 1, 9, 36–37; Chimen Abramsky, Maciej Jachimczyk, and Antony Polonsky, *The Jews in Poland,* pp. 1–3; Robert Chazan, *European Jewry and the First Crusade,* pp. 54, 63; Ben-Sasson, *History of the Jewish People,* pp. 1096–97; Martin Gilbert, *The Jews of Russia,* p. 37; Judah Gribetz, *The Timetables of Jewish History,* p. 110 passim; Magocsi, *History of the Ukraine,* pp. 146–47; Margolis and Marx, *History of the Jewish People,* p. 528; *Encyclopedia Britannica,* qv Poland [re Batu Khan], p. 639.

3. *Encyclopedia Britannica,* qv Christianity, vol. 4, p. 467; qv Crusades, vol. 5,

p. 299; Margolis and Marx, *History of the Jewish People,* pp. 359–63, 527–29; Rosman, *Lords' Jews,* pp. 36–37.

4. Rosman, *Lords' Jews,* p. 36; Abramsky, Jachimczyk, and Polonsky, *Jews in Poland,* pp.1–3.

5. Margolis and Marx, *History of the Jewish People,* pp. 528–29; *Encyclopedia Britannica,* qv Poland, History of, p. 639 and map p. 647.

6. Margolis and Marx, *History of the Jewish People,* p. 528.

7. Magocsi, *History of the Ukraine,* pp. 146–47; Gribetz, *Timetables of Jewish History,* p. 157; Margolis and Marx, *History of the Jewish People,* p. 527.

8. Celia S. Heller, *On the Edge of Destruction: Jews of Poland between the Two World Wars,* p. 20. Only two such Spanish physicians—Isaac Hispanus and Solomon Ashkenazi—are identified by Dubnow (*History of the Jews in Russia and Poland,* vol. 1, pp. 131–32). As for possible emigration to Poland by any other Jews who were expelled from Iberia in 1492–1497, clear evidence is lacking (Bernard D. Weinryb, *The Jews of Poland: A Social and Economic History of the Jewish Community in Poland from 1100 to 1800,* pp. 32, 114; Iwo Pogonowski, *Jews in Poland: A Documentary History,* p. 64).

9. Magocsi, *History of the Ukraine,* pp. 146–47.

10. Margolis and Marx, *History of the Jewish People,* p. 528.

11. The Ukraine had been under Polish rule from 1569, when the Kingdom of Poland united with the Grand Duchy of Lithuania to form the vast Commonwealth of Poland-Lithuania, whose territory ran from the Baltic nearly to the Black Sea. Most Ukrainian nobles had been Polonized (*Encyclopedia of Ukraine,* qv Poland; Lublin, Union of; Ukraine (Ukraina); Ben-Sasson, *History of the Jewish People,* p. 630).

12. The system of leasing was called, in Polish, *arenda* or *dzierzawa* (leasing). The lessee (renter), who obtained the lease (contract) from the magnate noble (lessor), was called *arrendator* in Polish and Russian, and also either *arendarz* or *dzierzawca* in Polish, and *arendar* in Russian. The Yiddish equivalent word, *randar,* came practically to mean "village Jew . . . since most were Jewish" (Dubnow, *History of the Jews in Russia and Poland,* vol. 1, p. 93; Rosman, *Lords' Jews,* pp. 106, 110, 114, 216).

13. Rosman, *Lords' Jews,* p. 10 ff.

14. Steven J. Zipperstein, "The Shtetl Revisited," p. 18; Pinchuk, "How Jewish Was the Shtetl?" p. 111; Adam Teller, "The Shtetl as an Arena for Polish-Jewish Integration in the Eighteenth Century," pp. 29, 39; Rosman, *Lord's Jews,* pp. ix, 37, 39–40, 71; Dubnow, *History of the Jews in Russia and Poland,* vol. 1, p. 55 ff; Margolis and Marx, *History of the Jewish People,* p. 529 ff). The anti-Semitic horrors persisted across the centuries, but one example will suffice. In 1399 the Archbishop of Posen had the rabbi and thirteen Jewish elders tried for allegedly obtaining and desecrating three hosts. The fourteen Jews were roasted alive (Dubnow, *History of the Jews in Russia and Poland,* vol. 1, p. 55; Margolis and Marx, *History of the Jewish People,* p. 529).

15. Abram L. Sachar, *A History of the Jews,* p. 311; Louis Greenberg, *The Jews in Russia,* p. 8; Rosman, *Lords' Jews,* pp. 4, 106, 110, 114, 115–16, 213, 216, map

p. 12; Dubnow, *History of the Jews in Russia and Poland,* vol. 1, pp. 93, 112. Jews also were dominant in some local and regional commerce, in contrast to the magnates' control over the export of the same material—for example, in the important grain export, in which the produce from the magnates' latifundia went down the Vistula River to the port of Gdansk (Rosman, *Lords' Jews,* pp. 87–89).

16. Abramsky, Jachimczyk, and Polonsky, *Jews in Poland,* p. 3. The limits of a Golden Age for Jews in Poland are given variously as 1580–1648; unknown date– 1586; and "the fifteenth and sixteenth centuries" by the following respective authors: Heller, *On the Edge of Destruction,* p. 24; Dubnow, *History of the Jews in Russia and Poland,* vol. 1, p. 89; and Lucjan Dobroszycki and Barbara Kirshenblatt-Gimblett, *Image before My Eyes: A Photographic History of Jewish Life in Poland, 1864–1939,* p. 41. Poland (the Polish-Lithuanian Commonwealth) was the largest country in Europe in 1634. Among the non-Polish ethnic groups living in Poland and making up 60 percent of the population were "Germans, Ruthenians or Ukrainians, Lithuanians, Belorussians, Armenians, Turks, Italians, Scots, and the largest concentration of Jews in the world at that time. . . . Protestant, Catholic, Orthodox, Armenian, Muslim, and Jew . . . [lived] in close proximity. . . . Poland [was] the main supplier of food and natural products to Western Europe" (Rosman, *Lords' Jews,* p. 1).

17. The *kahal,* however, had been established by the Crown to facilitate the levying of taxes (Daniel Tollet, "Merchants and Businessmen in Poznan and Cracow, 1588–1668," pp. 28–29; Bridger, ed., *The New Jewish Encyclopedia,* qv Kahal). The four regions of the Polish-Lithuanian Commonwealth were Great Poland, Little Poland, Lithuania, and the Ukraine (Abramsky, Jachimczyk, and Polonsky, *Jews in Poland,* p. 3).

18. Magocsi, *History of the Ukraine,* pp. 200–02; Stampfer, "What Actually Happened to the Jews"; Margolis and Marx, *History of the Jewish People,* p. 555–56. In Ukrainian history, the period of "disintegration of Ukrainian statehood and general decline" from 1657 (death of Khmelnytsky), or earlier to 1687 (rise of Mazepa) is known as "the Ruin" (*Encyclopedia of Ukraine,* qv Poland; Ruin).

19. Heller, *On the Edge of Destruction,* p. 27; *Encyclopedia Britannica,* qv Shaabetai Tzevi; Margolis and Marx, *History of the Jewish People,* p. 565.

20. Heller, *On the Edge of Destruction,* p. 27.

21. Margolis and Marx, *History of the Jewish People,* pp. 578–79, 581.

22. Rosman, *Lords' Jews,* p. 210.

23. Ibid., p. 39.

24. Heller, *On the Edge of Destruction,* p. 28.

25. Magocsi, *History of the Ukraine,* p. 295. See *Encyclopedia of Ukraine,* qv Poland; Haidamaka Uprisings; Dubnow, *History of the Jews in Russia and Poland,* vol. 1, p. 182–86; Rosman, *Lords' Jews,* p. 4.

26. Rosman's study of Polish latifundia leads him to the following conclusion about Hasidism that is contrary to the common view: "The picture of Jewish life on the eighteenth-century magnate latifundia presented here cannot support the idea that Hasidism was a response of downtrodden people seeking a mystical release from the desperation of everyday life, or of disillusioned messianists needing

an outlet to diffuse their frustrated beliefs. Hasidism did not begin in the wake of 1648, nor in response to the abolition of the Council of Four Lands, nor in the aftermath of Frankism" (Rosman, *Lords' Jews*, p. 211).

27. Bridger, ed., *New Jewish Encyclopedia*, qv Gaon of Vilna; qv Hasidism.

28. Abramsky, Jachimczyk, and Polonsky, *Jews in Poland*, map, p. x.

29. Lucy S. Dawidowicz, ed., *The Golden Tradition: Jewish Life and Thought in Eastern Europe*, p. 13. After the Judaizing heresy in Russia in the last quarter of the fifteenth century was suppressed, Jews were to be denied entrance into Russia. The Russian army also routinely exterminated Jews in territories they conquered, until the end of the Polish partitions at the end of the eighteenth century (Ben-Sasson, *History of the Jewish People*, p. 571).

30. The Pale, formed by Catherine, was effectively abolished by Alexander Kerensky in 1917, in his first act as head of the Provisional Government (Henry Abramson, *A Prayer for the Government: Ukrainians and Jews in Revolutionary Times, 1917–1920*, pp. 3, 4, 34.

31. Howard M. Sachar, *The Course of Modern Jewish History*, pp. 73, 74; Daniel Beauvois, "Polish-Jewish Relations in the Territories Annexed by the Russian Empire in the First Half of the Nineteenth Century," pp. 78–90; Abramsky, Jachimczyk, and Polonsky, *Jews in Poland*, p. 78.

32. Ben-Sasson, *History of the Jewish People*, p. 790.

33. Rosman, *Lords' Jews*, p. 212; *Encyclopedia Britannica*, qv Poland.

34. Ibid.

35. Martin Gilbert states that 14 to 20 percent of Jews in any province in the Pale of Settlement received poor relief from the Jewish community (Gilbert, *Jews of Russia*, p. 25). Joachim Schoenfeld estimates that in his shtetl, 20 percent of the Jews were extremely poor, and "many" of these "depended on charity" (Schoenfeld, *Shtetl Memories: Jewish Life in Galicia under the Austro-Hungarian Empire and in the Reborn Poland, 1898–1939*, pp. 22–23).

36. Ben-Sasson, *History of the Jewish People*, p. 794.

37. Ibid., p. 773.

38. When Tsar Alexander II was assassinated in 1881 (March 1), one of the six conspirators sentenced to death was a Jew. The government abetted a series of pogroms beginning in Elizavetgrad in mid-April and spreading rapidly to more than one hundred other Ukrainian towns and cities, including Kiev and Odessa. Scattered pogroms continued through 1884. A deadlier kind of pogrom would begin in April 1903 in Kishinev, Bessarabia (Greenberg, *Jews in Russia*, p. 151; Ben-Sasson, *History of the Jewish People*, pp. 881–83, 886–87).

39. Roth and Wigoder, *New Standard Jewish Encyclopedia*, qv Hasidism; Catherine; Bridger, ed., *New Jewish Encyclopedia*, qv Hasidism; Haskalah; Ben-Sasson, *History of the Jewish People*, pp. 782, 790, 794. The first Zionist Congress met in Basel, Switzerland, in 1897 (*Encyclopedia Britannica*, qv Zionism).

40. Ruth Wisse, *A Shtetl and Other Yiddish Novellas*, pp. ix, x, 16, 25, 252–53. Zipperstein, "The Shtetl Revisited," pp. 19–21. Pinchuk, in a set of articles in preparation for his promised book about the shtetl, contends that the shtetl was a distinctively Jewish town that not only did not deteriorate from the late nineteenth

century onward, but in fact was reinvigorated (Pinchuk, "The Shtetl: An Ethnic Town"; "How Jewish Was the Shtetl?"; "Jewish Discourse and the Shtetl"; and "The East European Shtetl"). The prevailing concept of the disappearing shtetl appears to be based on the view that the preeminence of Orthodox Jewish practice and its accompanying community were disappearing. In contrast, the challenge is based on the view that population numbers were stable, and the "Jewishness" of both the shtetl community and its individuals remained, because it "consisted of many elements, most of them not related to religion (e.g., language, social structure, external appearance, etc.) whose sum total was distinctiveness relative to the surrounding society" (Pinchuk, "The East European Shtetl," p. 196).

Appendix B

1. For example, Roskies and Roskies, *Shtetl Book;* Levitats, *Jewish Community in Russia,* p. 214.

2. "For by the beginning of the early twentieth century the web had been broken; exit was possible; contacts had been established; new ideas had prepared young Jews for transition to another civilization" (Samuel, *World of Sholom Aleichem,* p. 285). The period from 1920 to 1945 was a time of change and modernization, almost entirely coinciding with Stalin's rule.

3. As of June 2004, the number of memorial books (*Yizkor Bikher*) at Yad Vashem was 1293. Of these, 202 (15.6 percent) were written in English, in whole or in part; for example, Bisberg-Youkelson and Youkelson, *The Life and Death of a Polish Shtetl* (Yad Vashem Reference and Information Services, personal communication).

4. Yaffa Eliach, *There Once Was a World: A Nine-Hundred-Year Chronicle of the Shtetl of Eishyshok;* Theo Richmond, *Konin: One Man's Quest for a Vanished Jewish Community;* Roskies, *Jewish Search for a Usable Past,* p. 61.

5. Kirshenblatt-Gimblett, "Introduction," in Zborowski and Herzog, *Life Is with People,* pp. xii–xiii, xl; Dan Miron, "Introduction," in S. Y. Abramovitsh (Mendele Mocher Seforim) *Tales of Mendele the Book Peddler; Fishke the Lame and Benjamin the Third,* pp. xxvii, xxxviii–xl; Miron, *Image of the Shtetl,* pp. 4, 6, 12–13; Roskies, *Jewish Search for a Usable Past,* pp. 41, 69. Kirshenblatt-Gimblett, in her excellent introduction to the book *Life Is with People* (1995) argued that the influential movie *Fiddler on the Roof,* together with its two progenitors—the Tevye the dairyman stories by Sholem Aleichem, and the book *Life Is with People,* by Zborowski and Herzog—had fostered a popular image of the shtetl that was false. She saw *Life Is with People,* forty years after its debut, to be a romanticized, idealized, or sentimental description of the shtetl (p. xxxviii). She recognized that "Several books were written as correctives to the image of East European Jewish life represented in *Life Is with People*" (p. xxiv, note 34, p. xliv). These are the following seven texts written from 1967 to 1994: Dawidowicz, *Golden Tradition;* Roskies and Roskies, *Shtetl Book;* Dobroszycki and Kirshenblatt-Gimblett, *Image before My Eyes;* Heller, *On the Edge of Destruction;* Ghitta Sternberg, *Stefanesti: Portrait of a Romanian Shtetl;* Zipperstein, "The Shtetl Revisited," pp. 17–24; Orla-Bukowska, "Shtetl Communities," pp. 89–113.

6. Hillel Halkin, "Introduction," in Sholom Aleichem, *Tevye the Dairyman and the Railroad Stories,* pp. xxxiii–xxxvi.

7. The six instances and their locations in the present text are as follows: (a) potato lamp: note 1 (chapter 10); (b) Kiev residence permit raids: note 5 (chapter 13); (c) "hooligan": note 4 (chapter 21); (d) cursing by Jewish women: note 2 (chapter 23); (e) Jewish women read secular books: note 8 (appendix B); and (f) Jewish women married Christian men in the shtetl: note 10 (appendix B).

8. Sholom Aleichem mentions the Arabian Nights tales as "*toysend-ayn-nakht*" ("one thousand and one nights"), in his complete works (Sholem Aleykhem, *Ale Verk Fun Sholom Aleykhem,* vol. 5, p. 190). (English translation in: "Tevye Goes to Palestine" in Marvin S. Zuckerman and Marion Herbst, *Selected Works of Sholem-Aleykhem,* pp. xvii, 454.)

9. Eva Hoffman, *Shtetl: The Life and Death of a Small Town and the World of Polish Jews,* p. 145; Irving Howe and Eliezer Greenberg, *A Treasury of Yiddish Stories,* p. 73; Roth and Wigoder, *New Standard Jewish Encyclopedia,* qv chapbooks; Charlotte Baum, Paula Hyman, and Sonya Michel, *The Jewish Woman in America,* p. 6; Zborowski and Herzog, *Life Is with People: The Jewish Little Town of Eastern Europe,* pp. 126–27; Roskies, *Jewish Search for a Usable Past,* p. 5; Pauline Wengeroff, *Rememberings: The World of a Russian-Jewish Woman in the Nineteenth Century,* p. 122; Joachim Neugroschel, *The Shtetl,* p. 266; Iris Parush, *Reading Jewish Women: Marginality and Modernization in Nineteenth-Century Eastern European Jewish Society,* pp. 133, 140.

10. Chava, daughter of Tevye the dairyman, marries Chvedka, a village peasant (Sholem Aleichem, *Tevye the Dairyman and the Railroad Stories,* pp. 69–82).

11. Joseph Morgenstern, *I Have Considered My Days,* p. 59.

12. Morrie Feller and Leonard Prager, "Dreyfus in kasrilevke" (Sholem-Aleykhem); Howe and Greenberg, *Treasury of Yiddish Stories,* p. 189.

13. Lincoln, *In War's Dark Shadow,* p. 27. In Russian, "*zhid*" is pejorative and vulgar for "Jew" (Wheeler, *Oxford Russian-English Dictionary;* Louis Segal, ed., *New Complete Russian-English Dictionary,* qv *zhid*) (feminine, "zhidovka.") In Yiddish, Harkavy gives "Jew (in contempt)" for "*zhid*"; "Jewess (in contempt)" for "*zhidovkeh*"; and "Jewish (in contempt)" for "*zhidovskeh.*"(Harkavy, *Yiddish-English and English-Yiddish Dictionary*).

14. The "third bell" is mentioned in Sholom Aleichem, "Cnards," p. 425.

15. Karl Baedeker, *Baedeker's Russia,* pp. xx–xxiv.

16. Sholom Aleichem, "Sticks and Stones May Break My Bones," pp. 145, 147; Sholem Aleichem, *Bloody Hoax,* p. 113.

17. For *oblavy,* see chapter 13, note 5.

18. Sholom Aleichem, "Sticks and Stones May Break My Bones," pp. 145, 147.

19. Dawidowicz, *Golden Tradition,* p. 311. In possible confirmation (I have not yet been able to trace the actual article of Russian law described), the following passage occurs in 2004 in an essay in Russian about nineteenth century Russian law: "Policemen received money awards for every person detained due to passport violations. If a person with an expired passport was detained, he or she would be punished by 2 or 3 days of incarceration and sent to the place of permanent residence. If the detained person did not have any identification, but could prove his

identity by other means, this person would be sent home with the transport of prisoners. If the identity could not be proven, he would be treated as a common vagrant. Vagrancy was considered a crime, punishable by deportation to Siberia" (Vassily Dybel, *Pasportnaya Sistema Rossii: Istoricheskiy Aspekt [Russian Passport Systems: Historical Perspective]*.

20. Miron, "Introduction," p. xxxix; Halkin, "Introduction," p. xxxiv; Sholem Aleichem, *Bloody Hoax*, pp. xi, xiii; Ken Frieden, *Classic Yiddish Fiction: Abramovitsh, Sholem Aleichem, and Peretz*, p. 112.

21. Frieden, *Classic Yiddish Fiction*, pp. 122–24.

22. Zborowski and Herzog, *Life Is with People* (1995); Sternberg, *Stefanesti*; Orla-Bukowska, "Shtetl Communities," 89–113; Sydney Stahl Weinberg, *The World of Our Mothers: The Lives of Jewish Immigrant Women*.

23. Kirshenblatt-Gimblett, "Introduction," ix–xlviii.

24. "[M]uch of what had been written on shtetl life for English-speaking readers understands such literary representation [the literary world of Mendele Mocher Seforim, Sholom Aleichem, and Peretz], as history." "Clearly this is the case for the most influential of all such work, Mark Zborowski and Elizabeth Herzog's 1952 anthropological study *Life Is with People* . . . the Broadway play's producers admitted that *Life Is with People* was a primary inspiration . . . on the making of *Fiddler on the Roof*" (Zipperstein, "The Shtetl Revisited," p. 22).

25. Abraham Ain, "Swislocz: Portrait of a Jewish Community in Eastern Europe," in Deborah Dash Moore, ed., *East European Jews in Two Worlds: Studies from the YIVO Annual*, pp. 1–21.

26. Hirsch Abramovicz, "Rural Jewish Occupations in Lithuania," in Hirsz Abramowicz, *Profiles of a Lost World: Memoirs of East European Jewish Life before World War II*, pp. 9, 24–25, 41–76.

27. Memoirs about shtetl life are uneven in total length, and in the proportion of the total in which information about a shtetl is contained. The section about the shtetl in these memoirs may occupy fewer than 30 pages (Abe Koosis, *Child of War and Revolution: The Memoirs of Abe Koosis*), or more than 250 (Edith LaZebnik, *Such a Life*; Bella Chagall, *Burning Lights: Thirty-Six Drawings by Marc Chagall*). Koosis's entire memoir occupies only 63 pages, Leibenson's has 77. LaZebnik's has 287 pages; Chagall's, 262 pages. Five regions within the Pale of Settlement contain the shtetls mentioned in the 27 memoirs by men and women: (1) Congress Poland, four memoirs (Asch, Peretz, Shapiro, Shtern); (2) Galicia, two memoirs (Miller, Schoenfeld); (3) Lithuania, four memoirs (Abramowicz, Aronson, Leibenson, Lown); (4) Ukraine, nine memoirs (Burroughs, Charnofsky, Gannes, Gray, Koosis, LaZebnik, Leonard, Sholom Aleichem, Wilcher); and (5) White Russia, seven memoirs (Assaf, Chagall, Laikin, Lisitsky, Mendele, Morgenstern, Zunser); and multiple authors, one memoir (Sogolow). See bibliography for full titles and publication information.

28. Schoenfeld, *Shtetl Memories*.

29. LaZebnik's "son Jack, an English professor . . . turned the disorganized manuscript into a publishable memoir" (n.p., book review by Jakki Savan, n.d.).

30. The nineteen autobiographical memoirs by men are Abramowicz, 1999,

pp. 9, 41–76, 24–25; Aronson, 1983; Asch, 1948; Burroughs, 1930; Charnofsky, 1965; Gannes, 1993; Koosis, 1984; Kotik, 2002; Laikin, 1971; Leibenson, 1991; Lisitzky, 2001; Mendele Mocher Seforim, 1986, pp. 254–358; Morgenstern, 1964; Miller, 1980; Peretz, 2002, pp. 263–359; Schoenfeld, 1985; Sholom Aleichem, 1985; Shtern, 1990, pp. 51–70; and Wilcher, 1992. Five of the nineteen books can be considered full-length, with 250 or more pages that concern a shtetl (Aronson, 1983; Burroughs, 1930; Charnofsky, 1965; Kotik, 2002; and Sholom Aleichem, 1985). See bibliography for full titles and publication information.

31. Aronson, Charnofsky, Kotik, Lisitzky, Mendele Mocher Seforim (1836–1917), Morgenstern, Isaac Leib Peretz (1851–1915), Sholom Aleichem (1859–1916), and Sholem Asch (1880–1957).

32. Burroughs, Gannes, Koosis, Laikin, Leibenson, Schoenfeld, Shtern, Wilcher.

33. Abramowicz, Miller.

34. The eight autobiographical memoirs by women are: Chagall, 1996; Gray, 1978; Lazebnik, 1978; Leonard, 2000; Lown, 1991; Shapiro, 2002; Sogolow, 1996; and Zunser, 1978. Four of the autobiographical memoirs by women are full-length (250 pages or more) books about life in a shtetl (Chagall, 1996; LaZebnik, 1978; Shapiro, 2002; Zunser, 1978). See bibliography for full titles and publication information.

Appendix C

1. My approach to Anna's story has been shaped both by an interest in historical accuracy and by personal experience as a neurologist with a research interest in dementia. As a member of the Washington University in St. Louis Memory and Aging Project, I had the opportunity to interview the healthy elderly as well as those with memory impairment and to participate in the development and validation of the Washington University in St. Louis Clinical Dementia Rating assessment for the early diagnosis and staging of Alzheimer's disease.

2. Anna probably went ice-skating in February, judging from the fact that she arrived in Petrograd in winter (in February, she said), and that she was still on a crutch and in a cast when she saw Trotsky speak early in March. Fractured bones heal in children in about two-thirds the time taken in adults of eighteen years and older. Thus, a fracture in a child's foot heals on average in four weeks (adults six weeks), and in the lower leg in eight weeks (adults twelve) (H. Gary Parker, *Sports Medicine Primer*, http://www.mainebones.com/Articles/article19.htm).

3. Klavdia Kolesnikova, personal communication, August 10, 1998.

4. Pasternak, *Doctor Zhivago*, pp. 164–65.

5. Got'e, *Time of Troubles*, pp. 307, 316.

6. Jean Meeus, Carl C. Grosjean, and Willy Vanderleen, *Canon of Solar Eclipses*.

7. Chekhov, *The Oxford Chekhov*, vol. 8, pp. 3–5; Chekhov, *Anton Chekhov: Selected Stories*, p. xvi.

8. Anna may well have read Chekhov's story "Peasants." I did not ask her about this, but I would be surprised if she had not read it. She once suggested that I read Gogol's "Dead Souls" for its portrayal of peasant bondage. It is likely that

she had read other descriptions of peasant life by the Russian masters. Even so, she had been inside peasant homes in Korsun, had seen the icon corner, had been to the wedding of a schoolmate who came from a family of house servants, had observed peasant schoolmates, and had worked with Khveodora the maid and with Domakho the milk lady.

9. The ship manifest shows that Leya Spector and her three daughters departed Bremen, Germany, for New York on February 21, 1922, on the SS *America*.

10. Norman Sims and Mark Kramer, eds., *Literary Journalism: A New Collection of the Best American Nonfiction,* pp. 22–33.

Bibliography

Abramowicz, Hirsch. "Rural Jewish Occupations in Lithuania." In Hirsz Abramowicz, *Profiles of a Lost World: Memoirs of East European Jewish Life before World War II*. Trans. Eva Zeitlin Dobkin. Ed. Dina Abramowicz and Jeffrey Shandler. Detroit: Wayne State University Press, 1999.

Abramsky, Chimen, Maciej Jachimczyk, and Antony Polonsky. "Introduction." *The Jews in Poland*. Oxford: Basil Blackwell, 1986.

Abramson, Henry. *A Prayer for the Government: Ukrainians and Jews in Revolutionary Times, 1917–1920*. Cambridge, MA: Harvard University Press, 1999.

Adler, Ruth. *Women of the Shtetl—Through the Eyes of Y. L. Peretz*. Cranbury, NJ: Fairleigh Associated University Presses, 1980.

Ain, Abraham. "Swislocz: Portrait of a Jewish Community in Eastern Europe." In Deborah Dash Moore, ed., *East European Jews in Two Worlds: Studies from the YIVO Annual*. Evanston, IL: Northwestern University Press, 1990.

American Heritage Dictionary of the English Language, 4th ed. Boston: Houghton Mifflin, 2002.

Andrusyshen, C. H. and J. N. Krett. *Ukrainian-English Dictionary*. Toronto: University of Toronto Press, 2001.

Armstrong, John H. *The Railroad, What It Is, What It Does: The Introduction to Railroading*, 3rd ed. Omaha: Simmons-Boardman, 1990.

Aronson, Chaim. *A Jewish Life under the Tsars: The Autobiography of Chaim Aronson, 1825–1888*. Trans. Norman Marsden. Totowa, NJ: Allanheld and Osmun, 1983.

Arshinov, Peter. *History of the Makhnovist Movement, 1918–1921*. Trans. Lorraine and Fredy Perlman. Detroit: Black and Red, 1974.

Asch, Sholem. "The Little Town." In *Tales of My People*. Trans. Meyer Levin. New York: Putnam, 1948.

Augé, Gillon, ed. *Petit Larousse*. Paris: Libraire Larousse, 1963.

Babel, Isaac. "The Road." In *The Collected Stories of Isaac Babel*, ed. Nathalie Babel. Trans. Peter Constantine. New York: W. W. Norton, 2002.

Baker, A. B., and L. H. Baker. *Clinical Neurology.* Vol. 2. Philadelphia: J. B. Lippincott, 1991.

Bauernfeind, J. Christopher, ed. *Vitamin A Deficiency and Its Control.* Orlando: Academic Press, 1986.

Baum, Charlotte, Paula Hyman, and Sonya Michel. *The Jewish Woman in America.* New York: New American Library, 1976.

Beauvois, Daniel. "Polish-Jewish Relations in the Territories Annexed by the Russian Empire in the First Half of the Nineteenth Century." In Abramsky, Jachimczyk, and Polonsky, *The Jews in Poland.*

Ben-Sasson, H. H. *A History of the Jewish People.* Cambridge, MA: Harvard University Press, 1976.

Berkman, Alexander. *The Bolshevik Myth: Diary 1920–1922.* London: Pluto, 1989.

Bisberg-Youkelson, Feigl, and Rubin Youkelson, eds., *The Life and Death of a Polish Shtetl.* Trans. Gene Bluestein. Lincoln: University of Nebraska Press, 2000.

Bose, T. K., T. K. Das, and G. G. Maiti, eds. *Trees of the World.* Vol. 1. Bhubaneswar, Orissa, India: Regional Plant Resource Centre, 1998.

Bridger, David, ed. *The New Jewish Encyclopedia.* New York: Behrman, 1962.

Brown, Kate. *A Biography of No Place.* Cambridge, MA: Harvard University Press, 2004.

Bulgakov, Mikhail. "The Blizzard." In *A Country Doctor's Notebook.* Trans. Michael Glenny. London: Collins, 1975.

———. *Diaboliad, and Other Stories,* ed. Ellendea Proffer and Carl R. Proffer. Bloomington: Indiana University Press, 1972.

———. *The White Guard.* Trans. Michael Glenny. New York: McGraw-Hill, 1971.

Burroughs, Harry E. *Tale of a Vanished Land: Memories of a Childhood in Old Russia.* Boston: Houghton Mifflin, 1930.

Carpenter, Kenneth J. *The History of Scurvy and Vitamin C.* Cambridge: Cambridge University Press, 1986.

Cassell's French Dictionary. Ed. Ernest Baker. Rev. J. L. Manchon. New York: Funk and Wagnalls, 1965.

Cecil Textbook of Medicine, 17th ed. Ed. James B. Wyngaarden and Lloyd H. Smith Jr. Philadelphia: W. B. Saunders, 1985.

Chagall, Bella. *Burning Lights: Thirty-Six Drawings by Marc Chagall [Brenendike likht].* Trans. Norbert Guterman [from Yiddish]. New York: Biblio Press, 1996; Schocken Books, [1946; 1983; 1996].

Charnofsky, Michael. *Jewish Life in the Ukraine: A Family Saga.* New York: Exposition Press, 1965.

Chazan, Robert. *European Jewry and the First Crusade.* Berkeley: University of California Press, 1996.

Chekhov, Anton. *Anton Chekhov: Selected Stories.* Trans. Ann Dunnigan. New York: Signet, 1962.

———. "The Hollow." In *The Stories of Anton Chekhov.* Ed. Robert N. Linscott. New York: Modern Library, 1932.

———. "In the Ravine." In Avrahm Yarmolinsky, ed., *The Portable Chekhov.* New York: Penguin, 1977.

——. "On the Train." In *The Undiscovered Chekhov: Thirty-Eight New Stories*. Trans. Peter Constantine. New York: Seven Stories Press, 1998.

——. *The Oxford Chekhov,* Vol. 8: *Stories 1895–1897.* Trans. and ed. Ronald Hingley. London: Oxford University Press, 1965.

Cohen, Israel. *Vilna.* Philadelphia: Jewish Publication Society of America, 1992.

Dawidowicz, Lucy S., ed., *The Golden Tradition: Jewish Life and Thought in Eastern Europe.* New York: Holt, Rinehart and Winston, 1967.

Decter, Moshe. "The Old Country Way of Life: The Rediscovery of the Shtetl." *Commentary* 13 (Jan.–June 1952): 604.

Dirr, Michael A. *Dirr's Hardy Trees and Shrubs: An Illustrated Encyclopedia.* Portland, OR: Timber Press, 1997.

Dobroszycki, Lucjan, and Barbara Kirshenblatt-Gimblett. *Image before My Eyes: A Photographic History of Jewish Life in Poland, 1864–1939.* New York: Schocken Books, 1977.

Dubnow, Simon M. *History of the Jews.* [*Istoriia evreiskogo naroda na Vostoka*]. Vol. 5. Trans. Moshe Spiegel. New York: Thomas Yoseloff, 1973.

——. *History of the Jews in Russia and Poland: From the Earliest Times until the Present Day.* Vols. 1, 2, 3. Trans. I. Friedlander. Philadelphia: Jewish Publication Society of America, 1918, 1920.

Duranty, Walter. *Duranty Reports Russia.* New York: Viking Press, 1934.

Dybel, Vassily. *Pasportnaya Sistema Rossii:Istoricheskiy Aspekt* [*Russian Passport Systems: Historical Perspective*] http://www.nasledie.ru/oboz/05_03/5_15.HTM. Trans. Vladimir Feldman.

Eliach, Yaffa. *There Once Was a World: A Nine-Hundred-Year Chronicle of the Shtetl of Eishyshok.* New York: Little Brown, 1998.

Ellis, Cuthbert Hamilton. *The Pictorial Encyclopedia of Railways.* London: Hamlyn, 1968.

Encyclopedia Britannica, 15th ed. Vols. 4, 5. Chicago: Helen H. Benton, 1974.

Encyclopaedia Judaica. [New York] Macmillan, 1971–1972.

Encyclopedia of Ukraine. Vol. 1. Ed. Danylo H. Struk. Toronto: University of Toronto Press, 1988.

Espenak, Fred. *Maps of "Total and Annular Solar Eclipse Paths."* http://sunearth. gsfc.nasa.gov/eclipse/SEatlas/SEatlas2.html. Planetary Systems Branch, Code 693 NASA/Goddard Space Flight Center Greenbelt, MD 20771.

——. Personal communication, e-mail, August 20, 2002.

Estraikh, Gennady, and Mikhail Krutikov. "Preface." In Gennady Estraikh and Mikhail Krutikov, "Shtetl Image and Reality." Papers of the Second Mendel Friedman International Conference on Yiddish. Oxford: Legenda, 2000.

Feller, Morrie, and Leonard Prager. "Dreyfus in kasrilevke" (Sholem-Aleykhem). *The Mendele Review: Yiddish Literature and Language* 5, no. 4 (April 13, 2001).

Figes, Orlando. *A People's Tragedy: The Russian Revolution, 1891–1924.* New York: Penguin, 1996.

Fodor's 91 Soviet Union. Map, p. 130. New York: Fodor's Travel Publications, 1991.

Frieden, Ken. *Classic Yiddish Fiction: Abramovitsh, Sholem Aleichem, and Peretz.* Albany: State University of New York Press, 1995.

Frishman, David. Quoted in Dan Miron, "Introduction." S. Y. Abramovitsh (Mendele Mokher Sforim), *Tales of Mendele the Book Peddler; Fishke the Lame and Benjamin the Third.* Ed. Dan Miron and Ken Frieden. New York: Schocken Books, 1996.

Gannes, Abraham P. *Childhood in a Shtetl.* Cupertino, CA: Ganton Books, 1993.

Gilbert, Martin. *The Jews of Russia,* 3rd ed. Israel: Steimatzky and the *Jerusalem Post,* 1979.

Gogol, Nikolai. *The Collected Tales of Nikolai Gogol.* Trans. Richard Pevear, Larissa Volokhonsky. New York, Pantheon, 1998.

Got'e, Iurii Vladimirovich. *Time of Troubles, The Diary of Iurii Vladimirovich Got'e: Moscow, July 8, 1917, to July 23, 1922.* Trans. Terrence Emmons. Princeton, NJ: Princeton University Press, 1988.

Gray, Bettyanne. *Manya's Story.* Minneapolis: Lerner Publications, 1978.

Greenberg, Louis. *The Jews in Russia.* New Haven, CT: Yale University Press, 1944; 1965.

Gribetz, Judah. *The Timetables of Jewish History.* New York: Simon and Schuster, 1993.

Gross, Max. "Traveling Back to a Place of the Past." Review of Andrew Goldberg's *A Yiddish World Remembered,* a film documentary to be shown on PBS. In *Forward,* August 9, 2002.

Guillermier, Pierre, and Serge Koutchmy. *Total Eclipses: Science, Observations, Myths, and Legends.* New York: Springer, 1999.

Halkin, Hillel. "Introduction." In Sholom Aleichem, *Tevye the Dairyman and the Railroad Stories.* Trans. Hillel Halkin. New York: Schocken Books, 1987.

Hamm, Michael F. *Kiev: A Portrait, 1800–1917.* Princeton, NJ: Princeton University Press, 1993.

Harkavy, Alexander. *Yiddish-English and English-Yiddish Dictionary,* 22nd ed. New York: Hebrew Publishing Co., 1928.

Harrison, T. R., et al., eds. *Principles of Internal Medicine,* 3rd ed. New York: McGraw-Hill, 1958.

Heller, Celia S. *On the Edge of Destruction: Jews of Poland between the Two World Wars.* New York: Columbia University Press, 1977.

Heschel, Abraham Joshua. *The Earth Is the Lord's.* New York: H. Schuman, 1950; New York: Jewish Lights, 1995.

Hoffman, Eva. *Shtetl: The Life and Death of a Small Town and the World of Polish Jews.* Boston: Houghton Mifflin, 1997.

Howe, Irving, and Eliezer Greenberg, eds. *A Treasury of Yiddish Stories.* New York: Meridian Books, 1956.

———. *A Treasury of Yiddish Stories.* New York: Schocken Books, 1973.

Hunczak, Taras. *Symon Petliura and the Jews: A Reappraisal.* Toronto: Ukrainian Historical Association, 1985.

Kaffka, Stephen. Personal communication, e-mail, January 28, 2002.

Karl Baedeker. *Baedeker's Handbook for Travellers: Russia, with Teheran, Port Arthur, and Peking 1914.* n.p.: Arno Press, Random House, 1971 reprint).

———. *St. Petersburg.* Modern series, 2nd edition, n.d.

Katz, Jacob. *Exclusiveness and Tolerance: Studies in Jewish-Gentile Relations in Medieval and Modern Times.* New York: Schocken Books, 1962.

Kenez, Peter. "Pogroms and White Ideology in the Russian Civil War." In Klier and Lambroza, ed.s, *Pogroms: Anti-Jewish Violence in Modern Russian History.*

Khorol-Sharal, Jenny. Quoted in Rosalie Sogolow, ed., *Memories from a Russian Kitchen: From Shtetl to Golden Land.* Santa Barbara, CA: Fithian Press, 1996.

Kirshenblatt-Gimblett, Barbara. "Introduction." In Zborowski and Herzog, *Life Is with People.*

Klepfisz, Heszel. *The Inexhaustible Wellspring.* Jerusalem: Devora, 2003.

Klier, John, D. "What Exactly Was a Shtetl?" In Estraikh and Krutikov, "Shtetl Image and Reality."

Klier, John D., and Shlomo Lambroza, ed.s. *Pogroms: Anti-Jewish Violence in Modern Russian History.* Cambridge: Cambridge University Press, 1992.

Kolesnikova, Klavdia. Personal communication (letter of August 10, 1998), in English, from Klavdia Kolesnikova, a resident of Korsun and an employee at the Korsun-Shevchenkovsky Historical Cultural Preservation Park.

Koosis, Abe. *Child of War and Revolution: The Memoirs of Abe Koosis.* Oakland, CA: Sea Urchin Press, 1984.

Kotik, Yekhezkel. *Journey to a Nineteenth-Century Shtetl: The Memoirs of Yekhezkel Kotik.* Ed. David Assaf. Detroit: Wayne State University Press, 2002.

Kubijovyc, Volodymyr, ed. *Ukraine: A Concise Encyclopaedia.* Vol. 1. Foreword by Ernest J. Simmons. Toronto: Published for the Ukrainian National Association, University of Toronto, 1963.

Laikin, Benjamin. *Memoirs of a Practical Dreamer: From a Russian Shtetl to an American Suburb.* Trans. Murray Kass and Moshe Starkman [Yiddish]. New York: Bloch, 1971.

LaZebnik, Edith. *Such a Life.* New York: William Morrow, 1978.

Lehmann, Rosa. "Jewish Patrons and Polish Clients: Patronage in a Small Galician Town." *Polin* 17 (2004): 153–70.

Leibenson, Joseph. *Shtetl Memoirs and Others.* Contributors, Sam Levenson et al. n.p., 1991.

Leonard, Joann Rose. *The Soup Has Many Eyes: From Shtetl to Chicago: A Memoir of One Family's Journey through History.* New York: Bantam Books, 2000.

Lerski, George J., and Halina T. Lerski. *Jewish-Polish Coexistence, 1772–1939: A Topical Bibliography.* Foreword by Lucjan Dobroszycki. New York: Greenwood Press, 1986.

Levitats, Isaac. *The Jewish Community in Russia, 1844–1917.* Jerusalem: Posner and Sons, 1981.

Liberman, Anatoly. *Michail Lermontov: Major Poetical Works.* Minneapolis: University of Minnesota Press, 1983.

Library of Congress. "Transportation: The Empire That Was Russia; The Prokudin-

Gorskii Photographic Record Recreated." http://www.loc.gov/exhibits/empire/transport.html.

Lih, Lars T. *Bread and Authority in Russia, 1914–1921*. Berkeley: University of California Press, 1990.

Lincoln, W. Bruce. *In War's Dark Shadow: The Russians before the Great War*. New York: Dial Press, 1983.

———. *Passage through Armageddon: The Russians in War and Revolution, 1914–1918*. New York: Simon and Schuster, 1986.

———. *Red Victory: A History of the Russian Civil War, 1918–1921*. New York: Da Capo, 1999.

Linscott, Robert N., ed. *The Stories of Anton Chekhov*. New York: Modern Library, 1932.

Lisitzky, Ephraim E. *In the Grip of Cross-Currents*. Trans. Moshe Kohn and Jacob Sloan [Hebrew]. Rev. by the author. New York: Bloch, 2001.

Littman, Mark, Ken Willcox, and Fred Espenak. *Totality: Eclipses of the Sun*, 2nd ed. New York: Oxford University Press, 1999.

Lown, Bella. *Memories of My Life: A Personal History of a Lithuanian Shtetl*. Malibu, CA: Joseph Simon, Pangloss Press, 1991.

Magocsi, Paul Robert. *A History of the Ukraine*. Toronto: University of Toronto Press, 1996.

———. Personal communication, letter, December 17, 2002.

Margolis, Max L., and Alexander Marks. *A History of the Jewish People*. Philadelphia: Jewish Publication Society of America, 1927.

Matossian, Mary. "The Peasant Way of Life." In Wayne S. Vucinich, ed. *The Peasant in Nineteenth-Century Russia*. Stanford, CA: Stanford University Press, 1968.

Matusoff, James A. *Blessings, Curses, Hopes, and Fears: Psycho-ostensive Expressions in Yiddish*. Stanford, CA: Stanford University Press, 2000.

Mawdsley, Evan. *The Russian Civil War*. Boston: Allen and Unwin, 1987.

Meeus, Jean, Carl C. Grosjean, and Willy Vanderleen. *Canon of Solar Eclipses*. New York: Pergamon Press, 1966.

Meltzer, Milton. *World of Our Fathers*. New York: Farrar Straus and Giroux, 1974.

Mendele Mocher Seforim. "Of Bygone Days." In Ruth Wisse, ed., *A Shtetl and Other Yiddish Novellas*.

Metzer, J. "Railroad Development and Market Integration: The Case of Tsarist Russia." *Journal of Economic History* 34, no. 3 (1974): 529–50, 535.

Miller, Saul. *Dobromil: Life in a Galician Shtetl*. New York: Loewenthal Press, 1980.

Milne, Leslie. *Mikhail Bulgakov: A Critical Biography*. Cambridge: Cambridge University Press, 1990.

Miron, Dan. *The Image of the Shtetl and Other Studies of Modern Jewish Literary Imagination*. Syracuse, NY: Syracuse University Press, 2000.

———. "Introduction." In S. Y. Abramovitsh (Mendele Mocher Seforim) *Tales of Mendele the Book Peddler; Fishke the Lame and Benjamin the Third*, ed. Dan Miron and Ken Frieden. New York: Schocken Books, 1996.

Moorehead, Alan. *The Russian Revolution*. New York: Harper and Bros., 1958.

Morgenstern, Joseph. *I Have Considered My Days*. New York: Yiddisher Kultur Farband, 1964.

Mosyakin, Sergei, and N. M. Fedoronchuk. *Ukrainian Flora: Vascular Plants of Ukraine: A Nomenclatural Checklist*. Kiev: National Academy of Sciences of Ukraine, n.d.

Neugroschel, Joachim. *The Shtetl*. Trans. Joachim Neugroschel. New York: Richard Marek, 1979.

Nuntius Russia. Personal communication, e-mail, March 24, 2000.

Orla-Bukowska, Annamaria. "Maintaining Borders, Crossing Borders: Social Relationships in the Shtetl." *Polin* 17 (2004): 171–96.

———. "Shtetl Communities: Another Image." *Polin* 8 (1994): 89–113.

Parker, H. Gary. *Sports Medicine Primer*, http://www.mainebones.com/Articles/article19.htm).

Parush, Iris. *Reading Jewish Women: Marginality and Modernization in Nineteenth-Century Eastern European Jewish Society* [*Nashim kor'ot*.] Trans. Saadya Sternberg. Waltham, MA: Brandeis University Press, Hanover: University Press of New England, 2004.

Pasternak, Boris. *Dr. Zhivago*. New York: Pantheon, 1958.

Peretz, Isaac Leib. "My Memoirs." In Ruth R. Wisse, ed. *The I. L. Peretz Reader*. New Haven, CT: Yale University Press, 2002.

Philologos. "Fusion without Confusion." *Forward*, July 19, 2002, p. 13. Available at http://www.forward.com/issues/2002/02.07.19/arts4.html.

Pinchuk, Ben-Cion. "The East European Shtetl and Its Place in Jewish History." *Revue des études juives* 164, no. 1 (2005): 187–212.

———. "How Jewish Was the Shtetl?" *Polin* 17 (2004): 109–18.

———. "Jewish Discourse and the Shtetl." *Jewish History* 15, no. 2 (2001): 169–79.

———. "The Shtetl: An Ethnic Town in the Russian Empire." *Cahiers du Monde Russe* 41, no. 4 (Oct.–Dec. 2000): 495–504, 637–38.

Pipes, Richard. *The Russian Revolution*. New York: Alfred A. Knopf, 1990.

———. *Russia Under the Old Regime*. New York: Scribner, 1974.

Podvesko, M. L., ed., *Ukrainian-English Dictionary*. n.p.: Peredrook Offset Drookom, 1962.

Pogonowski, Iwo. *Jews in Poland: A Documentary History*. New York: Hippocrene Books, 1993.

Polonsky, Antony, ed. "The Shtetl: Myth and Reality." *Polin* 17 (2004): 3–278.

Pushkin, Alexander. *The Collected Stories*. Trans. Paul Debreczeny. New York: Alfred A. Knopf, 1999.

Rabinowitch, Alexander. *The Bolsheviks Come to Power: The Revolutions of 1917 in Petrograd*. New York: W. W. Norton, 1976.

Ransome, Arthur. *Six Weeks in Russia in 1919*. London: Allen and Unwin, 1919.

Richmond, Theo. *Konin: One Man's Quest for a Vanished Jewish Community*. New York: Pantheon, 1995.

Roskies, David G. *The Jewish Search for a Usable Past*. Bloomington: Indiana University Press, 1999.

Roskies, Diane K., and David G. Roskies. *The Shtetl Book.* n.p.: KTAV Publishing House, 1975.

Roslund, Roger. Personal communication, e-mail, March–October 2002, citing *Big Chief News* 15, no. 1 (Fall 1995).

Rosman, Murray J. *The Lords' Jews: Magnate-Jewish Relations in the Polish-Lithuanian Commonwealth during the Eighteenth Century.* Cambridge, MA: Center for Jewish Studies, Harvard University Press, 1993.

Roth, Cecil, and Geoffrey Wigoder, eds. *The New Standard Jewish Encyclopedia,* 4th ed. New York: Doubleday, 1970.

Ruhl, Arthur. *White Nights and Other Russian Impressions.* New York: C. Scribner's Sons, 1917.

Sachar, Abram L. *A History of the Jews,* 5th ed. New York: Alfred Knopf, 1965.

Sachar, Howard M. *The Course of Modern Jewish History.* New York: Vintage, 1990.

Samuel, Maurice. *The World of Sholom Aleichem.* New York: Schocken Books, 1943, 1965.

Schoenfeld, Joachim. *Shtetl Memories: Jewish Life in Galicia under the Austro-Hungarian Empire and in the Reborn Poland, 1898–1939.* Hoboken, NJ: Ktav, 1985.

Segal, Louis, ed. *New Complete Russian-English Dictionary.* New York: G. E. Stechert and Co., 1942.

Shapiro, Malkah. *The Rebbe's Daughter: Memoir of a Hasidic Childhood.* Philadelphia: Jewish Publication Society, 2002.

Sholem Aleykhem. *Ale Verk Fun Sholom Aleykhem.* New York: Sholom Aleykhem Folksfond Oysgabe, 1917–1923.

Sholom Aleichem. "Benny's Luck." In *Holiday Tales of Sholom Aleichem.* Trans. Aliza Shifrin. New York: Scribner, 1979.

———. *The Bloody Hoax.* Trans. Aliza Shevrin. Bloomington: Indiana University Press, 1991.

———. "Cnards." In *Selected Stories of Sholom Aleichem.* Intro. Alfred Kazin. New York: Modern Library, 1956.

———. *From the Fair: The Autobiography of Sholom Aleichem.* Trans. and ed. Curt Leviant. New York: Viking, 1985.

———. "Gitl Purishkevitch." In *Old Country Tales.* Trans. Curt Leviant [from Hebrew]. New York: G. P. Putnam's Sons, 1969a.

———. "Millions." In *The Adventures of Menahem-Mendl.* Trans. Tamara Kahana. New York: G. P. Putnam's Sons, 1969b.

———. "Sticks and Stones May Break My Bones." In *Old Country Tales.* Trans. Curt Leviant [from Hebrew]. New York: G. P. Putnam's Sons, 1969a.

———. *Tevye the Dairyman and the Railroad Stories.* Trans. Hillel Halkin. New York: Schocken, 1987.

———. "Third Class." Glossary entry in *Collected Stories of Sholem Aleichem: Tevye's Daughters.* Trans. Frances Butwin. New York: Crown, 1949.

Shtern, Yekhiel "A Kheder in Tyszowce." In Deborah Dash Moore, ed., *East Euro-*

pean Jews in Two Worlds: Studies from the YIVO Annual. Evanston, IL: Northwestern University Press, 1990.

Shtif, Nahum. *Pogromy na Ukraine: Period Dobrovolcheskoi Armii*. Berlin: Izdatelstvo "Vostok," 1922.

Sims, Norman, and Mark Kramer, eds., *Literary Journalism: A New Collection of the Best American Nonfiction*. New York: Ballantine, 1995.

Singer, Isaac Bashevis. "Big and Little." In *Short Friday and Other Stories*. New York: Farrar, Straus, and Giroux, 1964.

——. *In My Father's Court*. New York: Farrar, Straus, Giroux, 1966.

Sogolow, Rosalie, ed. *Memories from a Russian Kitchen: From Shtetl to Golden Land*. Santa Barbara: Fithian Press, 1996.

Stampfer, Shaul. "What Actually Happened to the Jews of Ukraine in 1648?" *Jewish History* 17 (2003): 207–227. [Kluwer Academic Publishers, the Netherlands].

Steel, Duncan. *Eclipse*. Washington, DC: Joseph Henry Press, 2001.

Sternberg, Ghitta. *Stefanesti: Portrait of a Romanian Shtetl*. New York: Pergamon Press, 1984.

Stiff, Nahum. *Pogromen in Ukraine: Di Tsayt Fun der Frayviliger Armey*. Berlin: Vostok, 1923.

Teller, Adam. "The Shtetl as an Arena for Polish-Jewish Integration in the Eighteenth Century." *Polin* 17 (2004): 25–40.

Tollet, Daniel. "Merchants and Businessmen in Poznan and Cracow, 1588–1668." In Abramsky, Jachimczyk, and Polonsky, *The Jews in Poland*.

Tolstoy, Leo. "Lost On the Steppe; or, The Snowstorm." In *Tolstoy's Tales of Courage and Conflict*. Garden City, NY: Hanover House, 1958.

Troinitskago, N. A., ed. *Goroda i poseleniya v uezdakh, imeiushchie 2.000 i bolee zhitelei/pod redaktsieiu N. A. Troinitskago*. St. Petersburg: N. L. Nyrkin, 1905a.108 p.; 27 cm.p. 90 [Widener Slav 3091. HOLLIS number 003538381].

——. *Naselennyiya mesta Rossiiskoi imperii:v 500 i bolee zhitelei:s ukazaniem vsego nalichnago v nikh naseleniya i chisla zhitelei preobladiushchikh veroispovedanii, po dannym Pervoi vseobshchei perepisi naseleniya 1897 g.pod redaktsieiu N. A. Troinitskago*. St. Peterburg: Tipografia. Obshchestvennaya pol'za, 1905b.269,119 p. 28cm. p. 82. [Widener|Slav 3091.6 Photoreproduction of original HCL copy. HOLLIS number 006493410].

Tsherikover, A. *Antisemitizm un pogromen in Ukrayne, 1917–1918*. Berlin: Oysgabe Funm "Mizre-Yiddishn Historischn Arkhiv," 1923.

U.S. Army Map Service (AMTT) *Corps of Engineers Map, The Belaya-Tserkov, USSR Section*, 1953 "compiled in 1953 from USSR 1:100,000, General Staff of the Red Army, 1936–43."

Weigel, William F. *Yiddish*. Jewish Language Research Web site. Jewish-languages. org/Yiddish.html.

Weinberg, Sydney Stahl. *The World of Our Mothers: The Lives of Jewish Immigrant Women*. Chapel Hill: University of North Caroline Press, 1988.

Weinreich, Uriel. *Modern English-Yiddish, Yiddish-English Dictionary*. New York: Schocken Books, 1977.

Weinryb, Bernard D. *The Jews of Poland: A Social and Economic History of the Jewish Community in Poland from 1100 to 1800*. Philadelphia: Jewish Publication Society of America, 1973.

Wengeroff, Pauline. *Rememberings: The World of a Russian-Jewish Woman in the Nineteenth Century*. Trans. Henny Wenkart. Ed. Bernard D. Cooperman. Potomac: University Press of Maryland, 2000.

Westwood, J. N. *Geschichte Der Russischen Eisenbahnen*. Zurich: Orell Fussli Verlag, 1966.

Wheeler, Marcus. *Oxford Russian-English Dictionary*. Oxford: Clarendon Press, 1972.

Wilcher, Abrasha. *Mother and Son: Tales of a Shtetle, 1908–1923*. Swampscott, MA: First Person Press, 1992.

Williamson, Samuel R. Jr. "The Origins of the War." In Hew Strachan, ed., *World War I: A History*. New York: Oxford University Press, 1998.

Wisse, Ruth, ed. *A Shtetl and Other Yiddish Novellas*. New York: Behrman House, 1973, 1986.

Wolf, Lucien, ed. *The Legal Sufferings of the Jews in Russia: A Survey of Their Present Situation, and a Summary of Laws*. London: T. F. Unwin, 1912.

Yad Vashem Reference and Information Services. Jerusalem, Israel. Personal communication, e-mails, June 14, 2004, and June 10, 2004.

Yarmolinsky, Avrahm, ed. *The Portable Chekhov*. New York: Penguin, 1977.

Zborowski, Mark, and Elizabeth Herzog. *Life Is with People: The Culture of the Shtetl*. Foreword by Margaret Mead. New York: Schocken Books, 1995.

—— *Life Is with People: The Jewish Little Town of Eastern Europe*. Foreword by Margaret Mead. New York: International Universities Press, 1952.

Zipperstein, Steven J. "The Shtetl Revisited." In *Shtetl Life: The Nathan and Faye Hurvitz Collection*. Berkeley, CA: Judah L. Magnes Museum, 1993.

Zuckerman, Marvin S., and Marion Herbst, eds. *Selected Works of Sholem-Aleykhem*. Malibu, CA: Joseph Simon, Pangloss Press, 1994.

Zunser, Miriam Shomer. *Yesterday: A Memoir of a Russian Jewish Family*. Emily Wortis Leider, ed. New York: Harper and Row, 1978.

Index